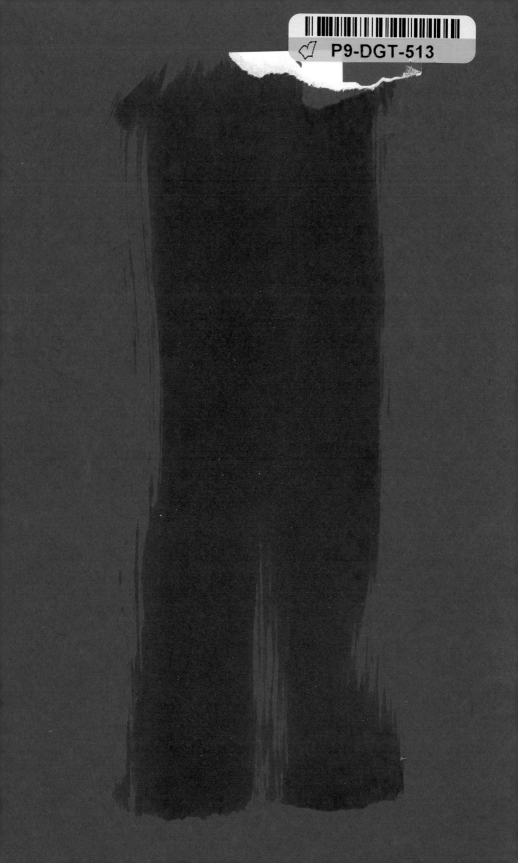

Apple

PRESS

Education and Technology

Charles Fisher
David C. Dwyer
Keith Yocam
Editors

Education and Technology

Reflections on
Computing in Classrooms

Apple
PRESS

Jossey-Bass Publishers
San Francisco

This book can be ordered from Jossey-Bass Inc., Publishers at 1-800-956-7739.

Substantial discounts on bulk quantities of Jossey-Bass books are available to corporations, professional associations, and other organizations. For details and discount information, contact the special sales department at Jossey-Bass Inc., Publishers. (415) 433–1740; Fax (800) 605–2665.

For sales outside the United States, please contact your local Simon & Schuster International office.

Jossey-Bass Web address: http://www.josseybass.com

Manufactured in the United States of America on Lyons Falls Turin Book. This paper is acid free and 100 percent totally chlorine free.

Library of Congress Cataloging-in-Publication Data

Education and technology : reflections on computing in classrooms / Charles Fisher, David C. Dwyer, Keith Yocam, editors. — 1st ed.
    p.   cm. — (The Jossey-Bass education series)
  Includes index.
  ISBN 0-7879-0238-1 (cloth : acid-free paper)
    1. Computer-assisted instruction—United States. 2. Educational technology—United States. I. Fisher, Charles, date.
II. Dwyer, David C. III. Yocam, Keith. IV. Series.
LB1028.5.E295 1996
371.3'34—dc20   96–10105

FIRST EDITION
HB Printing   10 9 8 7 6 5 4 3

The Jossey-Bass Education Series

Contents

Preface

In September 1985, Apple Computer, Inc., in partnership with a handful of far-flung school districts, launched the Apple Classrooms of Tomorrow (ACOT) project. At the time, personal computers were just beginning to appear in schools. At first, personal computers—like the dumb terminals that preceded them—were usually located in labs run by specially trained teachers and used primarily for instruction in computer programming or delivery of programmed instruction. Limitations on student access to machines, typically a few minutes a week in the few schools that had labs, were viewed as the major constraint on increased use. Against this background, the ACOT project was an extraordinary development because it simultaneously razed the access barrier and put computers into the hands of teachers and students in their regular classrooms. From the outset, ACOT worked in real classrooms with real teachers and real students. Access to machines was not an issue. The original classrooms had two computers for each student and teacher, one at his or her desk at school and one at home, all day every day. No constricting curriculum was imposed by the project as local educators used the new technology to create innovative learning environments. And ACOT's duration was open-ended; not a two-week trial, not a one-semester foray, but a long-term commitment.

At a time when personal computers were still rare except in specialized workplaces, these were exciting, imaginative innovations in schools. Since those heady days, ACOT has evolved into a sustained attempt to find useful ways to support students' learning with a wide variety of digital tools. In 1995, ACOT began its second decade, having worked with hundreds of teachers and thousands of students while incorporating modems, networks, multimedia, the Internet, and a host of other technologies into a substantial program of research and development.

This book is intended to be viewed from three successively larger perspectives: in the foreground, as a celebration of the first decade of ACOT's continuing inquiry into classroom learning; in the middle ground, as an early report on the widespread use of digital technologies in schools; and in the background, as commentary on the larger drama of educational change at the dawn of a new century. Many of the chapters provide glimpses of what can occur by using technology in education, and also provide sobering views of the time and resources required to accomplish desired gains. Through background, experience, and professional specialization, contributors to this volume have had somewhat different vantage points from which to see the drama—but all were close to the action.

The initial purpose of this book is to celebrate ACOT's first decade of pioneering work in elementary and secondary school classrooms. The contributors were invited to write personal essays on the roles and functions of digital technologies in school-based learning. In addition to reflecting on the past decade or two, authors were invited to speculate on the future of technology in education. Many of the contributors are educational researchers who have worked at one time or another in one or more of the ACOT sites. The majority of the authors are university faculty members or senior staff from well-known educational research and development agencies. About a third of the contributors are Apple staff members, most of whom worked directly on the ACOT project in research, development, and management roles for a substantial portion of its first decade. One chapter is contributed by teachers who have participated in the project since its inception. All the contributors have substantial experience with technology in education outside the ACOT project and, in many cases, have drawn on those wider experiences in their essays. For the most part, the work in this volume concerns learning in public schools as educators search for productive ways in which technology can support common intellectual, cultural, and educational experiences in a democratic and increasingly diverse society.

The second and broader purpose of the book is to portray a unique period in the evolving story of technology in education. The decade from 1985 to 1995 can be viewed as the first period of widespread use of personal computers in schools. At the beginning of the decade, computers were relatively rare in U.S. classrooms; by the end of the decade, practically all schools had computers for instructional purposes, and many classrooms were likely to have several machines. Over a remarkably short period of time, digital technologies and all that they have spawned—a transformation of the workplace, introduction of multimedia to offices and homes, a veritable revolution in local and global communications—are inexorably changing our perceptions of time, place, and knowledge itself. The last decade represents a punctuation point in the sense of Gould's theory of punctuated evolution. In terms of educational uses of technology, there was excitement in the air, a frontier mentality, a sense of speed—and ACOT was an early and persistent participant in these turbulent educational times. The essays in this book provide insights into this remarkable period and meanings drawn from the events. Although the introduction of digital technologies in classrooms is still in its infancy, and there is much ambiguity about whether or not technology's role will continue to increase, several of the essays outline possible futures. The initial decade of widespread use of computers in classrooms is fundamental to understanding how the emerging story is likely to develop.

The introduction of digital technologies into schools cannot be fully appreciated without also considering the much larger and very dynamic general field of education. While the chapters in this book constitute early reports on educational uses of technology, the field of education was crowded with other powerful forces vying for the attention of educators, students, and the general public. In 1983, the publication of A Nation at Risk heralded a new wave of educational reform. The Cold War was very much alive, with no end in sight. In the next decade, the educational stage was cluttered with a profusion of scenes and acts focusing on performance standards, cooperative learning, constructivism, outcomes-based education, the evolution of middle schools, site-based management, and teacher empowerment—among many others. These thrusts were not coordinated at the local, state, or national levels; they were often not mutually supportive, and were generally competing for dwindling economic resources. Unflattering international comparisons fueled growing dissatisfaction with public education by both the richest and the poorest segments of the population. By the end of the decade, charter schools were on the rise and, following other sectors, education seemed headed for an extended period of deregulation.

In this maze of reform efforts, the role of technology in education remains unclear, even as it is championed (or denounced) by contending forces. As is often pointed out, educational technology, like education itself, can be thought of as a tool and, as such, can be used for quite contradictory purposes. The point here is that the introduction of digital technology in schools is occurring against a background of dynamic change in education, and that powerful political, social, and economic interests are bound to affect both direction and speed during the next decades. But it is still the early days for digital technologies in school settings, and the recent prodigious development of communications systems may signal new surprises just ahead.

The book begins with an overview of the ACOT project followed by three thematic sections. The first section presents five contrasting views of the recent past and possible futures. The second section contains seven chapters exploring the evolving story of tools, practice, and student learning. The third section includes four accounts of programs designed to prepare teachers to work in the new environment.

The development and production of this book depended on the talent and goodwill of numerous colleagues. All of us involved in the project thank them for their unstinting efforts. We are especially grateful to Lesley Iura and Lorraine Aochi and their staffs at Jossey-Bass and Apple Press respectively for graceful support during the project, and also to Connie Troy-Downing for administrative support. We acknowledge the courage and commitment of teachers and students, especially those at ACOT sites, in exploring new tools and pedagogies to improve teaching and learning in schools. Finally, we acknowledge the sustained support of Apple Computer for research and development on uses of technology in schools. Without this support, it is unlikely that much of the work discussed in this book would have been attempted.

Ann Arbor, Michigan   *Charles Fisher*
April 1996   *David C. Dwyer*
                                       Keith Yocam

Education and Technology

1

The Apple Classrooms of Tomorrow

An Overview

For the past ten years, Apple Computer, Inc., in partnership with several school districts, has sponsored a research and development project called Apple Classrooms of Tomorrow (ACOT). The mission of the ACOT project is to deepen understanding of how technology can be used as a learning tool. Since its inception, the project's primary work has been intentionally situated in classrooms with the attendant authenticity and complications of everyday schooling. By operating in schools all year every year, ACOT has stayed close to the concerns of practicing educators and maintained a strong action orientation. The project operates as a partnership between Apple and individual school districts and this reliance on collaborative arrangements shapes both its approach to teaching and learning and its approach to research and development.

ACOT carries out a relatively large and eclectic program of research and development. Typically, these efforts are conducted by a small collaborative team with members from more than one institution addressing a particular issue. Team members are usually drawn from schools, universities, independent research agencies, and corporations. As a result, ACOT's growing body of work is more diverse than would be expected if it had all been conducted by a single agency.[1]

Within its broad mission, ACOT's objectives have evolved since the project began in 1985. Entering its second decade, ACOT intends to influence the general conversation about technology and education. Instead of talking narrowly about computers and other hardware, the project promotes conversations about learning by describing what happens when students use technology as a tool for building their own knowledge. The project studies how teachers use technology to create more challenging learning environments and how staff development can facilitate that process.

A Snapshot of the First Decade

The project began with a question: What happens to teaching and learning activities when students and teachers have access to technology whenever they want or need it? During the mid 1980s, a time of great excitement about using technology to enhance education, educators at Apple decided to pursue this question by creating environments in which technology was used as routinely as paper, pencils, and books. Descriptive research in these environments was expected to provide insights into how technology would affect teaching and learning.

The First Few Years

The ACOT project was initiated in 1985 when two classrooms, one in Eugene, Oregon, and one in Blue Earth, Minnesota, began fieldwork. Apple Computer supplied computers and training for the teachers who would use them; the school districts in the partnership provided staffing and made physical modifications to the classrooms. The initial notion of access to computers meant constant access to a personal machine as opposed to having a computer laboratory down the hall during school and no access after school. In these early days, portable machines were not yet available—but each student and teacher had two computers, one for school and one for home. After a year or two, the notion of access was redefined as *immediate access*, meaning that technology would be in the classroom but machines typically would be shared in some manner.

In ACOT's second year, five more sites were added in Columbus, Ohio; Cupertino, California; Houston, Texas; and Memphis and Nashville, Tennessee. Six of these fledgling sites were in elementary schools and one, at Columbus, was in a secondary school.

In 1987, the sites at Houston and Eugene were closed in favor of adding more classrooms at the other sites. The new configuration allowed cohorts of students to spend more years and grade levels in ACOT environments rather than giving students a one-year experience and then returning them to classrooms with little if any technology.

In July 1987, the first summer conference was convened in Cupertino, giving ACOT teachers an opportunity to meet each other, share experiences, and learn more about teaching with technology. These summer conferences continued for a number of years and proved to be important occasions both for refining and redefining program direction as well as for establishing a national identity for the project. Chapters Sixteen and Seventeen provide more information on these summer conferences and institutes.

Early Research

Although the project's primary efforts were directed to start-up activities during the first two years, ACOT (with advice from prominent educators and researchers) also developed an initial research agenda. From the beginning, there was systematic description of what was happening in classrooms. With encouragement to reflect on their experiences, ACOT teachers flooded the project staff with observations. In addition to weekly reports from each site, teachers sent monthly audiotaped journals in which they described instruction in their classrooms as well as their personal triumphs and frustrations. As the volume of communications grew, ACOT researchers developed a database for the anecdotal material (described in Chapter Seventeen) and began investigating themes related to technology and change.

By 1989, researchers from other institutions began to collect data in ACOT settings and, within a year, two longitudinal studies and a series of shorter investigations were launched. A research team at UCLA's Center for Technology Assessment led by Eva Baker began examining the impact of the program on students, staff, and parents. Robert Tierney, at Ohio State University, began a longitudinal study of ninth graders' thought processes at the site in Columbus. Chapters Ten and Eleven are partially based on these longitudinal studies.

In 1988, ACOT's first research studies were presented at annual meetings of the American Education Research Association, the International Reading Association, and the International Association of Computing Educators. The project was also featured in a report on use of technology in American schools published by the U.S. Office of Technology Assessment.[2]

Refining Program Focus and Expanding the Research Effort

In 1989, another decision was made to extend the length of time students spent in ACOT classroom environments. By adding classrooms at Columbus, Cupertino, and Nashville, the project began to follow students through still more grade levels. During the same year, an innovative outreach program was begun in the Nashville schools representing preliminary work on a teacher development model.

ACOT began to receive requests for information from other educators and from the press. Visitors from South America and the USSR toured the sites. ACOT was described in articles in *USA Today*, the *New York Times*, *Business Week*, the *Boston Globe*, and a Japanese counterpart of *PC Magazine*, and was also featured on NBC's *Nightly News*.

During 1988 and 1989, there was evidence that instructional practices were becoming more learner-centered as teachers gained experience with technology in their classrooms. Subsequently, ACOT began focusing staff development sessions to encourage a constructivist approach to teaching—a process described in Chapter

Two. A common language was developing in the project to help teachers collaborate more effectively. In the same period, multimedia was introduced at the sites. Also, classroom observations indicated that students were developing new competencies, some of which were not being captured by traditional assessment measures.

ACOT began expanding support for researchers at a variety of institutions whose projects addressed complementary research and development issues. For example, collaborative research projects were started on a language arts portfolio tool, writing instruction for students, telecommunications-based writing workshops for teachers, classroom task design, project-based learning, an innovative staff development model, and alternative assessment procedures. Early reports on the longitudinal research began to appear, including a two-year evaluation study, a four-year study of the evolution of teachers' beliefs and practices, and a study of classroom management.

Throughout the 1980s, the number of educators interested in teaching and learning with technology continued to increase. More schools and school districts were involved in implementing technology in their classrooms and, as a result, demand increased for information and training on using computers and other technologies for learning. ACOT had five years of experience in schools at this point, and—like other educational technology projects around the country—began to receive large numbers of inquiries about planning for and implementing technology in classrooms. ACOT staff began meeting with a wide array of educators and state and national policy makers. ACOT was especially responsive in cases where interests in educational technology extended to interests in new forms of assessment and approaches to staff development.

Between 1991 and 1993, ACOT made presentations to the U.S. Department of Education, the President's National Education Goals Committee, the National Governors' Association, the Education Commission of the States, the National Center for Education and the Economy, the Fortune Education Summit, the Federal Communications Commission, the California Business Roundtable, and the Smithsonian Computerworld program, among others. Formal presentations were made to the commissioners of education and their staffs for Kentucky, Vermont, New York, Indiana, Ohio, and several other states.

Since its early years, ACOT has hosted many international observers. Between 1991 and 1993, these international contacts also increased. Presentations were made to ministers of education for eleven former Soviet republics; briefings were provided for educators and policy makers from the United Kingdom, Singapore, Japan, Bulgaria, Saudi Arabia, Turkey, Portugal, Poland, United Arab Emirates, Hungary, and France. By the end of the decade, ACOT had distributed research summaries to more than 40,000 educators.

On the development side, recent technological advances had allowed developers to create tools for representing ideas in multiple formats, that is, in various combinations of text, images, video, graphics, tables, and charts. ACOT encouraged use of these new technologies, in part, by collaborating with developers on multi-representational tools. The project also participated in the development of software and curriculum materials. For example, ACOT developed hardware, software, and curriculum for using wireless technologies to demonstrate how students could use new technologies to support collaboration, communication, and expression of knowledge. In one project—known as Wireless Coyote—middle school students on a science field trip to the Arizona desert used wireless communications and mobile computers to collect and analyze data and to share their findings with colleagues at distant locations.

Still in the 1980s, Wireless Coyote was replicated in another project known as Cloud Forest Classroom. This project developed and tested an integrated data collection, data analysis, and messaging environment using Powerbooks connected by radio-frequency modems. The system was used by students on a biology field trip to Costa Rica's Monteverde cloud forest. A third project entitled MediaFusion was an early demonstration of how junior high students on opposite coasts of the United States shared thoughts and theories about global warming. Using Macintosh computers, students composed QuickTime movies with embedded graphs to express and support their positions. Then they exchanged these messages via satellite with peers across the country. ACOT classrooms were early and frequent users of local and wide area networks.

In the last half of its first decade, ACOT developed more—and more varied—partnerships. The project allocated additional resources for implementing and studying a new model of staff development. In 1992, with the National Science Foundation as a partner, ACOT Teacher Development Centers were established at three sites to explore the effectiveness of this new approach. Shortly thereafter, a network of ACOT Teacher Development Centers was established in partnership with the National Alliance for Restructuring Education. This arrangement allowed examination of the model on a larger scale and in environments where restructuring was already under way. By the end of the decade, ACOT's long-held view that the major challenge to supporting school learning with technology lay not with technology but in the professional development of educators was broadly shared among educational decision makers.

Technology as a Catalyst for Change

Over the decade, the ACOT project grew and changed. At the same time, the contexts of both technology and education were also changing. By the end of the decade, ACOT had worked with hundreds of teachers and thousands of students in several countries and continents. Throughout this experience, ACOT pursued an evolving research agenda, exploring outcomes for students and teachers as they used technological tools as a regular part of their school learning activities.

Not surprisingly, teachers and researchers found that having an array of tools for acquiring information, thinking, and communicating allows more children more ways to become successful learners. But they also found that the technology itself is a catalyst for change, encouraging fundamentally different forms of interactions among students and between students and teachers, engaging students in higher-order cognitive tasks, and prompting teachers to question old assumptions about instruction and learning. Mature ACOT sites tend to balance use of direct instruction with a collaborative and inquiry-driven knowledge-construction approach to teaching and learning. Teachers, with broad administrative support, appear to be the key to creating such learning environments.

Some Influences on Students and Teachers

Dispelling widespread myths, studies found that instead of isolating students, access to technology encouraged them to collaborate more than in traditional classrooms. And instead of becoming boring with use, technology continued to engage students as they gained in knowledge and skill in generating ideas and products. There was evidence that students were developing positive attitudes toward themselves and toward learning. Over time, researchers found that students in ACOT classrooms not only continued to perform well on standardized tests but also were developing a variety of competencies that are not usually measured.

As ACOT teachers became comfortable with the technology, they reported enjoying their work more and feeling more successful with their students. They also reported that they interacted differently with their students, more as guides or mentors and less as lecturers. In some cases, their personal efforts to make technology an integral part of their classrooms caused them to rethink basic beliefs about education and opened them to the possibility of redefining how they went about providing opportunities for students to learn.

Learning activities in ACOT classrooms increasingly incorporate interdisciplinary studies, team teaching, and accommodations for students with different learning styles. While these concepts are not new, they have proved difficult to implement in traditional classrooms. Introducing technology into the classroom appears to provide a catalyst for putting these concepts into practice and helping both students and teachers succeed, sometimes in dramatic fashion. Teachers appear to progress through stages (described in Chapter Seventeen) as they learn how to incorporate technology in classroom environments. As teachers become comfortable with a shift in classroom roles, they may extend their pedagogical repertoires. With appropriate support, they may also adjust their approach to teaching and learning from curriculum-centered to learner-centered, from individual tasks to collaborative work, and from passive learning to active learning.

Six Research Themes for Today and Tomorrow

In its first decade, research in ACOT classrooms included numerous topics and methodological approaches. Through widespread collaborations with more than forty educational researchers and developers, a diverse collection of studies has been completed, and more studies are under way. In addition to collecting data at its core sites, ACOT established additional short-term research sites in dozens of other classrooms. As the project enters its second decade, ACOT research is distributed over six interdependent themes. While not a comprehensive treatment, the remainder of this chapter outlines each theme, its driving question, and key examples of relevant research and development work. In these collaborative projects, ACOT staff sometimes play a leading role and sometimes a supporting role.

Collaboration. Technology both encourages students to collaborate and aids in collaborative work. What kinds of collaborative environments and tools are most helpful? Marlene Scardamalia and Carl Bereiter (Ontario Institute for Studies in Education) have created a computer-based environment that supports students in the manipulation and construction of information as they collaborate on projects. Brian Reilly (University of California, Berkeley, now at Apple) designed and tested a HyperCard stack that manages student work in a portfolio format and allows teachers and students to add comments.

Communication. In traditional classroom environments, learners have access to the teacher's knowledge and to information from textbooks or local library collections as their primary—and often only—sources. What happens when students have access to large numbers of experts, on-line sources of information, and remote colleagues? The Technical Education Research Center in Cambridge, the Public Broadcasting System, and ACOT created and developed MediaFusion. This project combined television (timely stories) with computers (interactivity) to create environments where students explore important issues and discuss their discoveries with students in other schools. Karla Kelly (Lucasfilm) developed an interdisciplinary curriculum, based on the Foxfire model, for middle school students to explore their own cultural heritage and to create interactive projects reflecting their life experiences. With the San Francisco Exploratorium and a local school district, ACOT is studying how elementary school teachers use media-rich environments to enhance communication, collaboration, and inquiry.

Multiple representation of ideas. How can the computer's power to represent ideas in multiple forms be used to support classroom learning? Jere Confrey (Cornell University) developed Function Probe as part of a discovery approach to teaching and learning calculus. The software tool allows students to construct relationships between tables, graphs, and equations easily and interactively. Barbara Buckley (Stanford University) created an interactive multimedia simulation to give high school students a deeper understanding of physiology. Roy Pea and Christina Allen (Institute for Research on Learning) created MediaWorks, a multimedia database and composing tool that allows students to research, create, analyze, and synthesize a wide array of multimedia information.

Intelligent applications and modeling. What are some of the ways to use computing power to support students when they're solving problems? John Anderson (Carnegie Mellon University) created an intelligent computer tutor for geometry that provides a visual tool kit for developing geometric proofs and gives feedback at each step. Bowen Loftin (University of Houston) developed Intelligent Physics Tutor, a physics-tutoring environment that observes each student solving problems and learns how best to respond to his or her errors and how to provide useful guidance through the curriculum.

Information analysis. What happens to motivation and learning when students use the same tools, or the same kinds of tools, that are used by experts? Chris Hancock (Technical Education Research Center) explored the use of TableTop, a visual database environment, to teach middle school students how to use data to solve real problems. Richard Greenberg (University of Arizona) developed materials and programs for teachers and students to use sophisticated digital image processing tools. Gene Stanley (Boston University) created hands-on activities and simulations for high school mathematics and science students to learn about probability and random processes in nature by studying fractals. Karen Price (Harvard University) developed a video manipulation tool allowing teachers and students to explore the context in which language occurs.

Assessment. If new tools are giving rise to new skills and competencies among students, how can these competencies be identified and assessed? Eva Baker and her colleagues (University of California, Los Angeles) developed portfolio assessment procedures and examined the effectiveness of traditional measures of student achievement and student self-concept in capturing changes in ACOT students. Robert Tierney (Ohio State University) studied developmental processes in learning to write, organize work, and frame problems among ACOT high school students. Allan Collins (Northwestern University and BBN Corporation) and Jan Hawkins (Center for Children and Technology) investigated the use of video in performance assessment of complex learning. Midian Kurland (Education Development Center, now at Apple) examined the use of TextBrowser, a technology-based language arts assessment tool allowing teachers to generate instructional activities based on students' own work. Roy Pea and Jeremy Roschelle (Institute for Research on Learning) created VideoNoter, a software tool that supports analysis of videotapes of classroom learning situations.

ACOT is a work in progress. As the second decade begins, ACOT continues its focus on both the technical and social underpinnings of effective technology-supported learning, but with a significantly expanded notion of *learning community*. ACOT has recently begun to include international sites and intends to add more—creating a distributed laboratory with partners in schools, universities, and ministries of education in many countries. On the technical side, ACOT will continue to develop and study the use of tools that provide access to information and expertise, create and express ideas and concepts, and support collaboration among learners at any time, anywhere. In the social and cognitive arenas, ACOT will focus on expanded roles for adults and students pursuing collaborative, project-based curricula in local communities and, through telecommunications, around the world.

Notes

1. ACOT research reports are available through Apple's Starting-Line materials distribution program and on the Internet at http://www.info.apple.com/education.

2. U.S. Congress, Office of Technology Assessment. *Power On! New Tools for Teaching and Learning.* Doc. no. OTA-SET-379. Washington, D.C.: U.S. Government Printing Office, September 1988.

Part I

Learning in the Age of Technology

The general context for thinking about technology as a learning tool continues to change with remarkable rapidity. The passing of a single decade has seen great changes not only in the numbers and kinds of technological tools that are currently being used in classrooms and schools but also in the kinds of tools that may become available in the future. The leading and trailing edges of technology are diverging with breathtaking speed, and schools are increasingly faced with new risks and opportunities as they attempt to plan and implement programs using technology. For example, the veritable revolution in telecommunications may offer possibilities that only yesterday were viewed as impractical. New technologies appear to be influencing how ideas are represented, communicated, stored, and interpreted. Part One explores some of these issues and their implications for education.

The chapters in this part provide reflections on and, in several cases, predictions about technology and education. While each chapter has implications for classroom practices, they all address broad areas of education and applications of technology. In Chapter Two, David Dwyer describes a major shift in schooling from what he calls *knowledge instruction* to *knowledge construction*, and posits a catalytic role for technology in this dynamic process. Drawing in part on observations of students and teachers in the ACOT project, Dwyer explores possible benefits from technology with cautious optimism. In Chapter Three, Jan Hawkins reflects on the apparently low productivity of direct transmission of information, the process of model development and dissemination in education, and initial classroom practices with technology. She points to new complexities in our social world and in our conceptions of knowledge that are giving rise to new challenges and dilemmas for both teaching and learning.

In Chapter Four, Allan Collins traces the developmental path from intelligent computer-aided instruction to intelligent tutoring systems to interactive learning environments. He identifies ten characteristics of interactive learning environments, explores their relevance for student learning, and outlines alternative scenarios for the future of technology in education. Kristina Hooper Woolsey's creative essay in Chapter Five recounts some hard-won learnings from extensive experience in the design and production of multimedia learning products. She provides insights into teaching, and comments on both new social structures and elements of designerly thinking. Part One closes with Decker Walker's essay in Chapter Six on using technologies appropriately in schools. Walker begins with a review of computer-assisted instruction as used by proponents of different theories of curriculum and learning. He concludes with a suggestion for improving the quality of technology use in classrooms that directly involves teachers in experimentation and subsequent sharing of preferred practices.

2

The Imperative to Change Our Schools

David C. Dwyer

"But it doesn't look like a classroom," said the reporter. "I've been here over an hour. I haven't seen a teacher teach yet. Children hardly sit still for two minutes. I don't see any textbooks. I mean, I'm kinda shocked!"

Laughing, the program's coordinator pointed to one of the adults in the room and said, "That's Barbara. She's the children's teacher, but she's also a mentor, helping four teachers get this kind of program started at their school. What seems most different to you?"

"I guess it's that everybody is so busy. It's not like pandemonium, though. It's the same kind of craziness you get in the newsroom right before deadline. Like those children over there. See them? Two of them just rushed in from somewhere carrying those notebook computers, and they went right over to that group and the whole bunch got really excited."

"Right, they're just back from the library. They were researching back copies of newspapers for information about hurricanes. Watch them, I think you're in for another surprise."

"Are they on line with that computer? I didn't know children could do that."

"The children are linked up with the university and can access satellite images and weather information from the National Weather Service. They're tracking the progress of a tropical depression in the Caribbean. And then that group over there, they're publishing a book. They've interviewed and videotaped people in various businesses—travel, agriculture, even the highway department—about how weather influences jobs and the economy. They want to research the topic worldwide over the Internet."

"Am I seeing right? It looks like they've got a color video running inside the text they're typing! How come twelve- and thirteen-year-olds can do all of this stuff? And what are those children doing? Look, they've made some kind of 3-D model of a tornado. . . ."

School Change: From What to What?

If you close your eyes and imagine a classroom, chances are great that you will *not* picture the scenario you just read. Instead, you most likely saw an adult standing at the front of a room that contains thirty or more students sitting in straight rows of desks. Chances are also good that students are doing one of three things: listening to the teacher talk, raising their hands to participate in a whole-class recitation, or working quietly and independently on some written exercise. Closely allied with this scene are assumptions about the basic organization of schools: textbooks and courses of study set by a central curriculum office, mandatory attendance, grade levels, bell schedules, and testing. This image, of course, does not just exist in our minds. It is, in fact, what most of our children encounter every day of their school lives. The opening vignette poses a different kind of learning opportunity for students. Computers, on-line systems, video cameras, multimedia, and simulation tools support students' activities, but what is most different is the underlying perspective about how children (or adults, for that matter) learn.

Knowledge Instruction and Knowledge Construction

In traditional settings, learning is viewed as the transfer of thoughts from one who is knowledgeable to one who is not—a view in which teacher work is perceived as direct instruction. The vignette is based on knowledge *construction*, a view in which learning is seen as a personal, reflective, and transformative process, in which teacher work is construed as facilitating students' abilities to integrate ideas, experiences, and points of view into something new. When applied in the context of schooling, this view of learning demands changes in deeply held beliefs about the form of classroom activities, the respective roles of teachers and students, the goals of education, the very concept of knowledge, and closely related positions on student success and means to measure student success. Even the role of technology changes.

In an instruction classroom, activity is usually the domain of teachers. They are the ones with freedom to move about, to initiate actions and interactions, to spend time and resources, to ask questions. They are the tellers of facts, the definers of important ideas. Students are, in the main, passive listeners and carefully choreographed followers. In the knowledge construction classroom, a teacher's activity and freedom are at least shared with students. Action becomes the domain of learners, whether teachers or students. Most times teachers are experts, but other sources of expertise are recognized, valued, and used—even student expertise. In stark contrast to the instruction classroom, students often work collaboratively, solving problems through conversation, inquiry, trial and error, and constant public comparison of one approximate solution against another.

In instruction-oriented classrooms, activity is focused on the transmission or transfer of facts. Common teaching methods include lecture, whole-class recitation, and seat work, where students work individually on drills from texts or workbooks. While students are often grouped by ability, their work is a private affair. Sharing what they know with anyone but the teacher is often construed as cheating and bears serious consequences. Evaluation, too, is an individual endeavor and takes the form of multiple-choice, short answer, and true-false quizzes or norm-referenced exams. Value is placed on students' abilities to recall and repeat facts on demand. Often the number of facts that can be recalled or discriminated is the basis for reward. The standards against which students are evaluated are generally secret.

In knowledge construction settings, facts are important, as well, but not so much for their own sake. Emphasis is on inquiry and invention. Investigations lead to the discovery of many and often conflicting facts. Students are encouraged to critically assess data, to discover relationships and patterns, to compare and contrast, to transform information into something new. Their work is varied. Groups of students may work at very different tasks, or they may find very different means to accomplish the same task. In sharp relief to instruction-based classes, collaboration stands out as a hallmark of knowledge construction settings. Students are encouraged to work in teams, to discuss their approaches to problems, to share information they have found, to critically review the ideas, models, drawings, and compositions of their peers. Evaluation may be criterion referenced; standards and responsibilities are made clear at the outset of activities. Tests may take the form of public performances (individual or group), expositions, or display of work before peers, parents, or expert panels charged with judging the quality of the work against rigorous standards. While the public nature of work in knowledge construction classrooms changes the dynamics of schoolwork, it also affects the quality. Public display ups the ante. It gives classwork purpose beyond drill or exercise. It introduces a sense of personal risk for students that encourages deeper inquiry and more careful invention.

Finally, I suggest that the role of technology varies in knowledge instruction and knowledge construction settings. It can be a patient, nonthreatening tutor for basic skill acquisition in the instruction setting, offering students infinite opportunity to repeat problems until process or content is mastered. It can help teachers with the administration and management of this kind of learning. Further, technology can enliven lectures and make them more effective by supporting the visualization of complex processes or unfamiliar and remote scenes. In the knowledge construction classroom, technology becomes a more general purpose tool, allowing access to information, communication with experts, more possibilities for collaboration, and a creative medium for thought and expression. These contrasting views of instruction and construction are summarized in Table 2.1.

Knowledge Instruction and Construction in Practice

As different as knowledge instruction and knowledge construction are, they are not incompatible as is often argued. They can be viewed as positions on a continuum of possible learning strategies. Instruction—that is, lecture, drill, and practice, is a great way to introduce skills or concepts, or build awareness, or reinforce some set of actions that can be replayed habitually. When breadth is valued over depth in curriculum, instruction is one way to make sure you cover the necessary content in a given amount of time.

When depth and understanding are the desired outcomes, however, knowledge construction is a better strategy to help learners personalize and deeply internalize ideas, to create situations where skills and concepts can be applied in different contexts to solve problems, to explore or generate ideas, and to generalize and synthesize knowledge. The point is for teachers or learning guides or facilitators or coaches—choose your favorite term—to reflect on their goals for children and for the tasks they set for children and to pick learning strategies that best accomplish those goals. I'm a pragmatist when it comes to classroom practice. As a veteran teacher and observer of learning practices, I believe the best-prepared professionals are those who can put a wide range of strategies to work for the benefit of their students.

While combining instruction and construction may seem a matter of common sense, it is not often done. The two approaches often raise serious debate, waged on philosophical, political, and even moral grounds.[1] The set of beliefs around instructionism builds up in us all through our own lives as students. As some train to become

Table 2.1. Attributes of Instruction and Construction Learning Environments.

	Knowledge Instruction	Knowledge Construction
Classroom Activity	Teacher centered (didactic)	Learner centered (interactive)
Teacher Role	Fact teller (always expert)	Collaborator (sometimes learner)
Student Role	Listener (always learner)	Collaborator (sometimes expert)
Instructional Emphasis	Facts (memorization)	Relationships (inquiry and invention)
Concept of Knowledge	Accumulation of facts	Transformation of facts
Demonstration of Success	Quantity	Quality of understanding
Assessment	Norm-referenced (multiple-choice items)	Criterion-referenced (portfolios and performances)
Technology Use	Drill and practice	Communication (collaboration, information access, expression)

Source: This table also appears in Dwyer, D. C., Ringstaff, C., & Sandholtz, J. H. (1991). Changes in teachers' beliefs and practices in technology-rich classrooms. *Educational Leadership, 48*(8), 45–52.

teachers, those beliefs are reinforced by the lecture-dominated pedagogy of universities. When new teachers arrive at their teaching assignments, the same beliefs are formally sanctioned by administrators through evaluation practices and informally in the faculty lounge by other teachers. This process explains the intransigence of traditional schooling to change. In the end, teachers most likely teach as they were taught, as observed by Dan Lortie two decades ago.[2]

Our beliefs about school run deep and they limit our ability to even think about alternatives. Getting started on the professional journey from instructionism to constructionism is a matter of obtaining a new stock of ideas and ways of operating. Putting these ideas to work in classrooms means dedicating oneself to trial and error and risk and to working with other teachers to critically review each trial. This kind of reflective practice is the mechanism that will eventually help old habits give way to new. It is a process of creating a new culture in our schools, one that offers a balanced diet of learning opportunities for students. It is a slow, difficult, and, I believe, critically important pursuit for teachers. It is just as important for parents, administrators, and policy makers to understand and support this goal. Just as teachers set the limits for students and their classrooms, so parents, administrators, and policy makers set boundaries for teachers, schools, and districts.

With the Advantage of Hindsight

For the past ten years, I worked with a team of teachers, researchers, and technologists who did have something different in mind for students and for schools. The "something" was the integration of computers into the routines of a half dozen experimental classrooms in varied settings throughout the United States. Under the auspices of the Apple Classrooms of Tomorrow project (ACOT) at Apple Computer, Inc., we set about trying to understand the impact of technology on teaching and learning. Today, ACOT schools are places where instruction is common but where children and teachers also engage in inquiry and invention, working at levels of sophistication that are surprising to many observers. In fact, the opening vignette is a composite of the kinds of construction activities that occur regularly in ACOT schools. The intervening years were action packed, messy, and learn-as-you-go. The integration of technology into the settings proved to be the simplest part of the effort. Applying new ideas about learning, on the other hand, was far more difficult.

No one in the early days of the effort knew what the contribution of various technologies in schools would be. Sometime in the

future, we thought, children and teachers might use technology as
routinely as paper, pencils, and books. What differences in teaching and learning would that change make? What problems would
students and teachers encounter? What assistance would they need?
In our own naiveté, we imagined improvements in traditional learning measures through individualized instructional approaches, improved student attitudes toward school, and lots more student and
teacher work getting done in less time. We had no idea about the
system-changing forces we were about to unleash.

We opened classrooms in seven schools, shipping enough technology to provide computers in the home and in the classroom for
each participating teacher and student. Various forms of chaos
ensued at the sites. For children, every day brought the excitement
of opening boxes of mysterious parts such as modems, CPUs, monitors, disk drives, printers, software, blank floppies, and cables—
miles and miles of cables. For teachers, those same boxes meant
countless hours of sorting, labeling, investigating, problem solving,
and planning—all on top of making sure classes kept progressing
and children kept learning. Sometimes the expectations seemed too
much and teachers worried about getting through the year and covering the basics. As one wrote, "I would feel a lot more comfortable
about some of the things that I do if I just knew that before the end
of the year I really was going to be able to meet all the objectives
and all the things that these children will need."

Computers, we discovered, neither made teachers' jobs easier
nor made their missions clearer. The confusion and uncertainty,
however, lessened as teachers witnessed positive changes in their
students. Changes in student attitude and engagement were per-
ceptible almost from the beginning.

Typical observations included: "We are finding that the students
are coming in to use the computers during lunch and staying late.
This degree of commitment and engagement is really unusual in a
group of quite ordinary kids." And: "My students are really involved.
They seem to be setting up standards for themselves to judge their
own work."

Other anxiety-reducing evidence began to mount. We worried early on about whether children would become socially isolated. In fact, cooperative and task-related interaction among students in the ACOT classrooms was spontaneous and more extensive than in traditional classrooms. We wondered if students' early enthusiasm for the technology would diminish over time. But we saw their interest in and engagement with technology grow steadily. They used it more frequently and imaginatively as their technical competence increased. A long-time ACOT teacher, looking back over many years, said: "The students don't get tired of working on the computer. They actually ask for things to do. In all of my years of teaching, I never had anyone ask for another ditto."

Even keyboards, which early on seemed a barrier for young children, proved to be a significant boon. With as little as fifteen minutes of keyboarding practice daily for six weeks, second and third graders commonly typed twenty words per minute with 95 percent accuracy—more than twice as fast as seven- and eight-year-olds write with pens or pencils.

By the end of the second year of the project, ACOT teachers had successfully translated traditional text-based, lecture-recitation-seatwork instructional approaches to the new electronic medium. Student deportment and attendance improved across all sites and student attitudes toward self and learning showed improvement. Test scores indicated that, at the very least, students were doing as well as they might without all the technology and some were clearly performing better.[3] At our site in Memphis, Tennessee, computers were used purposefully to raise student test scores. Two years in a row, the district reported ACOT students scored significantly higher on the California Achievement Test than non-ACOT students in vocabulary, reading comprehension, language mechanics, math computation, and mathematics concepts and application.[4] At other sites, students already performed well on achievement tests and no additional emphasis was placed on basic skill acquisition. Analysis of scores at those sites showed no significant increase or decrease even though students were spending far less time on standard curriculum as they developed keyboarding and word processing, database, graphics, and programming skills. Our research showed that ACOT students wrote more, more effectively, and with greater fluidity.[5] Teachers also found that their students finished whole units of study far more quickly than in past years. In one instance, a class completed the sixth-grade math curriculum by the beginning of April.[6]

I said that we had unwittingly unleashed system-changing forces. As pleased as we were with the results of the first two years, classrooms and classroom practice looked pretty traditional even though there was a lot of technology in use for much of each school day. The bigger story, the shift in teaching approach illustrated in Table 2.1, began after teachers themselves appropriated technology as a personal tool to accomplish their own tasks and acknowledged the purposeful and supportive collaboration of students who had spontaneously begun to help one another with the technology. Teachers' own growing prowess, coupled with the observable changes in their students' work and forms of interaction, opened the staff to the possibilities of redefining how they went about providing opportunities for students to learn. Technology was acknowledged as the catalyst for new perspectives and practices:

"As you work into using the computer in the classroom, you start questioning everything you have done in the past, and wonder how you can adapt it to the computer. Then, you start questioning the whole concept of what you originally did."

"Because of ACOT and the technology, I continue to be enthusiastic about being a teacher. But I am an altogether different teacher than I was before. I am now guiding the students. They are the masters of their own education now, creating their own knowledge and using their creativity to research and explain information to others."

"ACOT has revitalized the teaching process tremendously. It has also been the catalyst for a transition from blackboards and textbooks to a method of instruction where students can explore, discover, and construct their own knowledge."

Teachers began to experiment with more open-ended assignments, asking leading questions that were contemporary, meaningful to students—and ultimately unanswerable. The simple measure of right or wrong, therefore, had to give way to notions of quality, of depth of argument, of evidence brought to bear. In this process, technology became a tool for locating and accessing information, organizing and displaying data, creating persuasive arguments, and dynamically demonstrating ideas and conclusions to critical audiences of peers. Students needed bigger chunks of time to work on these kinds of tasks. The ACOT teachers responded by teaming, coordinating, and rearranging the school day. They adjusted, sometimes with personal difficulty, to noisier, messier classrooms. They had to learn new ways of evaluating student work as student work became much more complex—representative of students' personal styles and passions, collaborative, media intensive, and sometimes performance based. To my "teacher ears," the tempo and timbre of these classrooms evolved slowly but inexorably. Their rhythms became distinct. A district supervisor who worked with the project over several years wrote: "The ACOT classrooms have become a model for interdisciplinary studies, team teaching, and addressing individual learning styles. These are all concepts that have been around for many years, but that are not easily put into practice."

The teachers themselves, caught up in the day-to-day challenges of the project, were sometimes surprised by the changes in themselves and the learning environments they created. Infrequent opportunities to peek into other teachers' lives and classes were sometimes the only metric that helped them mark their own growth and empowerment.

"Being on hall duty this year, I had a chance to hear how, in class after class, the teachers' voices droned on and on and on. There is very little chance for the student to become an active participant. In today's schools there is little chance for the individual teacher to actually change the curriculum, but we can make the way we deliver the curriculum very different."

Another, with obvious pride, reflected: "I love walking through the math class this year. It is all individualized and there is such a businesslike hum going on. There is such a good feel to it. It seems like what schools ought to be."

A benchmark in ACOT's history was the conclusion of a longitudinal study of ACOT students at West High School in Columbus, Ohio. District data showed stark differences between the 1991 ACOT graduating class and their comparable West High, non-ACOT peers.[7] ACOT students' absentee rate was 50 percent less; they had a 0 percent drop-out rate compared to the school's 30 percent; and 90 percent of the ACOT students went on to college compared with 15 percent of the non-ACOT graduates. The college-bound rate was particularly important to us because half of the students who had joined ACOT as freshmen had not planned to go to college, perceiving themselves as incapable or seeing college as irrelevant to their lives. Further, this ACOT graduating class had amassed twenty-seven academic awards, including inductees into the National Honor Society and Who's Who Among High School Students and recognitions for outstanding accomplishments in history, calculus, foreign language, and writing. Differences of similar magnitude are typical of each of the seven ACOT graduating classes from the project's first decade.

Even more important, the longitudinal study of these students showed their greatest difference to be the manner in which they organized for and accomplished their work. They routinely employed inquiry, collaborative, technological, and problem-solving skills uncommon to graduates of traditional high school programs.[8] These skills are remarkably similar to a set of competencies argued for by the U.S. Department of Labor. Beyond basic language and computational literacy, it maintains that high school graduates must master the abilities to: organize resources; work with others; locate, evaluate, and use information; understand complex work systems; and work with a variety of technologies.[9]

It seems, then, that technology coupled with opportunities for teachers to learn about and apply new models of learning in schools is a powerful, system-altering one-two punch with very positive outcomes for students. While our reports and summaries tell the story at one level, it is still an interview with Billy James,[10] one of the project's elementary students, that for me makes this all very personal and sets the stage for the conundrum I believe we face as we think about the next decade.

Billy was a twelve-year-old in one of our urban elementary schools. He was the kind of child that teachers often dread. You sensed him immediately when he entered a room; a ball of energy, trouble with a capital T, a root cause of teacher migraine. And yet he was lots more, as we later learned; bright, verbal, funny, insightful, a leader. He was African-American. He was poor, at risk, underserved by the traditional education establishment. He was an artist and loved the skulls and flowers of Georgia O'Keeffe, whose work he had discovered on his own. He wanted to go to college and knew why that was important to him. And he was intensely and articulately aware of the way school usually frustrated him, as he shared in an interview.

"Last year when I was in a regular class, it was pretty boring. You'd do the regular stuff, you know, every day, day after day. The teachers were pretty strict. Sometimes, they were just ugly to you. And you didn't get to do anything. You know, you'd have to use a pencil all the time, and you'd be in a little wooden desk, just sitting there, all day long."

Billy stretched out the "all" in "all the time" for emphasis, like an evangelist on a roll. Then he described how his ACOT year was different, how he had found a friendlier and livelier place.

"This is the only school that I've been to where they have a gym and an art room. We get to sing and stuff, too, like in a chorus. It seems like in this school, we stop trying to be enemies with other kids. We ask around at lunch, and if you think somebody's not your friend, you try to convince them to be your friend and ask them what you did—you know."

Asked if technology in his classroom had made any difference in his life, he brightened and said: "Yeah, it's improved my, you know, my style!" He commented on other differences he saw when working with technology, like seeing examples, making choices, having some control over the level of challenge of his work. But he was most animated when he thought about how access to technology affected his own work in art.

"I'm a good artist without the computer, but it seems like the computer gives me more ideas about drawing. Since I came into ACOT, I even entered a contest. If you win, not only do you get to go to State college, but you get a hundred dollars! And then if you win, you go to Washington, D.C."

The art theme led Billy to share his thoughts about his future, including his view about the importance of college.

"At first I was thinking about being an architect. And then I thought archeologist. And now I want to be an artist. I think college is pretty important because if you try to get a job in an office, the first thing they're going to ask you is, 'Have you been to college?' If you say, 'I didn't think it was important' or 'I didn't want to,' something like that, well, they're going to think 'If he didn't think college is important, how's he going to think his job's important.' So I think it's important to go to college."

When asked what his new school and the ACOT program meant to him, Billy pondered a moment and then beamed, "It means, you can do it!"

We Can Do It! Or Can We?

Relative to the sixteen thousand school districts across the nation, ACOT is a modest effort. Through it, however, we have had a chance to demonstrate in a variety of schools that children and teachers can work differently and more effectively. The project has shown that technology is an engaging medium for student thought and collaboration. It has shown that the smart use of technology can increase student academic performance and support the acquisition of a whole new set of twenty-first-century competencies. Above all, ACOT has demonstrated that technology plays a catalytic role in opening the minds of teachers to new ideas about children, learning, and their own role in the education process. The inertia of schooling as we have known it, then, is not immutable. I am, however, uneasy as I look ahead to the next ten years. If we decide as a society to make a determined effort to modernize our schools through the addition of technology, the bits and wire part will be easy, just as it proved to be in ACOT's first ten years. It is our will as a society to apply and scale what we know about better learning that has me most troubled.

As I look to the next decade of technology in education, I see incredible potential. Portable devices could free children from the desk top, allowing them to capture data in their world, to reach out and ask questions of teachers and mentors when and where they need guidance and support. Connectivity through cable systems, satellites, or phone lines will offer the chance to expand our sense of learning community. Schools will remain an important center for learning, but they can be joined to information- and expertise-rich places like museums, zoos, libraries, community organizations, and homes. Parents may have an unprecedented opportunity to participate in their children's education through the use of technology.

The Internet, a meta computer in a way, and a vast communications system, is to today's schools what the microcomputer was in 1985 when the ACOT project began. It is *the* new technology that pundits now say will change the way we go about learning in the twenty-first century. Anyone who has even begun to tap the Net understands that words like vast, enormous, awesome, or revolutionary are, in this case, accurately descriptive and not exaggerations. But words like quirky, difficult, time consuming, and scary are also apt. The rate at which the Internet is evolving is just short of unimaginable. The Internet's World Wide Web makes more current information available on more topics to more people than anything in human history. It is rapidly transforming from a publishing system into a media- and information-rich communication and collaboration system. If we are accurate in our assessment that learning is fundamentally an active, social, and creative process, then the Web can play a major role as the avenue for learning. It can be used to support inquiry, information access, communication with experts, critical analysis of information, composition with varied media, and local and global collaboration among students. Finally, it provides a means for students to publish their work. They can reach audiences that are interested in their efforts, that can provide feedback, and that value student productions. Schoolwork, then, becomes real work. The opportunities it provides and the issues it raises should be the focus of much research in the coming decade.

My enthusiasm for this bright technology future is tempered by the knowledge that progress at school reform, improvement, or restructuring is painfully slow. In fact, we seem to take as many steps backward as forward. We know that since 1972, schools have showed a steady decline in the very kinds of classroom methods that engage children, with or without technology, like discussion, essay and theme writing, projects, and laboratory work.[11] Students' instructional diets consist overwhelmingly of drill and practice focused on literacy and computation skills. Yet a new report from the Public Agenda Foundation shows parents are still most concerned with the education basics.[12] Apparently, the recommendation of the SCANS report to extend the definition of educational basics to include twenty-first-century work skills and technology has not penetrated public opinion. Seventy percent of the parents who participated in the Public Agenda Foundation's focus groups indicated that they would be concerned if their children's pursuit of excellence in school interfered with their participation in social activities. Important large-scale experiments, like California's attempt to enhance the state assessment system for schools, are dropped for budgetary and political reasons. The debate over the merits of even having a federal Department of Education has begun, again. As a society, we seem unable to engage all the stakeholders in a sustained and informed conversation about our schools and build the necessary consensus to reform them.

All of this is happening when we know that the stakes are very high. The Carnegie Council on Adolescent Development, for example, reported that half of America's children between the ages of ten and seventeen engage in behaviors that place them in serious risk of alienation from society, even of death. The report clearly links school failure with the high risk behaviors. The Carnegie Council concluded: "The pervasiveness of intellectual underdevelopment strikes at the heart of our nation's future prosperity. . . . For many young children, the American dream ends with the recognition that they are not wanted and are of little value in this society.[13]

Technology is only the vehicle we may ride as we work to engage more children in the excitement and life-enhancing experience of learning. We will drive along a road that is paved by our public, collective will to build a modern, equitable, effective education system. Will it be a superhighway? Or a bumpy road of cobblestones—outmoded teaching strategies, low standards, out-of-date texts, limited assessment systems, and overburdened agendas? Will the drivers—the teachers—be the best they can be, supported with essential training and staff development? Will the passengers—the students—remain alienated or will the road take them to a new and challenging terrain, one on which they know they can build their futures? This is a democracy. We have a choice.

Notes

1. Cuban, L. (1990). Reforming again, again, and again. *Educational Researcher, 19*(1), 3–13.

2. Lortie, D. C. (1975). *Schoolteacher.* Chicago: University of Chicago Press.

3. Baker, E. L., Herman, J. L., & Gearhart, M. (1989). *The ACOT report card: Effects on complex performance and attitude.* Paper presented at the annual meeting of the American Educational Research Association, San Francisco.

4. Memphis Public Schools. (1987). "ACOT: Right here in Memphis." District newsletter, pp. 1–4.

5. Hiebert, E. (1987). *Report on the writing program at ACOT's Cupertino site.* Unpublished manuscript.

6. Similar results have since been reported in other projects with significant deployment of technology. Trends indicate 10 percent to 15 percent increases in achievement scores and 30 percent gains in student productivity when computers are routinely used in instruction. See Kulik, J. A., & Kulik, C.-L. (1991). *Effectiveness of computer-based instruction: An updated analysis.* Ann Arbor: Center for Research on Learning and Teaching, University of Michigan; Kulik, J. A., Kulik, C.-L., & Bangert-Drowns, R. L. (1985). Effectiveness of computer-based education in elementary schools. *Computers in Human Behavior, 1,* 59–74; and Bangert-Drowns, R. L., Kulik, J. A., & Kulik, C.-L. (1985). Effectiveness of computer-based education in secondary schools. *Journal of Computer-Based Instruction, 12*(3), 59–68.

7. The 1991 ACOT graduating class was not a technical random sample of West High School students. We believe, however, that it was representative of the school as a whole. The magnitude of difference between the ACOT students' performance and that of their peers is still provocative. Moreover, we have seen similar outcomes in each graduating cohort since 1991.

8. Tierney, R. J., Kieffer, R. D., Stowell, L., Desai, L. E., Whalin, K., & Moss, A. G. (1992). *Computer acquisition: A longitudinal study of the influence of high computer access on students' thinking, learning, and interactions.* ACOT Report Number 16. Cupertino, CA: Apple Computer.

9. Secretary's Commission on Achieving Necessary Skills. (1991). *What work requires of schools: A SCANS report for America 2000.* Washington, DC: U.S. Department of Labor.

10. Billy James is a pseudonym.

11. Darling-Hammond, L. (1990). Achieving our goals: Superficial or structural reforms. *Phi Delta Kappan, 72*(4), 286.

12. Public Agenda Foundation. (1994). *Assignment incomplete: The unfinished business of school reform.* New York: Author.

13. Carnegie Council on Adolescent Development. (1989). *Turning points: Preparing American youth for the 21st century.* New York: Author, pp. 27–28.

3

Dilemmas

Jan Hawkins

I think that educational technology is most interesting reflected in the sense that people make of it. In the case of education in the 1990s, it is most interesting in light of current dilemmas about teaching and learning. In spite of the fact that digital technology in education has a short history and a long future, I begin by reflecting on the recent past. So, this chapter will get to technology in a leisurely way, toward its end.

Education reform efforts have arisen and subsided a number of times over the last decades. The most recent ones have, among other things, tried to rework the deep-rooted transmission model of education. This is not just a struggle about means; it is also a struggle about the ends of education. While the challenges can be seen only imperfectly, it seems to me that at this point three major disappointments shape the challenges.

Disappointments

If we desire to educate all students to be thinkers and interpreters and open-minded colleagues, the way we have gone about it so far has been generally disappointing.

At the end of the twentieth century, at least three big disappointments are embedded in the background of many conversations about education. Insights underlying the disappointments are not, for the most part, new. John Dewey, for example, argued for a form of inquiry-based education at the beginning of this century, with only a narrow continuing thread of success across these decades. But old insights converge in a new way as the country now strives for changes in educational outcomes on a grand palette.

The first disappointment, I think, is that people don't learn much, or much of lasting use and significance, solely through direct transmission of information from persons or texts or technologies to learners. People seldom learn much in relatively silent herds organized for group absorption and fragmented exercise. The lecture needs to be reconceived as an art and, rather than dominating instruction as the premiere mode for transmission of knowledge, incorporated for its particular value into an expanded teaching repertoire.

Instruction, as we have individually and classically known it in our schools, is ineffective for the development of thoughtful persons. Certain bits and pieces of knowledge, like multiplication tables, are nicely acquired through rote or isolated exercises. I believe that for the most part people don't learn to use these bits well, or to grasp ideas that are at their root, or to alter their naive conceptions through passive receipt of information and decontextualized exercises.

We believe we know more now about how people learn well. Some features of successful learning environments include: thoughtful active engagement in meaningful tasks; being well-known by teachers and others; intense coaching that helps people to recognize their own commitments and preconceptions; carefully designed and sustained collaborative interactions among small groups of learners and experts; participation in cultures of practice; being inspired by or drawn into new ways of thinking; and ready access to many and varied resources.

In general, the strategy to distill the essences of discipline-based knowledge developed over centuries, to sequence this material over days and years in curricula, and to deliver it to large groups of students does not work for serious command of knowledge. This appears true not only for sophisticated material, but also for the basics like reading and elementary mathematics. A transmittal notion of education is buried in all of us, no matter how reformed, if only because we experienced it. And it is disappointing to realize that this efficient method is not sufficient. Traditional instruction formed us all.

The second disappointment, I think, is that the strategy of model development and dissemination—that is, designing and implementing new models of education in a few places and then reproducing them—does not work at all well for broad change in schooling.[1] There have been, and continue to be, wonderful schools and programs that are effective for educating thoughtful students. Focusing on delivering such models directly by distilling their features, creating wonderful materials, designing transmission programs for teachers and administrators, or attacking the assessment system, all prove frustratingly slow or inadequate in isolation. What are the alternatives to this sensible strategy of perfecting, proving, and transmitting?

The third disappointment, more recent and of seemingly less consequence, is that technology has more or less failed in its promise of the early 1980s to make, if not an educational revolution, at least serious innovation in practices. The introduction of microcomputers, artificial intelligence coupled with learning research, multimedia systems, and other technical advances were seen by many as means to solve formerly intractable problems. Many educators thought that newly introduced technologies would lead to individualized learning, more intense and faster learning through new cognitive tools, and emphasis on small-group and individual inquiry over lecture and rote exercises. Despite some wonderful materials and good classroom or school models, the technologies were far more commonly appropriated to the ways things are traditionally done. Dynamic technology-enhanced curriculum materials become rote exercises in the hands of those unable to exploit them well. Individualized education becomes mind-dulling drill when systems are built on distill-and-deliver ideas about learning. There are now echoes of the technology-driven promises for an education revolution in the recent dazzle of telecommunications, often discussed in terms of access to everything, and revolutionizing relationships. One conjecture is that schools have simply not yet had *enough* technology, or sufficiently powerful and connected technology to realize serious change. But this is at best only part of the problem.

Beneath the disappointments that digital and visual technologies themselves did not act as powerfully as anticipated is, I think, a deeper disappointment. The tacit and achingly optimistic American belief that wonderful technologies will make things better has run into rough water. The efforts to engineer broad change in education through designing the best materials, technologies, and programs have proved disappointing in many specific cases. It has proved disappointing in the general strategy beyond the particular technologies involved. Perfecting and replicating a product has not been an adequate conceptual framework for shaping change in this arena. If we can't put the essences into objects and use them to engineer systemic advance, how can such national change be conceived?

New Challenges

So, what are some ways to facilitate the transformation that is needed? Before exploring a few ways that digital technologies might play some role, I want to first explore the ways in which these technologies create new challenges, and increase the tensions between old and new ways of doing education.

Beyond educating students better in things-well-known, the late twentieth century brings new pressures to the conception and design of education. I will mention two that I believe are especially important.

Knowing in the Twentieth Century: Grappling with Complexity

Traditional schooling specifies goals of competence in literacies and discipline-based content. But throughout the twentieth century, many of the disciplines have been rattled in their assumptions about the nature of understanding. These problems of epistemology and method have not yet much affected K–12 education. Students are being ill prepared to handle the complexity and uncertainty they will confront each day in their lives and workplaces, in framing problems, making decisions, and understanding their worlds.[2]

A general view of the nature of knowledge developing throughout the twentieth century poses a key dilemma to schools. The unprecedented reach provided by information technologies into vast databases and around the world will eventually make it unavoidable.

This dilemma tends to be mistakenly posed as the problem of the explosion of the quantity of information now available and accelerating—too much for anyone to wrap her arms around. But the bigger issue for learning is one of *complexity*. There are many perspectives on much of the material students work with in school, certainly the most important ones. There always have been. But the broader intellectual context of the late twentieth century converges with increasing access to more stuff and places a new challenge squarely in classrooms. Students are awakening to the many histories, not just the one interpretation provided as an immutable set of facts; the many readings of a text as conversations between reader and author; significant scientific advances understood as revolutionary changes in interpretation and vision, not accretion of data; and different ways of knowing that can separate cultures, current and historical. This means making the difficult adjustment to chronic uncertainty. Because of changes in theory, methodologies, and framing of problems, both evidence and procedures for warranting evidence undergo constant tinkering.

Technology accelerates and popularizes this complexity. It is not limited to the upper reaches of the academy, but touches people in their daily lives. Images and ideas from around the world flash by on television screens, and through the new communications pipelines now snaking into homes. People experience competing perspectives, confront intractable problems, encounter conflicting facts, opinions, and solutions, experience competing demands for attention and authority. It is not necessary to seek this out; it is part of mundane business. And technology provides increasingly sophisticated tools for manipulating and representing complexity to ordinary people (for example, hypertext and hypermedia, mathematical tools, and visualization tools). Digital technologies have once again changed the relationships between reality and representation; for example, imaging technologies mean we can no longer be assured that what looks like a photograph is really a direct recording of light on film. Students must learn to read a complex array of representations, to use the tools well, to command them for their work and their lives. These technologies allow students to get closer to authentic complexity much earlier, demanding learning environments that help.

Beyond the tradition of instructing the fixed facts of disciplines and received knowledge, schools must now enable students to appreciate the complexities that bathe them—to develop sophisticated interpretation skills, tolerance for ambiguity and uncertainty, an appetite for difficult problems, and measured thoughtfulness in pursuit of solution. This requires creating habits of seeking out various perspectives and consulting multiple disciplines for any big question. It requires facility with the tools that help to find and make sense of evidence. It requires openness to conversation as a way to challenge one's assumptions, and a habit of remaining interested in new ways of conceiving of things. This, too, is not new, only more urgent.

In Each Other's Company

A second big challenge is to educate for the social complexity of the current world. We have always existed in diversity, nationally and globally. But the consequences of this, and the kind of education required for the perspectives, open-mindedness, and diplomacy to thrive in each other's company has not been common. Today's students must function in an increasingly connected globe that is created through media, interactive communications, interlaced economies, and technologies of travel. Schools need to support students who bring diverse perspectives to school; they will also need to help students grapple with their own and their fellows' otherness, to imagine their ways into other views.

Transitional Tensions

This is, we hope, a transition time in the development of education. Along with the disappointments and the new challenges, possibilities have grown like shoots, some from seeds dormant for decades. But there are many tensions as people try to keep their bearings in the course of redesign. A discussion of some of them follows.

Standards and Project-Based, Student-Centered Pedagogy

In light of the disappointments about the effectiveness of schooling and traditions of locally defined goals with room to differ, a great deal of effort has recently gone into defining common standards for learning in several of the disciplines. These are efforts to get everybody on the same page, to define rigorous standards for all students so that the extreme variability in expectations and outcomes for different schools can be brought into line. There is often tacit tension between these efforts to reach national or state consensus on outcomes and the belief that more effective education features highly individualized curriculum created and adapted for the individual and local needs of students.

The creation of standards can be seen as an effort to preserve what is valuable about the traditional strategy to distill the essences of disciplines as bases for the design of education. What should we all know? This can also serve as a strategy to address the second disappointment, that creation and delivery of models for change are not especially effective. If standards can act as blueprints, then everyone can build houses of their own materials. One problem with standards that depend on a process of dissemination-through-abstraction is that, like students, few adults learn well in this environment. Adults also need to engage in exploring and judging the specifics of concrete, extensive, and complicated materials to develop full understanding.

Thus, a tension exists between the need for standards that assure us there are common rigorous criteria and the relatively recent urge to eliminate *standardization* from the design of education in favor of complex and meaningful project-based tasks. If students learn best through in-depth engagement in meaningful tasks, then curriculum in each school is likely to be highly original. Project-based or problem-based learning tends to have too many messy strands to have much more than a compliance relationship with the grid of knowledge and skills associated with standards. The need for consensus to guide and to assure and the need for local generativity to foster real learning, for both students and adults, creates tensions that are not easily resolved.

Assessment for What?

A second tension follows naturally from the first. In light of the first disappointment, the ways in which student learning has been assessed for decades have been generally discredited. It is not that the ubiquitous tests are technically inadequate, but rather that many educators, and increasingly the general public as well, believe that these assessments do not give us the most important information about students' development. Considerable effort has been devoted to creating new ways to assess understanding. Among these, performance and portfolio approaches have gained favor in that they are believed to measure complex understanding and flexible use of knowledge. These new forms of assessment have proved to be technically more difficult and soberingly more expensive than was hoped. And they have also proved to be both conceptually and emotionally difficult to assimilate.

As a culture we are deeply wedded to number when it comes to grasping the meaning of measurements. Mathematics has had a deep effect. There is a tension between what these new forms of assessment measure and how they measure it on the one hand and our deep sense of how information about knowledge should be represented on the other. We are used to a crisp, clear, composite number (or letter) that assures, or alternatively worries, us about the ability and accomplishment of an individual student. A single grade that summarizes a year's work, an IQ score that flaunts or places a ceiling on learning potential, an SAT score that summarizes the accomplishments of a childhood; all have been deeply meaningful and emotionally powerful representations of ourselves. It is difficult to let go of symbols that have been so potent for knowing about our peers, ourselves, and our children.

The new forms of assessment ask that we transfer our grip on old symbols to new kinds of representations of accomplishment like rubrics, narratives, sequences of work in portfolios, and records of performances in specific contexts. Human judgments are a central feature bringing to the surface the difficult problems of bias and reduced reliability. The new forms shatter the myth of assessment as a distant, technical processing of objective information. Judgment occurs at the point of performance rather than in the design and vetting of test items. The representations of performance in the new assessments are more complex than single numbers. This asks not only that new symbols be embraced but also that different views of human learning and intelligence be taken. The new measures assume that learning is contextual, effortful, and developmental rather than fixed and revealed. The tension can be seen, for example, in those conversations where people embrace the new approaches yet ask, "What's her score?"

Professional Development, Community, and Distributed Teaching

One of the key aspects of educational change is helping teachers and administrators to alter the way they do their jobs. In light of the disappointments, both with respect to the nature of learning and the integration of technologies, resources are being allocated for teacher training. Traditionally, training experiences are short, circumscribed workshops to introduce new materials or a new practice.

Although schools of education that prepare young people to be teachers are currently little altered to reflect changed ideas about effective education, we are asking teachers to do radically re-designed jobs. Teachers are being asked to facilitate learning rather than deliver information, organize collaborative learning rather than competition, create effective small groups rather than whole-class instruction, assess complex development rather than administer tests, and command subject-matter knowledge in ways not traditionally required of this profession. More radically, in future years teaching is likely to be a distributed profession, involving a variety of adults and resources in different locations rather than one or two individuals in an isolated classroom.

A gap has arisen between the substantial changes in practice that are being asked of the teaching profession and the means and resources that are thus far available to address these changes. To provide even minimal support for teachers during the change process would require: intensive experiences that allow them to be immersed in the new ideas and approaches, including hands-on practice with the activities they will be asking of their students; follow-up mentoring for at least two years that focuses on problems that arise as they try things in their own circumstances; reflective dialogue with others who are doing the same job; and regular opportunities to see how other people and schools work. Do we really mean that we want a profession to change? The tension between how professional development is now structured and financed, and the conditions that are actually required to make substantial change, must be resolved.

Resources: Community and Global

Schooling in the United States for the last several decades has taken place in communities, but largely isolated from the dailiness of activities and resources in those communities. The occasional field trip or outside visitor highlights the relative isolation by the specialness of these occasions and the preparation they require. The materials available to teachers and students have, in many places, been dominated by textbooks, with some hands-on materials in the early grades and in science. Visit a richly appointed elementary school in the morning, and a high school in the afternoon, and the textbook-heavy passive bias of later education is palpable. In far too many schools, especially urban ones, libraries either have been closed for budgetary reasons or never existed in the first place.

The rapidly changing structure of telecommunications has been promised to change this, bringing a wealth and diversity of resources rapidly into schools. It is a vision now familiar to all of us through the popular press—futuristic stories imagine students cruising the Net and trolling for information they need for their projects, communicating with other students and with expert adults both in their communities and around the world. They will be able to link their homes with their schools, and with information resources whenever and wherever they are needed.

In addition to support from telecommunications, it is often envisioned that there will be substantially more community involvement in education. Beyond the occasional classroom visit from an expert or community member, the notion of distributed teaching enlists many more people in the education of children than the single teacher or cluster of teachers that is now the norm. This is now most frequently seen in projects that connect classrooms with scientists who can apply disciplinary expertise to students' queries, and in a few cases, to mentor students.

Tensions arise with the embodiment of this vision. Most classrooms and schools are soberingly resource poor for the kind of education that is being supposed. There are insufficient quantities, diversity, and richness of materials to support an education primarily focused on intensive student work. Beyond supplying more stuff, do we *really* mean that we want substantial community and global involvement? That requires a different kind of commitment than mere access, and raises many new challenges.

First, if more resources are to make a substantial difference, we need to think about the problem not as one of only access, but of complexity. For students to go beyond cruising and finding to interpreting and transforming, supportive environments and tools need to be created. This means environments that encourage students to query, consider, find patterns, and interpret the information they find in relation to the ideas and problems they bring to the encounters. Far too little attention has yet been paid to this dimension.

Second, are we going to make enough good stuff freely available? Beyond the now popular vision lies an ocean of expensive digitization. While many libraries are now on line, it is mostly their skeletons rather than their flesh that we find: catalogues of materials rather than the texts or images themselves. Slices of some library collections are subjects of current experimentation; to offer students deep browsing of entire libraries is an enormous step. The situation is similar for museums. While there is considerable desire to make our cultural collections widely available, it is a daunting task to do so. The problem of making lots of stuff available to students—and making it free for education—will require considerable ingenuity and resources to solve.

Third, there is a tension around making lots of stuff available to students that includes vetting its quality, appropriateness, and decency. Our traditional system of relatively closed classrooms, high levels of approval required for curriculum acquisition, and the editorial system of the existing education publishing industry has effectively screened materials that make it into classrooms. A more inquiry-driven educational model chafes at the intellectual limits of the closed classroom; on-line schools combined with the public-access design of the Net detour around the traditional editorial processes. Do we really mean we want relatively free access to materials for students? This would require equipping them much more rigorously with critical abilities to interpret and judge.

Fourth, distributed teaching means that more adults need to be equipped to participate appropriately in the educational process. As many have found, simply recruiting an expert to help with a science project is far from sufficient. It takes thought and effort to design methods to educate collaborating adults. And how can participation in education become a small but legitimate aspect of professional lives?

Finally, there is something disturbingly familiar about the current vision of on-line resources. It has some of the quality of the early arguments for technology revolutionizing education: if we just get the materials right, then substantial changes will naturally follow. It is a familiar American road, a belief that wonderful curriculum, or the engineering of technology, is the fundamental key to change. Access to all the resources will prove important but insufficient (and it remains to be seen just what the actual scope of resources will be, and how freely they will be distributed). They will be most powerful in combination with commitments to changing the goals (tinkering, thinking, interpreting, critical use), changing the tools (supports for considering and manipulating, not simply acquiring), and changing the education practices.

Questions and Opportunities

In light of the disappointments and tensions, what are possible roles for technologies in contributing to resolution? A fundamental issue is the conceptual stance we take toward technologies now; to be used to advantage, they are neither separate nor neutral. Their design and integration are intimately linked to particular conceptions of education; creation and deployment must be more deliberate in relation to the broader, more difficult problems of change.

Here are some conjectures about the contributions technologies might make to education.

Models and Scale-Up

The strategy of perfecting models, distilling key features, and reproduction is seldom satisfying. It appears that people in different locales benefit from these models as images, yet need to interpret how new ideas and approaches make sense in their own heads and their local systems. Conditions that help people take their own small steps of invention appear to characterize places and projects where changes take root. Sustained reflection and critical conversation appear to be basic conditions for reframing, reseeing, and adapting new approaches. There is little tradition of this kind of professional culture and exchange among education practitioners in this country. One important role for technologies is as backbone for an invigorated, vibrant professional community among educators. This will not happen, however, without considerable effort to design the technologies and the social structure of their use with this objective made explicit.

Complexity

As with distribution of models, the distillation and sequencing of information in curricula in order to reproduce it in lockstep herds of learners has proved inadequate. While complex, meaningful tasks are now popularly regarded as a better way, the problems associated with effective and sustained use of this difficult and less-practiced approach in most schools are far from solved. Much more material in much greater depth must be efficiently available to teachers and students. Digitized information flowing through cables and fibers may be the beginning of a solution. But it is much more difficult to develop and implement the supporting tools and conditions that will enable students to interpret, judge, and manipulate the information that flows to them. Well-designed computational tools that support these skills of inquiry and interpretation must be infused into the information wilderness as it comes on line. Beyond intelligent agents as information finders, students need sensemaking supports that enable them to become intelligent pathfinders. While there are examples of designs for these goals, the problem has barely begun to be solved.

Distributed Teaching and Learning

Adults who view knowledge as complex and open to interpretation are fundamentally needed to support new education practices. The best information resources and inquiry tools are still only technology and thus, in themselves, insufficient. While teachers' command of foundational knowledge will remain key, broader and deeper pedagogical repertoires are required to support learning for all students; especially when the teaching model is based on distributed resources. Distributed notions of teaching are now being explored that go beyond teaching teams in a single school to teams of teachers, experts, and student collaborators distributed across a country or, in some cases, the world.

Technological support is considered key to more broadly distributed teaching, particularly as text and visual communications capacities become increasingly available in coming years. Considerably more effort needs to be devoted to the social circumstances of distributed teaching. Who are the teachers? How are many trained? What are their responsibilities and obligations? What is the structure of activities that distributed participants do together? How are more broadly distributed resources to be designed so that they embody an interpretive stance toward knowledge? How can the personal connections that are hallmarks of effective education be realized? How are the distributed responsibilities and sustained collaborative work to be coordinated and managed?

New Forms of Assessment

Assessment procedures may appear to be a small and bothersome element of fundamentally reconceived education. But beyond a local and national accounting system of the intellectual debits and credits of students' progress, methods of assessment provide us with the terms, images, and emotions of what it is important to know. The kinds of representations and records that constitute the core of any assessment system fundamentally define the real stance toward knowledge that is in effect. Representations of student progress that are complex yet manageable are essential if we are to create a system in which the pedagogy is not in tacit conflict with the accounting. Likewise, records that respect complexity are essential for teachers to guide student learning in a system that is distributed.

Technologies have key roles to play. Those roles are only beginning to be explored. Currently, the critical roles for technology involve modeling and scaling up, complexity of knowledge, distributed teaching and learning, and new procedures for assessment. All of these will be necessary to help us to do the fundamental changing of our minds and schools.

Notes

1. Tyack, D., & Cuban, L. (1995). *Tinkering toward utopia*. Cambridge, MA: Harvard University Press; McLaughlin, M. W., & Talbert, J. (1993). *Contexts that matter for teaching and learning: Strategic opportunities for meeting the nation's goals*. Stanford, CA: Center for the Context of Secondary School Teaching; McLaughlin, M. (1976). Implementation as mutual adaptation: Change in classroom organization. *Teachers College Record, 77*, 342–343.

2. Toulmin, S. (1990). *Cosmopolis*. Chicago: University of Chicago Press. Offers a concise argument about the historical roots of the current climate of understanding.

4

Whither Technology and Schools?

Collected Thoughts on the Last and Next Quarter Centuries

Allan Collins

I slipped by accident into thinking about technology and education. Jaime Carbonell Sr. lured me into working on his SCHOLAR system, which was an attempt to apply Ross Quillian's idea of semantic networks to education. On that project, I started studying how human tutors carry on dialogues with students in order to embed their strategies in SCHOLAR. Then I tried to build my own system, WHY, that incorporated the best strategies of inquiry teachers. Eventually I abandoned building systems altogether and simply tried to understand how our best teachers teach. I even became reckless enough, with the help of Apple Classrooms of Tomorrow (ACOT), to try to teach fifth and sixth graders science using computers. Chastened, I now just think about how best to use computers for education, and I teach graduate students how to think about designing learning environments. So, herein I will recount what I think I have learned about what technology portends for the future of education during my journey of over a quarter century working in the field.

From ICAI to ITS to ILE

Carbonell called the SCHOLAR system an Intelligent Computer-Aided Instruction (ICAI) system to distinguish it from all the

---

Note: I thank Katerine Bielaczyc, Charles Fisher, Paul Horwitz, and John Richards for their comments on an earlier draft of this chapter.

computer-aided instruction systems, such as Plato and TICCIT, up to that time (circa 1970). SCHOLAR was intelligent in that it had knowledge of South American geography stored in a semantic network, which it used to answer student questions, to pose questions to students, and to evaluate their answers. The system took the initiative in asking students questions, much like a human tutor, but it could be interrupted at any time if the student asked a question. The tutorial dialogue took place in typed English, and the system had a primitive system for understanding and generating text, based on its semantic network. A second version of SCHOLAR was developed for an early text-editing system called NLS, developed at SRI by Doug Englebart. NLS-SCHOLAR included a simulation of the NLS system, tutorials on how to use different commands in NLS, and tasks for the student to carry out in the NLS simulator, together with its semantic network and language understanding capabilities.

Carbonell died in 1973, but not before he had recruited John Seely Brown to come to BBN Corporation, where we worked. Brown brought along Richard Burton and Alan Bell, and the three of them launched into the development of Sophie, an ICAI system for teaching electronic troubleshooting. Like NLS-SCHOLAR, Sophie had a simulator that allowed it to evaluate student hypotheses, and a semantic network that allowed it to answer student questions. But it also had a variety of heuristic strategies for evaluating student hypotheses and requests for tests, together with a very sophisticated language understanding system, based on a semantic grammar that Burton developed. Sophie was clearly one of the high points of ICAI history.

Around 1980, Brown started referring to these kinds of systems as Intelligent Tutoring Systems (ITSs). The emphasis on tutoring had been there from the start, but the name change highlighted the idea of personalized dialogue and the building up of a model of the student. SCHOLAR had a primitive model of the student in that it marked in its semantic network what the student had answered correctly, or not known when asked, or had asked about earlier. This was used to guide its questioning, and in a later version it tried to estimate the sophistication of the student and gear the level of difficulty accordingly. Sophie had a much more sophisticated model of the student that could remember the various tests that had been performed on the circuit and could deduce from that information what the student should be able to figure out about the circuit. This kind of inference was used to personalize the responses and feedback given the student.

The high points of student modeling in ITS history probably were the West coaching system and the Debuggy system that Burton and Brown developed (which may have provoked the name change to Intelligent Tutoring Systems). West was a coaching system built by Burton and Brown for the Plato game, How the West Was Won. The Plato game is modeled on Chutes and Ladders. The players rotate three spinners and have to take the three numbers that turn up on the spinners and form them into an arithmetic expression by using $+$, $-$, $*$, $/$, and appropriate parentheses—and then specify the value of the expression. So, for example, if a player gets a 1, 3, and 4 on the spinners, the numbers might form the expression $(1+3)*4 = 16$, allowing a forward move of sixteen spaces. A player who lands on a town (towns occur every ten spaces) moves forward to the next town. One who lands on a chute slides to the end of the chute. And landing on an opponent sends the opponent back two towns. The optimal strategy is to figure out all the possible moves you might make and take the one that puts you farthest ahead of your opponent or gets you to the end. But students do not use this strategy; they are much more likely to lock onto a strategy like adding the two smallest numbers and multiplying by the largest. They do not learn much from following such a rigid strategy.

The West coach analyzed students' moves in terms of the optimal strategy I described above and could rate the moves with respect to that strategy. The West coach watched to see if the students consistently followed a less-than-optimal strategy, such as not taking opportunities to land on a town or chute or opponent when such a move was very advantageous to them. If the West coach saw such a pattern, it would intervene at an opportune time, when the student's move was far from optimal, and it would point out how the student could have done much better. It then would give the student a chance to take the move over. West was a sophisticated coaching system that could diagnose which less-than-optimal strategies students were using.

Debuggy was even more complicated. It was developed to diagnose systematic errors that students make in applying addition and subtraction algorithms. For example, some students who do not know how to borrow will always subtract the smaller digit from the larger digit in a column. If faced with a problem like 423 minus 381, they will come up with the answer 162 when they follow their strategy perfectly. But of course they make slips, or occasional errors, just like the rest of us. Burton and Brown analyzed a huge corpus of arithmetic tests and identified over a hundred such systematic error strategies that students make. Debuggy was designed to pose problems to students in order to identify whether they were using one of these buggy strategies. The system was designed to identify such strategies even when students make a lot of slips as well. So it had to be quite sophisticated, particularly since many of the buggy strategies are slight variants of each other.

In 1978, Brown and Burton deserted BBN for the Xerox Palo Alto Research Center, but tutoring systems lived on at BBN. Albert Stevens and Bruce Roberts developed STEAMER, which was designed to help Navy seamen learn how to shut down shipboard steam plants under different conditions. These steam plants sometimes blow up, so it is good to practice in a safe environment. There were several new ideas in STEAMER. One was the notion of a visual simulation, where you could see what happens inside different pipes as you turn valves on and off. Another was the notion that the learner interacts with the system by clicking on visual icons, rather than by natural language. A third was the notion of a conceptual model of the system as opposed to a physical model. The Navy has a physical steam plant simulator, but it fills two rooms (like the real thing) and takes a crew of eight to operate it. STEAMER instead let a single person manipulate the system in layers; at the top was a system overview, and individual subsystems could be controlled by going down a level. This gave the learner a conceptual view of the system that the physical simulation did not provide.

A later system, called Quest, developed by Barbara White and John Frederiksen, was designed like Sophie to teach troubleshooting. In addition to presenting a visual model of the circuit, the system could explain both the behavior of a circuit and an optimal troubleshooting strategy for the learner using a voice synthesizer. Its simulation used the kind of qualitative simulation that had been developed in artificial intelligence by Johan De Kleer and others. In Quest's simulation, changes in voltage and current were passed along through different elements in a circuit, following qualitative rules for different elements when arranged in parallel or serial configurations. Furthermore, it systematically structured the problems the student faced, so that students would develop a first-order model of troubleshooting, followed in sequence by more and more sophisticated models, incorporating different kinds of circuit structures and elements.

Outside of BBN, various tutoring systems have been developed by the likes of Elliot Soloway, Bill Clancey, John Anderson, Beverly Woolf, Alan Lesgold, Roger Schank, and their colleagues. When a group of these people decided to start a journal around 1990, they called it Interactive Learning Environments (ILE), which signals a further change in the focus of the field. The most important change is from *tutoring system* to *learning environment*. This reflects a change in control from teacher-centered to learner-centered education: the designer attempts to create environments where learners are put in new situations and given appropriate tools and supports to learn how to deal with those situations. It also reflects a change away from personalized tutoring to an environment where several people may be learning together. Finally, the name change reflects a deemphasis on putting intelligence into the system in favor of an emphasis on interaction with the learners.

In the 1970s, there was an emphasis on natural language understanding and student modeling, designed to individualize instruction. This emphasis has been gradually fading away. My assessment is that while these may be interesting research issues, they do not have much to do with good pedagogy. As Richard Burton—who built perhaps the most sophisticated natural language understanding system in Sophie—has said, he probably could have done just as well with menus from an educational point of view. Natural language understanding does not provide much advantage unless someone is learning a language, and when a system misunderstands the learner, it destroys whatever value natural language communication may have. Until there are off-the-shelf language-understanding systems available, natural language processing is not worth the effort.

Similarly, as I tried to recount, there was much effort devoted to building student models in the late 1970s. But the possibility of misdiagnosis is ever present, especially given the limited bandwidth for communication between the learner and the system. As Brown points out, some learners using West adopt the goal of getting the tutor to talk to them. But whenever the goals of learners are different from the goals assumed by the system, there will be a mismatch between what the system does and what is appropriate. Furthermore, studies of human tutors reveal that for the most part they do not develop elaborate student models. It turns out that effective teaching depends mainly on other things besides diagnosis of learners' misconceptions. For example, if a tutoring system provides scaffolding when the student gets in trouble, the system does not need to know why the student is in trouble, it just needs to know what to do to get out of trouble. So like natural language processing, deep student modeling turns out not to be worth the effort involved. There does not need to be a lot of intelligence in the system, just in the design of the system.

If language processing and student modeling are fading away, then what is left? My answer is a list of characteristics of interactive learning environments that I think support learning in ways that schools can not easily provide: realistic situations, simulation, animation, voice, video, diverse knowledge sources, multiple representations, interaction, scaffolding, and reflection. Most of these characteristics evolved in the eras of ICAI and ITS, but they have become the bases for interactive learning environments. Let me elaborate on why they are important and how they affect learning.

Realistic situations force learners to figure out what to do. They may have to design a rocket ship, troubleshoot a malfunctioning circuit, or put together a television news program. They allow learners to take on roles in novel situations, something that is largely missing from school. The situations can be structured so that easier tasks arise before harder tasks.

Simulation is the key to letting learners explore new situations. Simulations allow learners to try out different courses of action, and provide flexibility to deal with many different situations.

Animation allows learners to see processes as they unfold—processes that they often cannot view otherwise. They can see blood circulating in the body or the center of mass of a set of objects changing as the objects move in space. That is, animation highlights important aspects of processes, downplays other aspects, and makes the invisible visible.

Voice can be used to explain what is happening and why at the same time as it happens. It can also present expert advice, hints, and cautions while learners are working on different tasks.

Video conveys what situations look like. It can help learners relate the abstractions of animation with real situations. It also provides rich contextual information essential for recognizing objects and places.

Diverse knowledge sources include digital resources available over electronic networks, adults who serve as mentors or experts, students from around the world, and the varieties of help that systems offer when students face difficulties they can not solve themselves. These systems provide a wide range of methods for bringing students the knowledge they need, when they need it.

Multiple representations refers to the ability of these systems to present different characterizations of the same situation or process simultaneously. This allows students to see how different representations capture different aspects of a situation or process, how the different representations are interrelated, and how the different representations change as the situation or process changes.

Interaction allows learners to see the consequences of their actions. In this way they have their expectations and predictions confirmed or disconfirmed, and can try different courses of action to evaluate their relative effectiveness. Interaction provides the feedback from the world that is crucial to all learning.

Scaffolding is the support the system gives learners in carrying out different activities in a problematic situation. This can take the form of structured or highly constrained tasks, hints when needed, buttons to click when help is needed, and so on. Scaffolding helps learners carry out tasks that are beyond their capabilities, until they are able to do them on their own. Scaffolding fades naturally as students need less support.

Reflection encourages learners to look back on their performance in a situation, and compare their performance to other performances, such as their own previous performances, and those of experts and others like themselves. Reflection can highlight the critical aspects of a performance and encourage learners to think about what makes for a good performance and how they might improve in the future.

These capabilities of interactive learning environments give them capabilities for teaching that human teachers do not have. Furthermore, they foster a constructivist approach to learning, where students, rather than teachers, do most of the work. Instead of modeling the design of systems on human tutors, we are learning how to design systems to exploit the strengths of the medium.

Why Technology Hasn't Revolutionized Schools

I have argued elsewhere that in the world outside of school, it is increasingly the case that communicating, calculating, and thinking are being carried out with powerful tools in technological environments. These are central concerns of education, and schools cannot ignore what is happening in the world outside. They simply cannot prepare people to live in a twenty-first-century world using nineteenth-century technology. My metaphor for educating children as schools now try to do, is that it is like trying to teach people to fly spaceships by helping them learn to ride bicycles. So why have the new technologies not revolutionized schools?

With the help of Denis Newman and ACOT in 1990, I tried teaching physical sciences to a fifth- and sixth-grade class for about twenty sessions each lasting two hours. The experiment took place at a public school in Cambridge with a very diverse student body. We had ten Mac IIs, a network linking them, a library of books about the physical world, and a variety of interactive learning environments, such as Physics Explorer and TableTop. Students were to investigate their questions about the physical world, such as why the moon appears to follow you around, how the earth formed, and why all the planets do not fall into the sun. They were supposed to write up their answers to such questions and put them together into a HyperCard stack for other kids to read.

One of the things I learned from this experience was how awkwardly current computer technology fits into schools. We first tried putting the Macs into the classroom where we were working. But they were too bulky for the space allotted to them by the teacher, so we could only fit seven of them in the classroom and even then there was not enough room for students to work together. It made it very difficult to figure out the logistics of who could use the computers when, and what the other students should do when they were off the computers. It did not support the kind of investigation that involves using a computer whenever you need it (even though our network allowed students to access their files from any computer). So after a while we moved the computers, along with the print materials, down to a lab room that was kept locked. This meant that the class had to move from their classroom whenever they wanted to work on their projects, which took time and caused confusion. In doing so they were leaving behind all the materials in their room: books, notebooks they had been keeping on their work, globes, and so on. It also meant they could not get to the computers except when a teacher was there to let them in. This arrangement seemed less than satisfactory from the point of view of someone like me, who was used to living in a technology-rich environment.

As a result of this experience, I think there are a host of outstanding problems with using technology in schools. Until these problems are solved, technology use will be rare in schools. As I suggested above, space is precious in most classrooms. Good teachers line the walls with student work and make lots of materials available to students in their classrooms. They will not turn over their classrooms to a lot of bulky machines—and proposed solutions, such as building computers into desks, are not likely to have widespread application. Nor will it be easy to manage a class in which the teacher must cope with a shortage of machines by arranging for simultaneous activities with some students working on computers and some not. Nor will many teachers be willing to take their students down to a computer lab, leaving all their classroom resources behind and having to compete for time with other teachers. Furthermore, students have to leave all their work at school when they go home, unless they have a computer at home or a portable they can take with them. But of course portables are likely to get broken, lost, or stolen on the way home from school. The unfortunate fact of life is that the design of the school and the design of the computer are not currently compatible with the widespread use of computers in schools.

Those are only a few of the problems that make schools and technology incompatible. Some of the problems will go away as a new generation of teachers who have grown up with the new technologies come into schools. But the structure and conception of school that evolved in the last century is quite incompatible with effective use of new technologies. The view of teaching as transmission of information from teachers to their students has little place for students using new technologies to accomplish meaningful tasks. The forty-five-minute period makes it difficult to accomplish anything substantial using technology. The curriculum specifies an overabundance of material that must be covered by the end of the year. The tests are designed to make sure that each individual student learns the knowledge and skills specified in the curriculum. All of these elements evolved together; if you change just one or two of them, the rest of the structure will work to change things back to the way they were. So the new technologies face a host of barriers that they must overcome. It will be a long and difficult struggle.

What the Educational Revolution May Be Like

Stephen Jay Gould is noted in biology for the theory of *punctuated equilibrium*. When you look at the fossil record, it turns out that there are long periods of stasis followed by rapid bursts of evolution. This view has replaced the earlier prevailing view of continuous evolutionary change. The bursts of evolutionary change in the punctuated equilibrium view are brought about by changes in the environment: for example, a meteor crashes to earth, two continents collide, or someone invents penicillin. After such dramatic events there are rapid changes in biological organisms until a new equilibrium is reached.

I believe that the evolution of social systems follows a similar pattern. For example, the modern corporation reached an equilibrium with the development of General Motors in the 1920s under Alfred P. Sloan. This model held sway in America until competition from Japanese corporations and changes in technology forced major restructuring in the 1980s (which is continuing to this day). Even General Motors has been forced to restructure itself, though it was the last of the large American automobile companies to do so. The buzzwords of total quality management, reengineering, and the virtual corporation reflect the many changes that are occurring in American corporations because of the changed environment they face. A similar change is occurring in the medical system, which for many years was based on fee-for-service personal physicians, an elite cadre of specialists, and medical insurance tied to the job. The medical system is under severe pressure, has already endured many changes, and is likely to keep evolving into the next century.

Likewise, a number of pressures have been combining to bring about change in the educational system. A major pressure arises from the introduction of technology into every aspect of life. Because technology can carry out the routine tasks in the world, there is less and less demand for people to do such tasks (such as bank tellers, typists, clerical workers, and production line workers) and more and more demand for people to do work that requires thinking and problem solving (such as analysts, information brokers, and technology support personnel). Even jobs that were once considered fairly routine (such as secretary and farmer) have come to require complex information processing.

But there are many other pressures converging on the education system in America that may jar it loose from the stasis reaching back to the early part of this century. Urban schools have become dangerous places where little learning goes on. With the aging of the population, taxpayers seem less and less willing to support public schools in the manner to which they have become accustomed. The teaching force has become unionized and is increasingly militant in the face of the pressures on the system. There is more concern over accountability of schools and general unhappiness with the use of multiple-choice testing to determine which students can go to prestigious colleges. Furthermore, it is clear that American students compare poorly to students in most other developed countries, which may make them less able to compete in a global economy. Finally, I should emphasize the unhappiness many people feel with the fact that the schools are not teaching students basic values, such as morality and responsibility. The public's sense of the failings of the American education system are only likely to increase as these pressures increase, making it likely that we are heading into a period of change in American education. But it is not at all clear what that change will be.

Let me offer a conjecture as to where all these pressures will lead. The thrust of new technology generally, particularly the communication technologies (computer networks, fax, voice mail, teleconferencing, and so on) is toward wider distribution of work and communities. This is readily apparent in the business world: companies are partnering with competitors all around the world, more and more meetings are taking place by teleconferencing, people are writing more and more documents with colleagues at remote sites, communication is more and more dependent on e-mail, on-line services, electronic bulletin boards, World Wide Web pages, and even multiuser environments, such as MUDs or MUSEs. Communities, which were once defined by location, are coming to be defined by common interests. My guess is that this growing redistribution of work and community will eventually encompass education.

What this means for K–12 education is that more of it will likely move to homes, churches, and other places outside of schools. It is estimated that home schooling as a movement has increased twentyfold over the last decade in America. What I sometimes refer to as my nightmare scenario is that the religious right will lead the way. In this scenario, they will develop a computer-based curriculum that incorporates the values they find missing from American schools. Then parents can get together with their friends in homes or church basements to educate their children using the new computer-based, interactive learning environments. This is the idea behind a charter school in Michigan that plans to support home schooling around the state. Once the religious right has figured out how to do this, then all the other groups that find the public schools subverting their values, such as the Black Muslims, the Catholic Church, the environmental movement, and even perhaps the labor movement and Native American groups, can make a similar investment in their children's education. That is, all the religious, ethnic, and political movements in America can create their own computer-based home-schooling curricula.

This scenario, if it comes true, will have profound effects on American education. A major goal of public education in America has been to integrate a diverse population into a common culture. If education is taken over by different interest groups, then that goal will be undermined. Furthermore, it will be the students whose parents care about their education that will be drawn out of the public school system, leaving behind the students whose parents are least interested in education. This will further reduce the public's desire to fund public education and draw many of the best students out of the system.

On the other hand, such a scenario may promote radical changes in a dysfunctional system. If there are successful models of student learning using new technologies, this would serve as a strong stimulus for change. Students in these settings would likely learn much more than their school-based counterparts for several reasons (as is currently the case with home-schooled children as measured by standardized test scores). First of all, the parents who choose computer-based out-of-school education will be those who care about education and they are likely to instill that concern in their children. Second, these students will not have to work against the strong peer culture that dominates most schools and that dismisses the value of education. Third, these students are free to pursue topics as long as they are interested and until they understand them. Fourth, the new technologies foster the kind of active, collaborative learning that constructivists advocate. Finally, such students will be forced to take responsibility for their own learning in a way that most schoolchildren are not. So if anything, education outside school is likely to enhance the learning of these children.

But what about the children left behind in the public schools? At first, I think things are likely to be worse for them as the schools lose many of their learning-oriented students and the base of support for public schools shrinks further. But eventually this will force the public schools to rethink their mission in the terms set by the out-of-school education movement. That is, they will be forced to think about how they can create smaller groupings of students who can work with new technologies under the guidance of paraprofessionals. Teachers will work with paraprofessionals much as doctors and dentists now work with large staffs. Ideally, this will bring more parents into the schools in the role of paraprofessionals, as Head Start has done. In any case, it is critical to the success of schooling in America to bring more adults into the schools to counter the dominance of the peer culture; an infusion of adults will make schools much safer places for learning to occur. These adults do not have to be subject-matter or teaching experts, but they do need to love children and care about their education. This will require a major change in the nature of schooling, but we have witnessed a similar change in health care over recent decades.

I do not know how education will change over the coming decades, but I am convinced that major changes will occur after eighty years of stasis. I have speculated on where the pressures are likely to lead, but I do not have much confidence in my predictions. I do not want to convey the impression that the changes I anticipate will be for the better. Many children, whose parents cannot afford computers and network connections, are likely to be ill served by the coming changes. Still, I think that the painful transition we are starting to go through will lead to a much more constructivist view of education and an emphasis on children taking more responsibility for their own education.

5

Hope and Joy in a Rational World

Kids, Learning, and Computers

Kristina Hooper Woolsey

Computers can mimic and stimulate thinking
They can enhance learning
They can provide storehouses of data
They bring an element of timing to interactions with
ideas
They encourage revision and communication
They enable individuals to collaborate remotely and to
form communities around ideas
They can change time and space constraints
They let us explore the behaviors of complex systems
They provide hope even with limited local expertise
They challenge us to be articulate, to model actions we
program
They encourage the development of a fluid and
sophisticated visual language
They offer us room to dream

These are some of the reasons computers are important for learning. They explain why I have spent so much time paying attention to the possibilities offered by these unique machines, even as these possibilities are often obscured by technical, social, and commercial constraints.

A Personal Perspective

The interaction of kids, learning, and computers seems always to have engaged me. I still vividly remember working with so-called teaching machines as a grammar school student at the Frederic Burk Lab school in San Francisco in about 1958. I wondered what the phrase "teaching machine" meant even then, and I enjoyed critiquing the design of the systems that I explored. I also remember wandering around the old Ventura Hall at Stanford, having fun working with friends who were creating some interactive math lessons in the innovative program that Pat Suppes and Richard Atkinson ran there.

I have especially detailed mental images of Dean Brown's Lab at the Stanford Research Institute in about 1968. I enjoyed the excitement of early invention and became intrigued by Doug Engelbart's latest developments. Doug's lab was nearby and as an undergraduate student I wondered whether these new devices would "augment the human intellect," as Doug suggested. I began to think of relationships between human thinking and computer processing even as I majored in biology.

> I am a machine
> I am not magic
> You bring what you are
> who you are
> how you work, play, see, imagine.
> You bring your fears
> your expectations
> your enthusiasm
> . . . and maybe something special can happen between us.
> I am a machine
> I won't tell you:
> "Stop it," "Be quiet," "Sit still,"
> I won't say

"You're wrong"
I won't say
"You must do things to please me or I won't like you."
I am a machine
I won't leave you when you want me. . . .[1]

My interest and spontaneous discoveries in this arena only increased when I was a graduate student studying cognition at the
University of California, San Diego (UCSD), with Don Norman.
Images from a conference at Lake Arrowhead in about 1972 still
bounce around in my mind. The conference brought together members of the UCSD research group and groups from Alan Kay's lab at
the Xerox Palo Alto Research Center and Seymour Papert's lab at
MIT. Somehow, the invention of computing systems, programming
languages, and theories of mind kept intersecting and emerging
from a study of kids' learning.

There are still many who do not understand why I am interested
in the study of cognition, the investigation of child development,
and the invention of new computer programming languages to
model human thinking, to represent complex schooling processes,
and to develop commercial products for computers. My neighbors
and colleagues alike are often confused about what I really do. Yet,
by engaging these ideas early in their development and thinking
about their intersections, I have seen new possibilities in their relationships. I get great satisfaction from studying children and learning from them.

If I were going to choose a best friend to work with
A colleague to help me understand computers and learning
I would choose a child
A child who can remind me of what is really going on
A child who is honest about what is good and bad
A child who can inspire me to make his life even better
A child who still has wonder and possibilities reflected in
    her eyes.

Yet, I do sometimes become confused about which direction to take in my work. I wonder whether I really do this work for my own entertainment, for my own three children (now ages nine, eleven, and thirteen), for the advancement of general scientific understanding, or for some more political goals of access to good learning for everyone. And I wonder what each of these points of view implies about what is important or where a contribution can be made. In considering all this, I vacillate a lot between doing very specific and pragmatic work that results in commercial learning products and doing work that sets forth general theories, policies, and understandings for incorporation in the work of others.

In all of this, I struggle with the relationships between the ideas of doing things faster, doing things better, doing new and better things, and having more people doing better things, which are all part of the opportunities and rhetoric of computers in learning. I grimace often at the bigness of the ideas in the conversation and the smallness of the examples offered to illustrate them. I wonder about the progress any of us has made in connecting our great ideas and the realities of our culture's learning enterprises. I wonder just what leverage technological opportunities really provide to most of our educational issues, and whether it is simply a diversion from intractable problems. And so, even as I am impressed with the certainty of others' convictions about the importance of technology for learning, there is a lot of questioning in my work as I explore all these avenues and wonder about various perspectives.

> When I was younger I worried about not knowing
>   everything
> I challenged myself to be clearer and clearer
> To become precise about the truth and the right directions
> As I get older I worry about keeping the arguments going
> I challenge myself to lay out possibilities and tensions
> To become helpful in community discussions of what we
>   all might do
> I've come to find honesty in debate

Healthiness in discord
Aliveness in systems that aren't neat and tidy
Maybe I am afraid of being bored by everyday dialogues
    and pat answers and simplistic platitudes
Or maybe I just need some drama in my life!

I came to Apple Computer more than ten years ago to move my ideas of multimedia (which had been developed in laboratory settings) into real products. I also came to investigate human interfaces, to understand the principles of the desktop interface, and to explore new multimedia interfaces. Most of my work in the last few years has been focused on media and interface issues. And yet children's learning keeps creeping in, or more specifically, what I consider to be my best ideas about media and interfaces keep emerging from my observations of children's learning and school settings.

Though I have not been a formal participant in ACOT, I celebrate this tenth anniversary of the program with seven general observations about opportunities for technology to enhance learning. I begin with the motivating goal, the *moments of joy* when learning occurs, and then consider *what I have learned* in pursuing this phenomenon. I step back a bit to acknowledge the *teachers* associated with this good learning, and step back even further to question just how any of what we learn can be *generalized*. I then step forward to outline a *design methodology* that may offer a paradigm shift to make digital technologies even more significant tools for learning. I linger a bit on my excitement about the intersection of distributed technologies and *new social possibilities*, and conclude with an assertion of *faith* that work on computers and learning will make a positive contribution to the culture.

Moments of Joy: The Motivation

Moments of joy are a daily occurrence in a good classroom. Things begin with a flurry of bewilderment. Closely following is a set of activities, intermingled with frustrations. Then, when it works, there is the moment of joy. It is the moment when a new concept is understood, or an old one reexamined. It is the moment when everything fits together and this new whole piece of cloth becomes part of ordinary experience. Moments of joy are what many teachers live for, what keep students working, what engage cognitive researchers in the mystery of learning.

For whatever set of reasons, it seems to me that these moments occur more often when students are using computers in their learning. It may seem this way because the learning process is often more explicit when surrounded by technology. Because of the presence of the computer, the learner must make explicit what he knows or what she wants to have elaborated. And the computer screen typically displays the current state of knowing—the results of a simulation, the draft of a paper, the progress in an activity—and student comments on this display are often very revealing of the state of learning.

It may be that more moments of joy occur because the computer offers permission for students to *not* know. There is no judgment by the computer of a student's brightness. This encourages active engagement and participation by the student. In turn, this can engender effective learning. Somehow there is an impedance match between the pace of learning and the responsiveness of computers.

Collaborative activity around computers may also explain why there seem to be frequent learning advances in a computer-centered environment. Students engage each other's ideas and the group keeps moving forward even when an isolated student gets stuck. Planning of projects and strategies for learning are made explicit in conversations.

> Is that a smile or a grimace on your face
> As you stare at that screen?
> Are things going right?
> Or are they going wrong?
> Just how does it feel to be so caught up in the process?
> To be part of the ideas

To be part of all the sense and the nonsense
Of what you now know and don't know.
And then how does it feel when the tension releases
When the tool works
When the paragraphs fit together
When your e-mail says what you want it to
When you finally understand the sound of a heartbeat
Or the bouncing of a ball
Or the rhythm of the stanza?
Just why do you call this the joy of learning?
It looks like work to me!

Whatever the reasons computers seem to encourage learning, it is very exciting to teach their use. It is exciting to get inside students' heads a bit more, to know what kind of guidance to offer and when to celebrate their learning. It is fun to know just where someone is on a task and to be free to talk about it, aiming remarks at the screen rather than the often fragile learners.

We need some basic research to find out whether the intense gaze and active reasoning we see in front of computer screens really indicate or presage effective learning. Interestingly, I have not seen much compelling data or engaging analysis of the relationship between computer use and learning. It could be just our imaginations or our wishful thinking or our joint fantasies that convinces us that learning is improved. And yet, even without much formal data, I see the connection between a thinking human and a computing device as something quite compelling and suggestive. It motivates me and many others to take these machines seriously when we think about learning.

Paying Attention: Learning with Experience

It is important to be guided by one's principles and one's theories. It lets one move past the single observations and into general and powerful ideas. Yet it is important to take account of what one sees and experiences to refine one's principles and theories. Otherwise one stands still, and often moves quite a distance away from original good ideas. In addition, newcomers to a field always need to start at the beginning, rather than building on the experience of others.

> Learning about learning is compelling
> Learning about learning systems is even more engaging
> The trick is to find ways to notice what one sees
> And passing the word on
> For if each of us keeps learning by ourselves
> And scurrying on from one great thing to another
> One great advocacy to the next
> We will continue to remain blind to what is going on
> Complacent in our preconceptions and personal beliefs
> Ignorant as to whether we are going forward or back
> Relying too much on what we know and not what is.

I've been paying attention to a large number of activities surrounding a very large number of different kinds of computing devices for more than twenty years. I've worked with powerful research machines whose power is now dwarfed by off-the-shelf Power Macintoshes. I've programmed first-generation personal computers like Apple IIs and Atari 800s to handle a range of different learning tasks. I've watched graduate students use computers in mathematics and preschoolers use them to understand narratives. I've spent many years in front of different word processors and almost as many making products that have still images and movies in them. In all this I have learned quite a lot. I list some of these learnings here, many of which developed contrary to my initial intuitions.

Sharing computers is good. It encourages conversations and collaborative work. Single machines for individuals oftentimes result in isolation.

Teachers offer the main opportunity for success. Kids are very engaging, and it is tempting to build computer systems that are completely independent of context and directed only to kids. Yet if teachers and other adults who work with children are not considered, the projects are doomed to failure. One should always consider adults in designing learning experiences for classrooms. When working in schools, more than half of technology resources should be directed to teacher professional development and support.

Word processors are revolutionary. Learning to write with word processors brings concepts of revision, editing, annotation, and critique into the learning process. These tools can remove much of the drudgery of writing and allow students to gain confidence in representing their ideas. Although outside the context of writing classes word processors too often function only as advanced typewriters, they offer much more.

Lots of people think images are important to learning. When I did image-based learning research twenty-five years ago, I could find few collaborators or believers. Now, although there is little more evidence that images support substantive learning, many people have accepted this approach. I still yearn for basic research on the topic, even as I am pleased by the momentum.

Commercialism and entertainment can easily dominate serious learning; money does not get attracted to good ideas naturally. Our culture seems to identify images as the property of the entertainment industry and is unable, in many cases, to focus on the use of images in multimedia products for learning. I am very depressed that even as more and more dollars are invested in multimedia products for general education, few really innovative or effective learning products are reaching the market.

Most great education takes place without computers, and is not very costly. I have spent many years researching, analyzing, and advocating the use of computers in education. And I believe that they can revolutionize the ways we think and learn and enliven schools at the same time. Yet I need to acknowledge that I learned a great deal as a young student, without technology. I also acknowledge that currently I learn most of what I do in conversations with colleagues, not necessarily via technological assistance. Also, as I watch my three children learn, I am most impressed with nontechnologically centered learning—saxophone lessons, dinner-table deliberations, art projects in social studies, discussions of plays or musicals, drawing and writing projects. Computers add to all these noncomputer activities; they are not a substitute for them.

There is a big gap between curricular guidelines and activity design. I have learned quite a bit about curricular issues, and having personally benefited from a good education, I understand most of the content presented in K–12. Yet, I am constantly impressed and amazed at the large distance between knowing the content and providing a set of activities from which students can and will learn. Good teachers are superb at designing activities, choreographing sets of tasks for students that, while appropriately constrained, encourage learning. This activity design, rather than simple content analysis, is a key to interactive computer-based learning.

Distributed computer systems have momentum. Netscape took off faster than I ever imagined. I think the fascination with the Internet is about product distribution, though, and not learning opportunities. I hope I am proven wrong.

There is limited insight and innovation in materials development for education. There are too few experts with passion involved in the development of educational materials. Even the superficial opportunities for using technology in learning are underexplored and rarely applied.

Simplicity is hard when opportunities are many. Many uses of computers are too flexible and general; many students and teachers would do better with a few concrete simple things.

General acceptance does not necessarily breed substantive success. In five years at the Apple Multimedia Lab (1987–1992), we did substantial work with a core team of six people. Similar levels of productivity have not been duplicated with much larger teams with many more dollars. Too often, the current hype and large investments in multimedia have detracted from the quality of products rather than added to them.

Anti-intellectualism is prevalent in the United States. America has not established an educational culture. While we have borrowed from the traditions of numerous immigrant populations, we are too pragmatic and have not yet evolved traditions that value ideas. We are completely unable to identify the intersection of equity and excellence, or to articulate whether learning is for financial or other less tangible rewards (to make a living or to make a life?). The manner in which we use computers may help us to evolve our intellectual culture, or it may completely freeze it; while the medium is excellent for presenting, elaborating, and exchanging ideas, too many current uses of computers are not about ideas at all.

Content and process are both important. What you learn and how you learn are equally important. Indeed, in the most interesting cases, they appear to be inseparable.

Learning one thing well offers great advantages. It gives a learner a feeling of success and an identity, and skills that can transfer to other domains.

Furniture arrangements in school are critical to activity design. Computers, especially when used for project-based work, quickly break down the traditional model of classroom organization with seats neatly in rows and a teacher at the front.

Humor and risk taking are key to effective innovation. Unless you can create a culture around technology use that encourages real involvement, you will not make any interesting progress. In this regard, we must be explicit about the downside—you can never say, "I know it is risky, but I'm sure it will work."

Many teachers don't think they have time to be learners. Teachers often feel that any gap in their own understanding needs to be hidden rather than built upon. Time must be made for teachers to learn continually about technology and about many other things so that they can maintain their liveliness, confidence, mastery, and relevance.

It is not surprising when technology doesn't work. One of the unfortunate by-products of technology is that most large-scale environments have many different kinds of technologies, many of which will be incompatible with one another. Even in homogenous situations, one learns quickly that technologies often don't work.

This means that you must be conservative about what to use when. It also means that everyone using technology needs to be comfortable troubleshooting equipment that doesn't work. In rare situations, broken technology can become a community project, cultivating problem solving and collaboration among students and teachers. Yet it should be acknowledged that there will be costs in time and aggravation to having working technology systems.

These kinds of observations do not tell you what kind of computer system to buy or how to include computers in your classroom or just why computers might support good education. Yet these notions are the kind of everyday knowing that people who have been exploring these arenas carry with them and that need to be passed along as context for future work. In fact, I suppose that the main thing I have learned in the last twenty years is that observations like these are valuable. I used to think that research and technical data would lead the computer revolution but I now think that we will move forward by building learning cultures based on these kinds of relatively simple observations. If this implicit knowledge were made explicit and shared with colleagues, improvement of education would be much more rapid.

Burdens of Teaching: The Context

It may well be that schools will be replaced by distributed networks of learners who are engaged with each other about ideas over space and time. This is the visionary advocacy of many.

And yet, I keep returning to an appreciation of real space and time and the interactions that can occur among teachers and learners in such a context. Perhaps I am still overly impressed that most kids manage to arrive at school early in the morning on most days in spite of the incredible logistics involved. There is something fundamentally good about having real spaces called schools that are dedicated to ideas. Even if this is sometimes only in principle, it pro-vides a foundation upon which we can build.

Early on, I was an unconscious advocate of designing computer-based learning systems independent of teacher involvement. This was partly because I knew more about interaction design on com-puters and the thinking of children than I did about teachers. I also thought of teachers as roadblocks to great new ideas, missing, as many of us did in our youth, the simple notion that great new ideas and great old ideas and an understanding of current logistics need to combine for anything effective to occur!

More critically, I didn't understand how interested many teach-ers are in supporting their students' learning, and how willing they are to help out in this, even when the methods may seem a bit strange (for example, technological). And I didn't understand teachers' perspectives on their role in learning.

I am your partner
I am your friend
I am here to help you include new things in your mind
And to learn that your not knowing provides us with a
　　great opportunity to work together.
I'm never going to be as good as you at this
I've made my mark on the world already
And learned a lot of what I will about ordinary things
And mostly I have done this without any electronic
　　contraptions
But for you the world is going to be different
And so I am here to learn some special things
Things about
taking risks
and learning together
and sharing the frustrations
and finding ways to learn who knows what

and inventing ways to connect with what we both want
Things about
media and computing
networking and technical troubleshooting
New things for me
That are becoming old hat to you.
Do have some patience with me
There are a lot of details involved in
changing one's entire life work!

Some argue that as long as we have schools as we know them, teachers must be central to instruction and learning. However, as we move into virtual worlds, the same people expect that computers can be used by students without the support of teachers. This argument seems as compelling to me as the arguments about automation creating paperless offices and a leisure class. In fact, I think teachers will become even more central to the learning experience with the incorporation of technologies. The more sophisticated the technology, the more important teachers' roles are likely to be. Furthermore, newly evolving distributed technologies for learning will support more and more social interaction, allowing teachers to interact with even more students rather than fewer. I think that these new technologies will successfully break down the isolation of single classrooms and thereby strengthen cultures for teacher professionalism and colleagueship. And the very technologies that can enhance the profession of teaching will then naturally become the tools of choice to sustain student learning.

There is a lot of work to do in this area. We need to figure out how technologies can lessen the burdens of teachers' everyday activities as well as encourage some innovative teaching. We need to find ways to represent technology as support for a new kind of culture, not simply a structure for managing low-level skill development. We need to encourage risk taking by teachers, even as we provide safety nets for them and for their students. And we need to encourage teachers to work as colleagues with other inventors of technology-rich educational systems, voicing their perspectives and adding their insights.

Scale and Generalization: The Realities

One wonderful property of most technologies that support learning is that they are extensible and generalizable. I can produce one CD-ROM product and then distribute this single version to thousands of sites. Similarly, we can design one multimedia computing system that a wide range of very different people can use successfully. And with the Internet emerging, I can quite easily find ways to distribute copies of my work; in theory it does not cost any more to give one friend a copy of a paper I have written or a movie I have made than it does to make copies available to hundreds of thousands of interested people.

In practice, however, it is difficult to take advantage of this generality and efforts are often unsuccessful. Like the transfer of educational innovation in general, transfer of innovations in educational technology is typically very slow, very ineffective, and oftentimes very ugly. Great ideas often turn to mush as they are scaled up for access by large numbers of people. Wonderful activities lose their punch when implemented outside the environments for which they were designed. Everyday realities including economics, entrenched social structures, racism, poverty, and neglect quickly get in the way of the theoretical possibilities of generalization inherent in computer-based learning.

Similarly, the huge gap between research demonstrations and practical widespread solutions is terrifying. Speaking with some experience, I know that it takes an enormous amount of concentration, collaboration, collective talent, and resources to develop innovative educational technology demonstrations. Whether it is developing multimedia CD-ROM projects in content areas or computer programs to facilitate remote video communications from classrooms, the logistical problems and technological challenges of any new approach are quite overwhelming.

And when the demonstration is done, there are devastating critiques implying it is insignificant, or even harmful. Some favorite themes of critics include: "What impact does this have on reading scores?" "Since computers will never be available to low-income groups, isn't this only adding to the differences between the haves and the have nots?" "How do you plan to distribute this?"

> She smiled quietly
> as she told me that I should
> show movies of black kids
> using computers.
> He argued loudly as he said that I was perpetuating
> the myth that boys do science in America.
> I listened to the next sentence from each one of these
> strangers.
> He said that unless everyone can do everything
> I shouldn't do anything.
> She said she wanted to be sure
> everyone who saw my movie
> would know that they could do it too.
> He was wrong.
> She wasn't.
> I told her that everyone could soon do what I was trying.
> She reminded me that most people didn't believe that.
> I learned from her.
> We must figure out a way to assure that everyone benefits
> from educational technology developments.
> It is not a simple puzzle.

And so I continue to struggle personally with just how I can make a large enough and general enough impact to justify my hard work. Frankly, it is depressing, and I am driven to thinking in larger and larger contexts. Yet, as I try to enter into policy conversations, major publishing scenarios, or general reform efforts, I lose the crispness and honesty of single demonstrations; demonstrations that are about certain tools, certain schools, and certain moments. This needs to be solved. We must do good work. We must show possibilities. We must enhance kids' realities, and not just *some* kids' realities. The potential is too great to waste, and yet we are doing this every day by not facing this generalization problem in a sophisticated and knowledgeable way that moves past mere rhetoric.

Designerly Thinking: The Fundamental Change

I've been the executive producer of a number of early multimedia titles, including the Visual Almanac, CountDown, Planetary Taxi, Life Story, Voices, and Interactive NOVA: Animal Pathfinders.[2] I produced these titles to show ways in which multimedia might be significant for learning. Along the way, I became very taken with the process of multimedia design. I love the collaboration of individuals with very different perspectives and skills. I find the transition from idea to prototype to product exhilarating. I like making a thing that exists in the world independently of me.

This has taken my work in two directions. On one hand, I now work extensively in the invention of new tools for the creation of *casual* multimedia—tools that allow you to focus on ideas rather than production, tools suitable for everyday work and not just professional media production. I learn so much each time I engage in a multimedia design process that I want others, including students and teachers, to have the tools to make things themselves and to learn as they do this. If we don't evolve a culture of multimedia tool-users, we may completely miss the possibilities for major cultural change in this arena.

On the other hand, I have become convinced that the process of design, a process familiar in the design disciplines but often unknown in other domains, is extremely important for learning. I find that making my ideas explicit and presenting them to others is healthy. I find that organizing my thoughts in diagrams and sketches is significant. I find that making prototypes refines my own thinking and that group critiques greatly increase my own insights.

> I never seem to get it right the first time
> I never can say what I mean until I try a few times
> And then making my ideas concrete takes so much
>   anxiety away
> I used to worry about being accurate all the time
> And finding *the* answer
> I used to hide my work from you until I was sure it was
>   complete
> And I sure never thought that helping you out was my
>   responsibility
> Now I sketch out ideas to see if I understand them
> And diagram projects to see that we have mutual
>   understandings
> Whiteboards and brightly colored montages surround
>   and inspire me
> And I look for one of many answers to the questions I
>   pose
> I've become a part of an idea-driven design culture
> And I look forward to having more of you to play with
> And I look forward to school kids using these methods
> For learning physics and history and math, and almost
>   everything else.

These two approaches, new media tools and a new design methodology, offer the greatest hope in the educational technology arena. Each approach takes us away from our unfortunate tendencies to use technologies to do what we are already doing, but with a bit more efficiency.

Recently I completed a new CD-ROM titled VizAbility[3] that

attempts to show how designerly environments and cultures can sustain important work in several domains, including schools. It provides basic training in seeing, drawing, diagramming, and imagining so that one can actively participate in a design culture.

Interestingly, this general design approach is not unfamiliar to schools. For example, the programs in teaching writing initiated by the Bay Area Writing Project reflect many of the values I have identified in design. Drafts are important, especially when accompanied by critiques and revisions between drafts. Organization of materials is important, both for the big picture and for the details. Self-communication is as critical as communication to particular audiences for particular purposes. Group collaboration is encouraged. This writing program has been very successful, in that it has been adopted by many teachers and many students have become successful writers.

I'm hoping we can effectively introduce design methodologies into our classrooms. I'm betting that if we truly enter the information age using computers in our schools, it will be because we introduce design cultures into the educational fabric. I'm betting that mental work can be truly augmented by computers when computers are used as tools within design contexts, contexts rich in problem solving, approximation, collaboration, and inventiveness.

It's rather counterintuitive, but as the world becomes more virtual, techniques originally developed for dealing with real objects will gain in importance. If it is at the intersection of realism and abstraction where our computers are most useful, then a methodology that allows exploration and expression is central to progress.

New Social Structures: The Opportunities

I used to think that the ultimate goal of computers in education was that more students would understand academic subjects more easily and that creative expression in both text and media would be enhanced. I have been infatuated with the idea that if graphics could be made quickly, we could enter into new kinds of conversations and new realms of understanding. I also find that simulations are magic and that thinking can be extended using computer programming concepts.

I still think that these ideas are important. Recently, though, I have—like many others—become enthralled with the communities of learners made possible with distributed on-line worlds where more information is available to more people. While we are only beginning to explore these communities, I now think their significance is in the new social structures that can be created. You don't have to be isolated with your own ideas; you can find someone else to discuss them with. We are not limited to one physical locality for expertise or engaging conversations. Experts on genetics or Shakespeare or the stock market can be available to a wide range of people. And expertise of retirees or individuals in remote locations, which was once skipped over, can become available to schoolchildren everywhere.

> I rather like living in the real world
> Especially when the sun shines and a friend smiles
> And yet these virtual worlds are becoming inviting
> Their abstraction matches the kinds of ideas I want to
>   exchange
> And their evolving reality lets me dream of traveling
>   everywhere, from here,
> And it lets me dream of a new utopia free of current
>   real-space limits and prejudices.

I have only begun to explore the significance of this. It seems to me, for example, that good schools do not need to be limited to a few special locations. Students can gain access to knowledge systems regardless of the school districts they live in. The incremental cost for an additional student will be negligible. Safe environments for exchanging ideas can be created in virtual communities and the currency of the exchange is not based on age, race, or economic status. Even if we can't break the cycles of segregation, racism, and ageism in our real-life environments, we have a chance of eliminating these in our virtual communities.

But there are other sides to this big dream. It requires that everyone have access to computer systems. For access will define participation in the learning culture, not simply access to one piece of data or one resource. In this scenario, computer use no longer offers an enhancement, it offers an entry into the world of ideas and the roads to success. It is no longer optional, it is required, much like textual literacy in the twentieth century.

And so, like so many great opportunities, this one has a dark side. It is imperative that we find methods to provide computer technologies, as imperfect as they sometimes are, to everyone. This next stage of evolution demands taking current successes from the few to the many, even as we continue to work on the next great idea. Distributed technologies must be designed to accomplish these goals without the exclusionary price tags that might be associated with virtual realities. If we don't do this, it will represent a failure of courage, will, and understanding, not technologies and resources. It will show that our current systems are motivated by local profit rather than the long-term general gain accomplished with an educated populace. Many reasons for past failures have been eliminated; the challenge is not to invent new excuses for new kinds of failures.

In Conclusion: Unfounded Optimism

Computers are really expensive. The difficulty of learning to use computers keeps many people away from them. Expecting students to use computers most of the school day simply doesn't make sense. We don't have much evidence that significant learning is enhanced with computing systems. Technological investments in schools are inevitable given current trends in politics and business, but, unfortunately, quality education is not at all inevitable.

It doesn't make any sense to think that things will get
    better
If one pays attention to all the complexities
and all the obstacles
it is clear that there are structural problems with the use
    of technology in learning
almost as many as there are in learning and schooling
    itself
And yet pessimists never get anything done
There's room for a couple of optimists
To shed our sense of the problems and look for the
    opportunities
Bringing them to the attention of those who are willing
    to use these opportunities
To address the problems head on
It is important to imagine and to invent and to try
And computers and education
Have a destiny to acknowledge
For which we must take some responsibility.

As a new generation takes leadership in research and development, innovation in technology and education may accelerate in
the next few years. These new leaders will have grown up with reasonable computer tools. The next generation will come to school
from inside the computer learning culture. They will be natives of
the culture and the language, so to speak. I look forward to an ac-
celerated wave of understanding and invention. I look forward to a
time where the early ACOT years and those that went before them
are taken for granted, and the struggles of the pioneers are forgotten in the glow of the integrated technologies for human learning.

I won't forget these years, because for me they have offered a
wonderful opportunity to learn and to create with valued colleagues.
Yet I do think that future generations will use computing resources
very naturally for learning, much as we use telephones to talk with
colleagues and friends.

The notions that computing resources require one to
Connect "typewriter looking" devices to the walls to gain
    power
Use text and numbers most frequently and wait many
    minutes for any media elements
Be avant-garde to have regular access to remote
    information resources
Set up complex personal or school-specific network
    administration systems
Rely on others to prepare media-rich programming
    resources
Provide training to teachers on how to use a mouse
Convince school administrators that computers have a
    role in learning
will be laughable.
I'm looking forward to the laughter!

Notes

1. This statement is taken from a 1969 brochure for a SRI Summer
   School directed by Dean Brown.

2. See Visual Almanac [Computer software], 1992, New York: Voy-
   ager; CountDown [Computer software], 1993, New York: Voyager;
   Planetary Taxi [Computer software], 1994, New York: Voyager;
   Life Story [Computer software], 1992, New York: Sunburst; and
   Voices [Computer software], 1994, New York: Sunburst; Interactive
   NOVA: Animal Pathfinders [Computer software], 1993, New York:
   Scholastic.

3. See VizAbility [Computer software], 1996, Boston: PWS Publishers.

6

Toward an ACOT of Tomorrow

Decker F. Walker

A decade ago, conventional wisdom held that American schools lagged so far behind other countries that they put the nation at risk. Yet at that time American schools were unquestionably first in the world at one thing: using computers. Virtually every American elementary and secondary school had at least a dozen computers and most had more. A broad movement for computer literacy had mushroomed virtually overnight, and nearly every child in school had some experience using computers. Logo, invented at MIT, became the center of a thriving international community of teachers and researchers. The world's three major computer-assisted instruction (CAI) systems had been developed at universities in Illinois (PLATO), Utah (TICCIT), and California (CCC). Intelligent tutoring systems were under development at several universities and research centers such as BBN Corporation; and the Xerox Palo Alto Research Center. New computer-based academic tools were being developed at the Technical Education Research Center, Bank Street College of Education, and the Education Technology Center at Harvard, in addition to many universities. A substantial market was developing in educational software and edutainment products for the home and school.

In the most recent decade, the pace of innovation has subsided. Networking and telecommunication have spread widely, it is true, and the CD-ROM has provided the memory needed for multimedia, but most classrooms still lack a telephone line and most school computers do not have CD-ROM drives. The first international assessment of achievement in computing[1] gave the United States a slim lead in computers per student, but not if we count only latest-generation systems capable of multimedia. The early mass media successes of *Where in the World is Carmen Sandiego?* and *Voyage of the Mimi* have not been duplicated. Probeware is still rarely used in science classes. The teaching of programming has become a routine high school elective hovering between academic and vocational programs.

American educators have had more than a decade in which to learn from our pioneering experiments with the use of computers. What have we learned? Not as much as we could have and should have, I fear. The rest of the world seems to have learned more from our experiments than we have. In a number of countries, whole national school systems have implemented computer education programs similar to those pioneered in a few U.S. schools.[2]

As I look at the events of the past decade, I see these major developments:

- Widespread excitement, verging on hysteria at times, about the promise of computers for education

- A fierce competitive struggle for leadership in this new area, waged mainly with sweeping educational ideas and visions

- Thousands of innovative school and classroom programs springing up that reflect these sweeping visions

- Widespread disappointment in the results of these innovative programs

- A turning away from these failed ideas and visions to search for new, still more innovative visions

ACOT has been an exception in many ways. Although it was founded in a period of great optimism, ACOT did not make its bid for leadership on the basis of sweeping new educational ideas and visions, but rather on a common-sense notion: give some teachers and students the kind of access to computing that we suppose all children might have one day and see what they are able to do with it. ACOT didn't insist that teachers adopt a particular educational vision. It invited them to use the one they had. ACOT funded a range of evaluation and research studies that enabled all concerned to learn more from their experience than would otherwise have been possible. In these and other ways ACOT blazed its own trail into the unknown territory of computer intensive education.

This chapter is my reflection on what we can learn from the experience of the past decade and on how we could do better at realizing the educative potential of computing in the decades to come. It begins with an account of the struggle for leadership in educational computing in the early years. It proceeds with an analysis showing why that struggle leads to innovations that are strong out of the gate but weak at the finish. It shows how ACOT was an exception to this pattern and blazed its own path. It closes with a sketch of an ACOT of tomorrow in which innovators, teachers, and researchers collaborate to orchestrate the crucial details that make an innovation successful.

Struggles for Leadership

I still recall my astonishment when it dawned on me that discussions of the educational uses of computers were rehashing old issues instead of breaking new ground. I had naively assumed that the sheer novelty of computing and its unprecedented powers of automation, symbol manipulation, simulation of complex systems, and expression in a variety of media, among others, would fuel an explosion of original ideas about education.

My enlightenment began when I read Robert Taylor's edited volume, *Computer in the School: Tutor, Tool, Tutee*.[3] The book was (and is) a marvelous introduction to the main currents of thought and innovation about computing in education prior to 1980. As I read essays in that volume by Papert, Suppes, and other pioneers of educational computing, I realized that I had heard these ideas before in the new curriculum movement of the 1960s. Seymour Papert's ideas about education expressed the same neoprogressive educational vision that Jerome Bruner and the Piagetians had expressed in the 1960s, and Logo was a logical extension of the hands-on science materials produced by the Elementary Science Study project at Education Development Corporation in the 1960s. Patrick Suppes's work on CAI expressed the same educational vision B. F. Skinner had advocated in programmed instruction in the 1960s, and CAI was a logical extension of the AAAS elementary science curriculum.

I had expected computing to loose a flood of new ideas on fresh topics like the educational value of learning to use different forms of representation, to manipulate symbol systems, and to internalize knowledge of complex systems through vicarious experience with computer models. What I found was an obvious and straightforward continuation of earlier debates between entrenched schools of thought. Suppes's commitment to traditional education could hardly be expressed more directly than in his claim (in the Taylor collection) that computers would make it possible for every child to have a tutor as great as the one Philip of Macedon arranged for his son Alexander two millennia earlier. Papert's commitment to progressive ideas is just as plain in his claim (also in the Taylor collection) that computers would make it possible at last to realize the visions of child-centered education. The impact of computing on educational discourse was not a revolution, not even a renewal, but just another battle in an ancient ideological war.

Why did this happen? Because the struggle for power over educational computing became the paramount issue. The most powerful interest groups in education aligned themselves with one or the other of these ideological camps, political and social conservatives with the traditional position and liberals with the progressive. Both camps saw it as most important to gain possession of this new educational territory, computing, for their side.

The participants made it quite clear that their educational visions and values were most important to them, and that technology was only a means to these ends. The notion that the technology itself should hold any intrinsic value or interest they considered technocratic and reprehensible. Interest in technology for the sake of one's educational ideology, on the other hand, was noble and humane.

Treating computing as simply a means to preconceived educational ends ignores the possibility that new means may make new ends achievable. Writing, history, science, music are all means to other valued human ends, but means that have profoundly affected our educational ends and our ideas about which ends are most important. Treating computing as merely a means toward the ends favored in their philosophy protected these groups against challenges to their educational views and values.

The new topic of computers and how we might use them for education was thus subsumed under the old controversies over education and how it should be done. The scary prospect of a fresh take on the old questions and the even scarier prospect of new questions and new voices expressing new visions and representing new political and social alignments were quickly dispelled. The old hands sighed with relief—even though the ground was new, the opponents were familiar. If you knew who your educational friends and enemies were before, you could still find them fighting under the old rhetorical flags.

In the ensuing years, the ideological battle for control of educational computing dwindled to an inconclusive draw. CAI, so promising in the sixties, was attacked by neoprogressives as mindless drill-and-kill directed at trivial educational goals. It never became popular with teachers and gradually lost its credibility as a panacea with the important leadership groups in education. Having failed as a reform, CAI settled into the role of a prosperous merchant with a substantial and growing market share. All along, evaluations of CAI programs had shown favorable but not spectacular results. Students who used CAI raised their standardized test scores an average of almost a letter grade on the conventional A–F normal grading curve and advanced a month or two more each academic year in normed tests. Nothing to sneeze at, but not a revolution.

Logo fared little better. Critics ridiculed the idea that children could get an education by figuring out for themselves how to move a tiny triangle around on a screen using instructions typed into a computer. Evaluations showed that after months of work with Logo many children still had not even learned the most basic commands and not many could make the turtle draw anything more complicated than a square. So Logo, too, lost its luster. A core of the Logo community keeps the faith but it now seems more like a user group than a religion, and most members have reached out for richer, fresher computer applications like games, robots, and multimedia construction kits. Logo is still a force, but not a revolution.

As the new/old battles wound down inconclusively, both ideological wings found new innovations to champion. The more traditionally inclined found computer literacy, computer programming, and Intelligent Tutoring Systems. The progressives found networking, constructivism, and communities of learners. Perhaps one of these will bring the promised revolution. More likely, they will suffer criticism, achieve mixed results, lose their credibility as a revolutionary force, and, in an endless wheel of innovation, give up their place to newer innovations.

I find a glimmer of hope in this bleak history, but it is one neither side is interested in highlighting. The research and evaluation done on pioneering computer education programs over the past couple of decades does not actually show unrelieved failure. While none of these innovations produced a revolution, they did produce some remarkable successes. It is much nearer the truth to say that the experience of the past decade shows that every innovative use of computers—CAI and Logo, to be sure—shows a mixture of successes and failures. Because a mixed record is not a revolution, however, neither side can claim victory in the ideological war, and so the search continues for the new panacea.

This search for panaceas is a marvelous spur to innovation but a serious barrier to real reform. As a society, we squander the limited resources available for innovation in education by overinvesting in the search for the next revolution and underinvesting in efforts to learn from and build on the achievements of the last one. In this never-ending ideological struggle no one has an incentive to look back, to study their failures, to salvage what worked, to fix what didn't, and to avoid making the same mistake next time. ACOT, by avoiding the smoke and noise of ideological combat, may have much to teach us about how to innovate more effectively.

Finding a Third Path

ACOT did not originate as a way of doing ideological battle—it had no official educational ideology. Although most of the program's staff leaned toward neoprogressive ideals, they supported teachers in using computers in more traditional ways, too. In its early stage, ACOT helped teachers work out their own program based on whatever ideas and intuitions they found most trustworthy and useful. The program arranged for teachers to have extra time to plan and encouraged teachers to work in teams and to plan jointly. It hired expert consultants to work with the teachers. It also funded a range of evaluation and research studies that enabled all concerned to learn more from the ACOT experience than would otherwise have been possible. ACOT encouraged leadership to emerge from teachers and consultants; it did not arrogate the leadership role to a charismatic figure heading a school of thought. Its managers took a long view, often taking classrooms of students through substantial portions of their precollege careers, and not hesitating to change course when unexpected problems arose or when someone found a better way.

One unfortunate result of all this ideological flexibility was that it was difficult to describe what ACOT's approach to educational computing really was. It could be described in general terms: computers were used routinely as tools for learning in a variety of academic areas; the use of computers was integrated intimately with whatever else went on in the classroom, under the teacher's direction; and computers were often used in projects and to prepare reports. But this description applied to many other computer-based innovations as well. The early ACOT approach, if there was such a thing, was more a matter of how teachers and students were supported than of how computers were used.

Evaluation reports show some impressive results. An Apple teleconference reported that nearly all students in the first ACOT class at West High School in Columbus, Ohio, went on to college, compared to roughly half of the high school class from which they were randomly chosen. Evaluation reports by the UCLA team[4] and from Ohio State[5] indicated impressive growth in a variety of important cognitive areas. Yet ACOT, too, failed to deliver the revolution everybody wanted. Readers of these evaluation reports and visitors to ACOT schools have generally been impressed but hardly overwhelmed.

What happened? I think ACOT stumbled at the same point as the other innovations, but over quite a different rock. ACOT, too, failed to learn from its early experience and to make adjustments to build on the early successes. ACOT, though, was not blinded by its ideology. Rather, it ran out of ideas for adventurous new ways of teaching with the technology. The first few years of the project were spent teaching teachers and students how to use the technology and how to make it do what they wanted. In the next few years, the ACOT teachers tried their best teaching ideas. While these were interesting and effective as far as they went, they were seldom revolutionary. Students apparently spent most of their time learning to use software and making computer-based reports on assigned academic projects.

When it began to seem that its initial teacher-centered strategy of innovation was not going to deliver a revolution, the ACOT staff turned away from it. They espoused constructivist pedagogy and brought in experts to help teachers develop more constructivist activities during summer workshops. In effect, ACOT came around to the prevailing view that the key to educational innovation is holding the right ideas. This is too bad, both for ACOT and for education. If the staff had renewed their commitment to their path of teacher-centered, close-to-the-classroom innovation, and rethought and revised their strategies for implementing this approach, I think the ACOT results would have been much more impressive by now.

Details Matter Most

The lesson I believe we should learn from these innovations in educational computing is not that they failed, not that the ideas behind them are wrong or weak, and certainly not that educational computing has little promise for education. I think we should learn that the genius lies in the details. To see what this means let us look briefly at the example of CAI, one of the earliest applications of computers to education and one that is still widespread. As it happens, an excellent comprehensive review of research on CAI was published recently in a special issue of the *International Journal of Educational Research*, edited by Henry J. Becker and Nira Hativa,[6] and I shall draw heavily from it.

CAI designers relied on a behaviorist psychology that emphasized the importance of learning in small steps, repetition, frequent practice, immediate knowledge of results, and reinforcement. CAI advocates promised improved productivity in achieving conventional goals of education, especially for lower achievers, who would be able to proceed at their own pace. Critics attacked the emphasis on rote learning at the expense of higher-order thinking and the boring, drill-and-kill nature of the experience.

When researchers studied what students actually do when they use CAI systems, however, they found something quite different from what advocates and critics predicted. In learning arithmetic by CAI, for instance, researchers found that benefits are greatest for those above average in arithmetic achievement. High achievers go twice as fast as low achievers and so the gap between high and low achievers widens over the years of using CAI. When high-ability students use CAI systems, they soon advance to topics their teachers have not yet taught them. From that point on, CAI becomes for them a kind of discovery learning as they figure out for themselves how to solve unfamiliar problems. They find this a stimulating challenge and seem to develop powerful strategies for independent learning and valuable attitudes of perseverance, initiative, and organization in learning.[7]

By contrast, many low achievers have difficulty adapting to the computer learning environment. They make frequent mistakes of many kinds, and the computer management system is unable to distinguish among the kinds of mistakes and prescribe appropriate help. As a result, these systems make low-ability students repeat problems they have already learned how to solve. For instance, low achievers make more keyboarding errors, more often get timed out for taking too much time to give an answer even when they know it, have a greater need to do scratch work before reaching a final answer, and have more trouble doing problems presented in an unfamiliar format (for example, arithmetic problems presented left to right instead of in columns). As a result, CAI systems often underestimate the arithmetic skills of low-achieving students and retain them at a level below their performance on paper-and-pencil problems. For them, the CAI experience is not one of discovery but of too little challenge in arithmetic and of repeated frustration with the mechanics of the system. Nevertheless, 75 percent of students using CAI report liking it and only 15 percent report disliking it.[8]

Designers and advocates of CAI systems cast teachers in the role of manager of learning—making sure students arrived on time, stayed on task, did their best, and progressed appropriately. Hativa summarizes the findings of research on the actual impact of the teacher in CAI this way (recall that ILS stands for Integrated Learning Systems, the contemporary term for CAI): "The teachers' behavior while students are on line appears to strongly affect students' gains from the ILS work. This is true for all students, but it is crucial in the case of the lower-achieving students. Low achievers need a lot of encouragement, help and support in their ILS work and having an apathetic or discouraging supervisor in the ILS lab, one who does not provide this support, is detrimental to these students' ILS work."[9]

In another unanticipated development, the use of CAI for only a few minutes per week changed the way teachers taught arithmetic the rest of the time. "The large discrepancies among students in the same class caused by the individualized computer work . . . make it much more difficult for the teacher to conduct the regular lessons in the traditional 'frontal,' whole-class teaching method."[10] In one study, "the introduction of computer-based individualized practice . . . has caused almost one half of the teachers . . . to switch from whole-class teaching to individualized and small-group methods of instruction."[11] It appears that CAI even affects education beyond the individual classroom. For instance, weekly class reports produced automatically by the computer management system can result in competition between teachers, and the use of weekly reports by principals to evaluate teachers can create additional evaluation pressure on teachers.[12]

In fact, the sweeping educational and psychological ideas that guided CAI designers offer surprisingly little help with any of the major design issues that this review found to be crucial, including:

- Whether to encourage competition or cooperation. (The former favors high-achieving males.)

- How forgiving to make time limits. (Short limits favor the able.)

- How frequently to use CAI. (More frequently is better for less able students.)

- What role to suggest for teachers. (More active and involved teaching turns out to be better for all students, no matter how effective the CAI programming.)

How could anyone have known before trying CAI that these details would be crucial? In a sensible approach to innovation, a new generation of ILS would be designed that capitalized on this hard-won knowledge of what is necessary to realize the promise of CAI in practice.

Although space does not permit similar reviews of findings about other applications of computers, I am confident that they would show similar results.

Neither powerful technology nor good ideas are enough to improve education. Success in using computers in education will come only as a result of the intelligent and artful orchestration of many details in the classroom. Once we look beyond partisan ideological loyalties, we realize that the ideas we use to make the case for educational computing are far too simplistic to serve as an adequate basis for designing a working educational program. They are too vague, they leave out too much, they extrapolate too far from too narrow a basis of prior experience, and they are not open enough to the possibility that something utterly unexpected might actually occur.

Any educational program is a complex social system. For a successful result, many factors must be made to work together. If we designed a machine that worked well some of the time and produced some valuable results but was inefficient and gave off some harmful emissions, we would keep working at it. We would troubleshoot, locate limiting factors and find ways around them, tinker and fine tune until we improved its performance. We would not give up on the idea because our first try failed to live up to our fondest hopes. Educational programs are not machines, but they are complex social systems and making them work is at least as difficult as making machines work.

Our mistake has been to suppose that talented people with good ideas could—in a few years and with a few million dollars—design revolutionary educational programs that work. It is this approach, rather than the innovations themselves, that has failed.

If the genius is in the details, then we squander valuable opportunities to learn when we give up on innovations because they failed to deliver revolutionary gains in their first decade. We must keep working to improve them.

An ACOT of Tomorrow

In this spirit, let us keep working to improve ACOT. Let us use what we learn from experience so far to help us design still better ways to innovate. Let us follow the original designers' example and invent an ACOT of Tomorrow as a way of exploring new approaches to innovation in educational computing. Here are some suggestions I would have for such a program:

First, to ensure a steady stream of innovative teaching ideas, make the ACOT classrooms national test sites for pedagogically adventurous uses of computer technology. Publish brief descriptions of the lessons used by ACOT teachers, so everyone who is interested can know what is already being tried. Invite educators from around the world to send in adventurous teaching ideas that might be used in ACOT classrooms. Have the on-site teachers review these teaching ideas, and also have a national advisory panel of distinguished teachers and educational experts review them. Arrange for the ideas considered most promising by both groups to be further developed, tried in classrooms, evaluated, and, if appropriate, revised and tried again.

Second, to maximize opportunities to learn from the adventurous teaching ideas used in ACOT classrooms, involve the education community in discussions of the innovative teaching experiments conducted there. Videotape class sessions and make these videotapes generally available. Record interviews with teachers and students and make these recordings available. Make available portfolios of student work. Hold meetings and establish on-line discussion groups to focus on the crucial details and find ways to improve each lesson and unit. Write up and publish what ACOT staff and teachers learned about the crucial details and how they must be orchestrated for trying these innovative ideas.

Third, to enable a range of crucial details to be tried, establish a network of ACOT-affiliated classrooms around the world. Why should ACOT teachers be the only ones to try these adventurous ideas? Invite other teachers also to try the most promising teaching innovations and to try others considered less promising by ACOT teachers but which they believe hold great promise. Affiliated classrooms and teachers would be independent of ACOT in funding and governance, but would belong to a sort of league that would keep them in regular communication with ACOT schools and make it easy to join in cooperative ventures. For instance, ACOT-affiliated classrooms might receive reports of teaching experiments earlier than others, they might be invited to join in teleconferences, participate in newsgroups, and join with ACOT classrooms in trials of adventurous teaching experiments. Some ACOT-affiliated sites would presumably dedicate themselves to a particular educational philosophy or ideology, while others will remain eclectic. Such a broad range of ideas will broaden the base of experience. Affiliates will also help to spread successful practice more rapidly.

Fourth, to improve the assessment of teaching experiments, invite teachers and experts of all kinds to contribute ideas for assessment procedures and instruments. Fund teams to develop the most interesting assessment ideas into workable instruments and procedures, and then use them in studies of the ACOT teaching experiments.

With such modifications as these, an ACOT of Tomorrow would certainly not run out of teaching ideas. It would encourage everyone to focus attention on the crucial details necessary to make innovative programs work. It would foster dialogue across the spectrum of educational philosophy. It would reward those who rally political support by using their ideas to develop effective practices, not just to engage the opposition in debate. It would encourage the development of more adequate assessment procedures. It would not revolutionize American education, but it might show us how to learn more from the bold experiments with technology we seem so good at initiating. And it might show us how to translate that knowledge into lasting and substantial improvements in the education of all American children.

Notes

1. Anderson, R. E. (1993). *Computers in American schools*. Minneapolis, MN: IEA Computers in Education Study.

2. Pelgrum, W. J., & Plomp, T. (1991). *The use of computers in education worldwide*. Oxford, England: Pergamon Press.

3. Taylor, R. L. (1980). *Computer in the school: Tutor, tool, tutee*. New York: Teachers College Press.

4. Baker, E. L., Gearhart, M., Herman, J. L. (1990). *Assessment—Apple Classrooms of Tomorrow (ACOT) evaluation study, first- and second-year findings*. ACOT Report Number 7. Cupertino, CA: Apple Computer.

5. Tierney, R. J., Kieffer, R. D., Stowell, L., Desai, L. E., Whalin, K., & Moss, A. G. (1992). *Computer acquisition: A longitudinal study of the influence of high computer access on students' thinking, learning, and interactions*. ACOT Report Number 16. Cupertino, CA: Apple Computer.

6. Hativa, N. (1994). What you design is not what you get (WYDINWYG): Cognitive, affective, and social impacts of learning with an ILS—An integration of findings from 6 years of qualitative and quantitative studies. *International Journal of Educational Research, 21*(1), 81–112.

7. Hativa, cited in note 6.

8. Hativa, cited in note 6.

9. Hativa, cited in note 6, p. 102.

10. Hativa, cited in note 6, pp. 102–103.

11. Hativa, cited in note 6, p. 103.

12. Hativa, cited in note 6, p. 103.

Part II

Tools, Tasks, Teaching, and Student Learning

The use of technology to support learning ultimately comes down to the use in classrooms of a repertoire of tools, tasks, and practices. Part Two consists of reflective essays on the development and use of a small sample of classroom tools and practices, and the influence of these tools and practices on student learning.

We begin with Charles Fisher's description in Chapter Seven of a sustained, cooperative task supported with computers and projection devices in an elementary school. Fisher reflects on everyday events in early ACOT classes and underscores the role of technology in developing student learning artifacts, composition environments, and cooperative learning. In Chapter Eight, Jere Confrey describes her experience in developing software that incorporates multiple representations of mathematical functions, builds student-centeredness, and supports inquiry. In her broad-ranging essay, Confrey questions the depth of understanding that students acquire by interacting with sophisticated software, and comments on software design processes that may marginalize some students. In Chapter Nine, Midian Kurland reflects on the development and use of computer-supported writing tools for teachers and students.

Chapters Ten and Eleven examine some influences of technology on classroom processes and student performance. In Chapter Ten, Robert Tierney describes the appropriation of classroom technologies by high school students during a longitudinal study of an

ACOT site. In Chapter Eleven, Eva Baker, Joan Herman, and Maryl Gearhart reflect on their extensive work on evaluation of technology programs in schools, including instrument development activities and field studies in the ACOT context.

In Chapter Twelve, Brian Reilly gives vivid portrayals of how technology is being used in three high schools by three innovative teachers to engage students in video production, animation, and multimedia projects. Finally, in Chapter Thirteen, Richard Greenberg describes the application of sophisticated image-processing tools to engage large numbers of middle and high school students in authentic science and mathematics activities.

7

Learning to Compute and Computing to Learn

Charles Fisher

"It's *show time!*" The words, spoken forcefully, were drawn out, the pitch rising on the middle syllable and coming down hard on the end. It reminded me of a television network announcer introducing a Lakers game during the Johnson-Jabbar era. From his tone, the speaker meant business—but there was also a promise of glee, as though whatever was about to begin would be fast paced, exciting, and replete with tantalizing moments of unpredictability. The sense of anticipation in the room was palpable.

It was a Thursday in April at precisely 10:00 A.M. when this unschool-like phrase shattered the stolid atmosphere of another late-week morning in elementary school. At this signal, twenty-five ten-year-olds, who a moment before were stuck in leaden poses, visibly relaxed and began moving about the classroom. Their movements were quick, their steps light. This was not the chaotic physical release one sees at recess when students noisily erupt from school buildings with no apparent purpose other than escape from whatever was going on inside. These students purposefully reorganized themselves into three-person work groups. There were no laggards, no one expressed resistance to the change by being just slow enough to be disruptive but fast enough to avoid a reprimand. Some students have a surgical ability to sense the boundaries of this zone of exaggerated compliance. In this case, students moved comfortably past one another with closed-mouth smiles and long-focused looks usually reserved by ten-year-olds for thoughts about their favorite foods. There was even a smattering of finger pops and a few discrete echoes of "Yesss!" as the new organization took shape.

Without another word from the teacher, each trio of students began working together on projects that had been started four days earlier. There was a buzz of activity, students matter-of-factly talking to one another about possibilities for the projects. After a few moments, the teacher began visiting one group after another asking students what they were trying to accomplish, then attentively listening to students struggle to articulate their ideas. I noticed that the teacher didn't offer many suggestions but usually responded with something like "And what will you be able to get done today?" Work continued for almost two hours, until lunch was announced at 11:50 A.M. The room had the tone of an energetic office in which people were fully committed to working on an important task.

The experience that gave rise to this memory occurred in 1988. I can still recall much of what was said, still see long shafts of light angling into the classroom, and still sense that quiet excitement that sometimes attends learning. The students in that classroom are seniors in high school now. It may seem odd, but this two-hour interval is my most vivid memory from numerous visits to several sites participating in the ACOT project.

Each group of students was creating a play about life and times in their local community. Their plays were planned, written, and simulated using Showtime.[1] The task culminated a few days later when each play premiered via an LCD panel projecting images and text on the classroom wall. Following each presentation, teams of authors were acknowledged for their efforts by a knowledgeable audience. The class discussed both the content of the drama and the process of making it. Each play represented about twenty-five to thirty person-hours of effort on a relatively open-ended complex task. Participation in such tasks is, in itself, far too extraordinary in the lives of most fourth graders in American schools.

As that Thursday morning scene unfolded, I knew that something very unusual was happening. I had been in more than a hundred elementary school classrooms in the previous twenty years and this two-hour stretch in the lives of some fourth graders and their teacher was special. What I found exciting was the way the teacher had orchestrated this large, cognitively complex task to actively engage students in thinking about their communities. Students produced interesting products and showed pride and joy in the process. In this case, there was more than mere mechanical orchestration, there were artistry and music worthy of the names.

I chose this anecdote to introduce these reflections for two reasons. First, the anecdote, like the ACOT project itself, puts students' learning in working classrooms at its center. The project's most visible mechanism for encouraging learning is the introduction of computers and other digital technologies. The ACOT story, however, is not adequately represented by focusing narrowly on technological tools. The instructional problems and learning issues to which the tools are applied, the responses of teachers and students to sustained educational change, and the interplay between ACOT classrooms and the larger educational and social contexts in which they are embedded are essential pieces of the puzzle. Innovations that do address these latter issues rarely last a decade. Several less visible, but complementary, mechanisms have also been put in place. The largest and most important of these is an extensive program of professional development that addresses much more than training on hardware and software. The classroom session described in the anecdote suggests a balance between technological and human capacity in the classroom.

The second reason for choosing the anecdote is that it illustrates three instructional themes that, from my classroom experiences, in ACOT and elsewhere, are increasingly important for focusing and intensifying students' academic work. These themes, outlined later in the chapter, are particularly well supported by digital technologies.

My interest in educational uses of computers began in the early 1980s when, with a group of colleagues, I studied some cognitive effects of learning to program computers among middle school students. A few years later, I participated in an early field study of an ACOT classroom and subsequently worked with several ACOT sites on a handful of research and professional development projects in elementary schools.

As an interested observer and sometime participant, I watched the project progress through several stages. What began as an open-ended exploration of what might happen in classrooms if access to computers were not a major constraint soon embraced and advocated tool uses of technology, a social constructivist view of learning, and ongoing professional development for teachers as primary planks in its educational reform platform. While these preferences are easily discernible, ACOT classrooms retain considerable flexibility regarding instructional programs for students. The project has also shown unusual flexibility in terms of the sometimes conflicting expectations that arise in the bureaucratic and corporate cultures of the partners. The project has adapted to several large- and small-scale changes in its corporate as well as educational contexts over the decade. This is a remarkable accomplishment for school-business relationships.

The ACOT project's tenth anniversary in 1995 provides an apt occasion for reflecting on both the project and the state of technology and education generally. Without the flexibilities mentioned earlier, there would be no occasion for these reflections. My comments, drawn primarily but not entirely from experiences in ACOT classrooms, are grouped around selected influences of technology on students and teachers, and the dynamics of change.

Some Early Influences of Digital Technologies on Students

It is useful to keep in mind that use of digital technologies in classrooms is still in its early days. The last decade definitely accounts for the majority of experience in this arena but, depending on the definition of digital technologies, perhaps activities could be traced back twenty or twenty-five years. While digital technologies themselves have developed at phenomenal rates, their use in schools has been comparatively slow. The Office of Technology Assessment[2] estimated that, in 1995, American schools had 5.8 million computers for use in instruction, approximately one for every nine students. In the same report, they suggest that very few teachers are actually using technology regularly for instruction. On the other hand, there are now several trade magazines and research journals devoted to educational technology, the most recent edition of the *Handbook of Research on Teaching* and the *Handbook of Research on Teacher Education* had chapters on technology and the most recent edition of the *Encyclopedia of Educational Research*[3] contained upwards of seventy-five references to technology. These indicators of educational respectability are increasing but we are still in the early days. While promises of earlier, nondigital technologies have typically failed to transform educational practices,[4] it is difficult for me to believe that digital technologies will not continue to make inroads into mainstream classrooms. I am less sanguine about our political will to extend ACOT-like educational environments in terms of both technology and professional development programs for teachers and administrators, to most of the country's two million or so classrooms any time soon.

In spite of the uneven progress of digital technologies in education generally, there have been sizable examples of sustained implementation where teachers and students have accomplished major shifts in classroom practices. The ACOT project is among the largest and most mature of these reform initiatives.

Valued Cognitive Outcomes

Classroom studies are beginning to indicate that students benefit from instruction supported with digital technologies. For example, students tend to produce longer, more complicated text compositions and revise their work more often, engage in larger and more cognitively complex tasks, and use higher-order thinking skills.[5] It will take much more research than is currently available to describe in detail just how and why technology influences learning but that it does is no longer the primary question. In addition to the cognitive benefits to students, there are other influences that make a difference in the day-to-day lives of students in schools.

Enthusiasm for Learning and Technology

In ACOT and other classrooms using technology, there is little doubt that most students are enthusiastic about their work. At the beginning, excitement may be associated with the novelty of new activities supported by technology but this effect soon subsides. The enthusiasm does not. Learning activities that are supported by technology often demand physical activity by students. This is especially true of learning activities that draw on constructivist principles. Increased activity, usually implying more student-to-student interaction and more noise, is generally attractive to students. Perhaps this accounts at least in part for students' continued enthusiasm.

New Niches for Students (and Teachers)

In ACOT classrooms, I noticed that the introduction of technology opened up a new set of niches in which students could develop expertise. These niches were usually associated with the official curriculum but sometimes they cropped up somewhere beyond state and district content guidelines.

I remember coming across two fourth graders bent intently over a piece of paper in a school hallway before class. Their discussion was animated and when asked about the excitement, they showed me a computer-generated drawing. It was a plan of a house. One of the students had developed the drawing at the request of the other. A description of what the house should look like had been provided a few days earlier and I had happened along just as the product was being delivered. I later discovered that this same student had provided analogous drawings for several classmates and was developing a reputation for computer drafting.

In another case from the same classroom, lots of students made computer-generated cartoons and submitted them to the newly initiated classroom newspaper. Soon the cartoons of two students were acknowledged informally by the rest to be most interesting. Both students continued to develop their expertise and clearly enjoyed their recognition. It's not that these students could not or would not have developed cartooning skills without technology, but I believe that the likelihood of developing these skills, especially in school, would have been far lower. The presence of technology no doubt made creation of cartoons easier in the first place and it supported exposure of the cartoons through the classroom newspaper (about which the same observations could be made). But there's more to it than making use of drawing programs, word processors, and desktop publishing at school. Public computer monitors allowed peers to see and interact about the cartoons while they were being created. This was true not only for the budding cartoonists in question but also for anyone who tried to produce one. As a result, many students had some idea of what it meant to create a good cartoon and contributed to the process of identifying which cartoons were interesting and which were not. This process, supported directly and indirectly by technology, is quite different from having students hand in cartoons to a teacher for grading, and it is intimately related to reshaping roles for both students and teachers.

Keyboarding

In the early days of digital technology in classrooms, there was concern over keyboarding. Could elementary school students be taught keyboarding? Were children's hands big enough to manage a standard keyboard? It turned out that students learned to use keyboards remarkably quickly and with relatively little instruction. With a little experience, most children typed at least as fast as they could write in longhand. Looking back, it now seems odd that this was ever a serious issue.

A Different Identity at School

ACOT kids were often considered special in the school and on the school yard. Perhaps this privileged status tended to decrease over time but in the first few years it was definitely present. Typically, only a few classrooms in a school were ACOT classes, thereby creating schools within schools. There was a selection procedure for admission and although other classrooms were likely to have some technology, it simply was not on the same scale with ACOT. In fact, there were very few classrooms in the world, at least in the early days, that provided anything like the quantity and quality of technology support for classroom teaching and learning.

Some Influences on Teachers and Teaching

When innovative programs are initiated in existing organizational structures, it is not easy to predict who will step forward to participate. If there are high levels of ambiguity about the structure and prospects of the program, then the risk to potential volunteers may be too high. After all, most schools as organizational entities are relatively conservative and teachers generally have placed high value in security.

When the idea of ACOT was first mentioned at a prospective school site, perhaps in a hallway between classes, the idea must have sounded outrageous. The notion that every student would have a personal computer on his or her desk and another one at home[6] must have lacked credibility to savvy teachers and elicited bad jokes from cynics. Who would accept this extraordinary challenge?

Who Were the ACOT Pioneers?

When I met the majority of the early participants, there were a few surprises. As a group, early participants were risk takers; they were searching for something. No surprise here. What did surprise me was that, for the most part, early ACOT teachers had little or no prior experience with digital technology. They were not techies. They were, in many cases, veteran teachers who knew their way around classrooms and schools. They were confident of their teaching skills and had achieved high levels of success in traditional teaching without digital technologies.

Another Side of the Coin

There were (and are) many benefits for ACOT teachers but participants often had to go the extra mile to make the project work. Some teachers' contributions to the project were easy to see. Teachers worked long hours and committed substantial portions of their summers to ACOT activities.

Some implications for the day-to-day work were more subtle; not all of the local conditions were necessarily supportive of the innovation. For example, some sites were located in states or districts with highly specified curriculum content requirements and grading policies. These conditions made it awkward to reorganize the school day in terms of time or curriculum. In one case, an early morning session was instituted allowing teachers and students to try innovative activities before the official school day began. This initiative was undertaken by local teachers in part to avoid criticism that ACOT classes might be stretching the boundaries of the official curriculum too far. This practice went on for months and effectively extended the school day by an hour. The early morning session was voluntary for students but most of the class attended regularly.

This addition to the school day required teachers to negotiate a number of the school's surprisingly powerful subsystems that so often slow innovative projects to a crawl—or, in all too many cases, stop them permanently. Alternative transportation had to be arranged for students without increasing the cost to the district. The custodial staff of the school had to agree to having the building open early in the morning, the teachers themselves had to vouch for the security of the equipment in the face of increased risk of theft or vandalism, and there were many similar obstacles.

Any number of everyday factors attending this very high-profile project were double-edged swords. For example, there was the prestige and excitement of being on the cutting edge but increased attention gave rise to resentments in some quarters. ACOT teachers sometimes got large or, in a few cases, double classrooms to accommodate the new equipment. Getting adequate power supply to the room sometimes disrupted teachers and students in other classrooms and incurred an unanticipated expense. The ACOT project, like most innovations, often had a local champion in the district hierarchy resulting in good news as long as the champion maintained high status in the district. Visitors to ACOT classrooms—television crews, parents, researchers, educators from near and far—increased dramatically, causing wear and tear on the bureaucratic fabric once the novelty wore off.

In spite of the workload and sometimes draining local politics, ACOT teachers have tended to stay with the project, some for the entire decade. This is by no means a common occurrence among high-profile, labor-intensive innovations in education.

Professional Development

While the inventory of hardware and software at ACOT sites garnered the attention of most visitors, the participating teachers were and are the heart of ACOT. As we have seen, they worked hard in their classrooms and from the inception of the project, they were supported by a sustained professional development program. In the early years, the entire teacher cadre attended extensive residential summer programs in Cupertino where, among other things, they shared successes and failures from the previous year, worked with emerging technologies, designed and exchanged curriculum units, interacted with an array of university-based teachers and researchers, and mounted extensive demonstrations of educational applications of technology for designers and engineers at Apple's corporate headquarters.

Summer institutes were also powerful social occasions that forged a clear identity for ACOT teachers as a group. The project involved participants from widely separated parts of the country. This fact gave the group a national status and erased any tendency to parochialism.

Each academic year also included a number of professional development activities. Participating teachers communicated via America Online and AppleLink from the inception of the project.

Whether they knew it or not, when teachers joined the project, they embarked on an intense and practically continuous program of development that in one way or another touched every aspect of their lives as teachers. Over the decade, ACOT teachers became a community of practice, a term that was not in common parlance while they were doing it. In the process, ACOT foreshadowed much of what is now considered best practice in professional development circles.[7] The Office of Technology Assessment is only now raising awareness of the need to spend substantial portions of resources on staff development when implementing technology in classrooms.[8]

The ACOT project also sponsored a broad array of research and development projects that engaged classroom teachers, university-based educators, and students in working classrooms. In some cases, these projects were exemplars of what school-university partnerships can be.

While it may not have been an explicit part of the ACOT design, many teachers began an authentic kind of team teaching in the context of the project. By *team* teaching, I mean an arrangement for joint planning, enactment, and reflection on instruction—as distinguished from *turn* teaching, where teachers simply alternate their presentations. Turn teaching does not often lead to significant instructional change. As anyone who has engaged in authentic team teaching knows, it is a potent context for thoughtful examination of teaching and learning. Like most—perhaps all—activities that have the potential to generate and productively channel the high levels of intellectual and emotional intensity that seem to attend nontrivial changes in teaching performances, team teaching is labor intensive and therefore expensive. ACOT sites, at least in the early days, usually had both sufficient resources and the innovative attitudes to foster team teaching.

Through these direct efforts (summer institutes, on-line networking, and classroom research and development projects) and indirect efforts (team teaching), ACOT teachers found themselves at the center of multiple influences for change. It was as though ACOT had helped organize an incubator for change by saturating, even oversaturating the teaching environment with opportunities for development. Although there was a core of shared experiences, the overall matrix of influences was quite different from site to site. To some extent, these large differences among sites made it difficult to give a concise description of the ACOT program. But regardless of site to site variations, most sites had more than a handful of other initiatives operating and thereby approximated an incubator for change. I am not implying that individual elements of a program do not matter, far from it. I am saying that regardless of the content of individual program elements, if you do not have enough of them to reach some dimly seen threshold, then the program may hold no possibility of change for the majority of participants. If there is any validity to this speculation, then it is sobering news to the single-solution, silver-bullet programs that typically promise lasting change and six months later leave nary a trace in classrooms. While it remains somewhat problematic to separate the effects of the professional development matrix from the hardware and software that were also central to the project, ACOT's decade of work provides education with a valuable example of long-term, broad-spectrum professional development.

This complex, sustained, multistranded program gave researchers an unusual opportunity to follow the development of a cadre of practicing teachers over several years. One analysis of data on ACOT teachers yielded a descriptive model of change.[9] The model posits a sequence of stages or phases that tend to typify teacher practice in using technology to support teaching and learning. The sequence progresses from an entry stage to adoption, adaptation, appropriation, and invention. This model also suggests that high levels of intensity and extended time periods are required to realize nontrivial changes in teaching beliefs, skills, and practices.

Emergent Themes for Classroom Learning

During ACOT's first decade, educators' views about learning were increasingly influenced by social constructivism. At the beginning of the decade, constructivism was already making major inroads among American academics; by the end of the decade, it constituted the mainstream view. In public school classrooms, however, even at the end of the decade, constructivist pedagogy is still more discussed than practiced.

At its outset, ACOT was blatantly nonsectarian in terms of learning theory, but after a few years it adopted the by-then prevailing view in the literature. Well before the end of the decade, visitors to ACOT classrooms could often see organizational patterns and discourse practices that, influenced by principles of social constructivist pedagogy, were in marked contrast to traditional practices. While digital technologies have been used to support a range of pedagogies, ACOT chose to explore the broad constructivist path. In the classrooms themselves one sees a mixture of practices as teachers and students negotiate the flood of demands that influence individual classrooms. Students probably still spend more time on traditional tasks but the distribution of activities is moving steadily in a constructivist direction.

Against this background, three interdependent learning themes stand out in my perceptions of ACOT classrooms over the decade. While each theme is conceptually independent of technology, technology has demonstrated that it can adapt to and support each theme exquisitely. At the beginning of the decade, I might have included these items in a laundry list of potential influences on learning but would not have singled them out as being more salient than others. From experiences in ACOT and other classrooms, they now appear to be much more important and relatively accessible paths to student as well as teacher learning.

First, I think the power of composition environments as contexts for learning has been underestimated and underused. The classic example is writing. Contemporary theories of reading give a much greater role to writing than was commonly the case only a decade or two ago. The ascendancy of writing has been greatly supported by the development of personal computers and word processing software. But ACOT classrooms are replete with composition environments, most of which are strongly supported by digital technologies. Drawing, painting, music, architecture, video—all of these domains now have sophisticated software that allows learners to design, compose, manipulate, revise, and exchange ideas. Where students and teachers are composing, cognitive engagement is focused and intense.

A second theme is the importance of artifacts in the learning process. Although this point is deceptively close to the first point, it can hardly be overemphasized. Digital technologies are exceptional in their capacity to create, manipulate, transport, and store artifacts of learning activities. When students work with these technologies they usually come away with a physical representation of their work. The house drawings, cartoons, robots, and plays mentioned earlier constitute physical entities that students can examine, demonstrate, talk about, and exchange. In a profound way, physical products make learning public. Having a physical product during as well as after a learning activity keeps learners thinking, communicating, and speculating about what might come next.

The third theme is the utility of collaborative or cooperative tasks in elaborating and deepening learning. This theme began gaining adherents in schools well before digital technologies came on the scene. These tasks are noisier, more difficult to manage in the classroom, and sometimes characterized by overt conflict, running directly counter to characteristics that have for too long been the shibboleths of good instruction. However, the intensity of engagement and quality of artifacts produced in collaborative tasks suggests they are potent contexts for learning for large numbers of students and teachers. Digital technologies have had some direct impact on collaborative tasks, for example through networking, but the larger impact has been indirect. Where digital technologies have been used to support constructivist pedagogy, as they have in ACOT, more group projects have been introduced and hence more cooperative learning.

In recalling experiences in ACOT classrooms, these three themes seemed especially important for students' sustained productive engagement in learning. The opening anecdote is one example that involves all three. Students were working on a collaborative task that involved extensive composition and at every stage had a physical product. In the example, students' energetic engagement in learning was in the foreground but their activity was supported at several levels by an array of digital technologies.

While I think that these three themes made important changes in the classrooms I visited, they did not characterize all or even most of the learning activities. This may not be bad news, since learning may in some sense be optimized when a variety of learning conditions are present. For example, while I favor neoprogressive pedagogies, I do not think that direct instruction is anathema to learning.

Perhaps a diet metaphor can be invoked. In the case of diet, health is a function of the distribution of proteins, carbohydrates, fats, vitamins, and so on. Too much or too little of particular elements leads to certain kinds of pathologies. In this crude analogy I am suggesting that in the main interventions in ACOT classrooms increased opportunities for collaborative, compositional tasks with physical artifacts shifted the learning activity diet in a useful direction. By implication, exclusive dependence on a narrowly defined regimen of collaborative, compositional tasks would probably lead to inferior learning. Trying to understand what the elementary ingredients are and in what combinations they facilitate learning for particular learners is the challenge that all thoughtful teachers face. The ACOT project, by not becoming too doctrinaire, seems to be addressing this concern productively.

In my thinking about classrooms' using technology to support teaching and learning over the past decade, the notion of connectivity and its implications for education seem, oddly enough, to be missing. Several years of the decade were past before schools had even a few machines connected in local area networks. ACOT, for example, had several participants who invested inordinate amounts of time trying to get early networks to perform even elementary functions. Since then, major progress has been made in terms of connectivity within ACOT and most sites have developed cutting-edge applications. However, the potential effects of connectivity on education are enormous and may soon rearrange the way educators think about instruction. But that seems to be a story for the next decade. To this point, connectivity has had very little impact on American classrooms. Given the barriers presented by inadequate infrastructure in schools, education may react very slowly or not at all to faster and more powerful information transfer. I, for one, looked ahead from 1985 and did not see the World Wide Web.

Change and Overdetermination

The practices described in the anecdote at the beginning of this chapter represent a change in the kinds of activities that students in one class undertook as part of their pursuit of learning. It might be more accurate to say that, among other things, the distribution of tasks changed. After a few years in the ACOT project, students were spending more time on larger, more complex collaborative tasks involving physical products than had been the case in previous years. By now, that distribution will have changed yet again.

If we ask what caused or at least influenced these changes, there is no simple answer. A lot of different things happened that influenced the direction and magnitude of the changes. Some may be traced directly to the introduction of digital technologies, while others may have had little or nothing to do with technology. For complex phenomena—and classroom learning is certainly a complex phenomenon—there invariably seem to be many potentially causal influences for any particular outcome. Furthermore, most if not all of these influences taken singly are neither necessary nor sufficient to achieve a given outcome. This implies that if we are examining potential influences one at a time, or even two or three at a time, we may or may not detect effects. To the extent that this situation holds for classroom learning, we may describe it as overdetermined. My experiences in ACOT have instructed me yet again on this point. It would appear that many things in the realm of the social sciences are overdetermined. Perhaps I should pin a note to this effect on my sleeve since I seem destined to have to learn it repeatedly.

When it comes to innovation and change, educators too often act as though they too have forgotten this notion. If educational systems are overdetermined, then there are likely to be multiple reasons any given practice exists. By the same token, to change an existing practice is probably going to require changing several things. However, too many change efforts proceed as though a single factor will be sufficient to establish a new practice. This is rarely the case. In fact, we should assume that many causes are the norm and we should design change efforts accordingly. In this sense, ACOT may have succeeded in part because it made a variety of interventions and sustained them for long periods of time. Now, let's see, what does that note on my sleeve say?

It is remarkable that the ACOT project is in its second decade. Who would have thought that this partnership, juxtaposing the bureaucratic culture of schools and the faster, rough-and-tumble corporate culture of a major corporation, would survive a decade—let alone develop a broad range of educational innovations that have demonstrated new possibilities for classroom practice. This project has given American educators many examples of how to proceed and some examples of how not to. Tomorrow's students would be well served if new partnerships were founded to expand on what this pioneering effort has shown is possible. Some will say that technology and education are doomed as partners for the one moves too quickly and the other too slowly, leaving education with perpetually outmoded machines. The gap that is created, however, is not to be eradicated so much as managed. For after all, the play's the thing.

Notes

1. Software introduced by Minnesota Educational Computing Consortium in the mid 1980s.

2. Office of Technology Assessment (1995, March). *Teachers and technology: Making the connection*. Washington, DC: Author.

3. See Clark, R. E., & Salomon, G. (1986). Media in teaching. In M. C. Wittrock (Ed.), *Handbook of research on teaching* (3rd ed.). New York: Macmillan; Brooks, D., & Kopp, T. (1990). Technology and teacher education. In W. R. Houston (Ed.), *The handbook of research on teacher education*. New York: Macmillan; and Alkin, M. (Ed.). (1992). *Encyclopedia of educational research* (6th ed.). New York: Macmillan.

4. See Cuban, L. (1986). *Teachers and machines: Classroom use of technology since 1920*. New York: Teachers College Press; and Cuban, L. (1990). Reforming again, again, and again. *Educational Researcher, 19*(1), 3–13.

5. See for example, Galindo, R., Tierney, R. J., & Stowell, L. (1989). Multimedia and multilayers in multiple texts. In J. Zutell & S. McCormick (Eds.), *Cognitive and social perspectives for literacy research and instruction*. Proceedings of the National Reading Conference, Tucson, Arizona; and Fisher, C. (1991). Some influences of classroom computers on academic tasks. *Journal of Computing in Childhood Education, 2*(2), 3–15.

6. Two computers per child was one of several original design conditions in ACOT that were modified as the project developed.

7. See, for example, Hargreaves, A., & Fullan, M. (Eds.). (1992). *Understanding teacher development*. New York: Teachers College Press; Lieberman, A. (Ed.) (1992). *The changing contexts of teaching*. Chicago: National Society for the Study of Education; and Little, J., & McLaughlin, M. (Eds.) (1993). *Teachers' work: Individuals, colleagues, and contexts*. New York: Teachers College Press.

8. Office of Technology Assessment (1995, March). *Teachers and technology: Making the connection*. Washington, DC: Author.

9. Dwyer, D. C., Ringstaff, C., & Sandholtz, J. H. (1991). Changes in teachers' beliefs and practices in technology-rich classrooms. *Educational Leadership*, 48(8), 45–52.

8

The Role of New Technologies in Designing Mathematics Education

Jere Confrey

Computers are clearly cultural artifacts. They express our beliefs, hopes, and convictions, embedding them in a pliable and receptive medium. When we design technologies, we design them for communities to use with potential audiences in mind and other audiences out of mind. Once built, our inventions create feedback loops in which the screen objects, commands, and resources become familiar parlance among the user communities, while other potential decisions about objects and users recede in importance. The enterprise of use commands our attention. Thus, computers are tools—tools to accomplish human tasks—and those tools can be designed either to reinforce or to modify social and cultural configurations. To those of us who design, our software products are creations for which we must take responsibility, while admitting that we never really knew quite where they would lead. In a very real sense, our software products are our personal experiments.

The Role of Design

A comparison between design and experimentation bears some deeper consideration. As a researcher engaged in the production of academic scholarship through experimentation, I work in a tightly disciplined way to make studies fit within accepted methodologies, connecting them to existing work and articulating the connections between the experiments and the theories I hold through explicit conjectures. When designing, I give myself more freedom. My intuitions are allowed fuller play; serendipitous occurrences are viewed as resources for the process of creation, and my own experience with students, the knowledge of the literature and research, as well as my own imagination are all invested in the products. I desire structural integrity by seeking the perfect design that works and relates all the parts. Design folds back on itself. It is its own justification, even before it is modified, tinkered with, experimented on, improved, streamlined, or scrapped. Like an experiment, a design is testable, and its refutation seldom surfaces immediately with results; rather, it is re-viewed in light of an array of experiments and situations of use. For these reasons, I would describe designs as speculative experiments of a personal nature. They serve to express deep and often subconscious beliefs.

When design activities are shared between programmer and designer, the communications acts are themselves an integral part of the process. A language develops that guides design and captures a thought. In our design work, three discussions resurface repeatedly. What choices do we want to make as designers, and what choices should be left to the control of the user? How should we design this to be true to a multiple representational view? And how can we build in and legitimize student approaches that might appear on the surface to be nontraditional or awkward?

I begin by discussing design, because much of the excitement of the last ten years has occurred in the design sessions, and because it was during these sessions that my own understanding of mathematics was challenged, refined, and matured. Designing tools for doing mathematics may seem to be a technical process of building in algorithms and hooking them to an interface. In fact, much more than this is possible.

Design is discussed for three additional reasons. It is the speculative nature of the changes made possible by design of computer technologies that has made them such a provocative vehicle for change in mathematics education and education in general. These changes allow us to create a vision less fettered by the constraints and limitations of schools. A focus on design will also be justified in the concluding section, where I propose that student involvement in design processes in mathematics-related activities needs to be more vigorously pursued.

Finally, by viewing learning technologies as personal design experiments, I can structure these reflections toward confirmations, toward surprises and revelations, worries and resistances. When you design for educating, your act can be likened to drawing in wax on an Easter egg and then dipping it in dye to reveal the design. It never looks just like what you planned, for the egg surface and shape, the wax, and the dyes all exert their influences on it, shaping the results. So, if I view the technological work as design, then I can reflect on the ways in which the culture of mathematics, the culture of schools, and the personal idiosyncrasies of the actors all influenced the directions of our initiatives. And, in design, one is always hatching a new plan—and so I will end this chapter with predictions!

Reflecting on the impact of technology on mathematics education is challenging. Computers express our culture's love affair with technology, as they tempt us into a technological determinism, sighing and gulping as we accept changes as inevitable, and accept the speed of change as obligatory. The pace is dizzying and by itself can disorient us into losing our wits, our perspective, and our critical faculties. It's harder to make reflective and critical decisions than it is to be pushed, embarrassed, stunned, or edged into the use of metaphor, analogy, assumption, activity, all permeated and transformed, subtly changed, with technological description. To reflect over the past ten years, I will try to step away from simple preoccupation with the sweep of technological change and think hard about what is best for educating our children.

Background

My involvement in designing software for use in ACOT began in 1988, when Wayne Grant asked me to propose a project at West High School in Columbus, Ohio, using our software, Function Probe, and our materials for a precalculus course, *Learning about Functions Through Contextual Problems*. An experienced teacher agreed to participate in the research using a precalculus class. A five-person research team implemented a curriculum using contextual problems and our software. The curriculum and software has been used at Cornell University since 1987 but it had to be adapted for a secondary school environment and an ACOT classroom. Local networking software was just beginning to emerge, and instability in the software and hardware haunted the students and the teacher. Providing sufficient teacher development and support left us all scrambling, as we sought to implement our fledgling ideas. The teacher, who had to learn a new approach to content and instruction on the fly, courageously and capably kept the class progressing, and struggled to meet our expectations (which evolved daily). Everyone's patience and tolerance were sorely tried; however, with determination on everyone's parts, instructors, students, graduate students and programmers, we all survived. As we were in the early stages of trying to study classrooms in their complexity, data gathering was a constant challenge.[1] Overall, the project was quite successful. The students learned a lot and we were learning about reform-based instruction in a technology-rich classroom.

The software was used later in the context of integrated mathematics and science with a model of experiment, simulation, and analysis. Since then, we have engaged in an extensive tool-based investigations project with third to fifth graders and from that project we are developing geometry software called Shape Shifter for elementary children to learn design while deepening their understanding of ratio and proportion.[2]

Confirmations

What happened that we[3] expected? Not everything was a surprise. We had designed the software to allow students to work flexibly among different representations, and that goal was achieved, with fascinating performances by the students. For instance, perhaps earlier than for any other software for functions, we anticipated the value of a table window as a means to explore functions.

A memorable moment was set up when a local teacher who was going to use the software in his class initially expressed his belief that tables were an unnecessary resource for students. As he put it, "If they can figure out how to go from the x-value to the y-value in the table numerically, it's just a small step to writing that in the form of an equation." To the contrary, however, we witnessed students using the table as an integral and essential part of problem solving. By putting in values first, they were able to identify, select, and define their variables. Selecting particular numerical values revealed hidden qualities; for example, in finding an unknown function such as $y = 3x + 4$, substituting large values for x (for example, $x = 100$, $x = 1,000$) could separate the additive factor (+4) and the multiplicative factor (3) in the function (by producing values such as 304, 3,004, and so on). This was one example of students independently inventing a test that is introduced much later in traditional mathematics instruction, when one studies polynomial functions and learns it as the "test of the leading coefficient of the highest degree term."

In another case in the ACOT class, researchers and teachers sat stumped as a student, typically sullen and uninvolved, generated an original method for finding an equation of a linear function by taking two consecutive points (x_1, y_1) and (x_2, y_2) from the table; multiplying $x_1 {}^* y_2$ and $x_2 {}^* y_1$; subtracting those products; and dividing by the difference $(x_2 - x_1)$. This produces the b term, which can be subtracted from the y values to yield the m value and the equation. The team was thankful that after his proposal, there was a fire drill that gave them time to puzzle out the basis for the method.

By the end of a semester of work with the software, the same teacher mentioned earlier had become an outspoken advocate of the use of the table as an essential resource for student work. Our development of the table as a computer resource led us to examine its role in the historical development of the concept of function. We found that its pivotal role in the generation of the function concept had been in fact obscured and neglected due to the current tendency to rely solely on modern notation in algebraic symbolism.[4]

Our predictions of the importance of listening to students in order to modify our designs proved indispensable to our success. For instance, once it was clear that students could describe the vertical pattern of the covariation of two columns before they could find a linking correspondence or rule, we created a distinction between covariation and correspondence views of function.[5] And we built in a resource so that columns that were not dependent on each other could behave as if they were linked, for sorting, cutting, and pasting. Watching students also led us to build a ratio command into the table, the first of its kind and an original notational contribution to mathematics. This command parallels a difference command and allows patterns of ratio in covariation $\circledR y = y_2/y_1$ to emerge, and thus it allows students to work more flexibly with growth rates in exponential and logarithmic functions. In our calculator, we built resources to allow taking logarithms to any base, still the only calculator we have seen that permits this. It required that we reconsider the design of the y^x key, splitting it operationally in a^x and x^a, to separate logarithms and roots as distinct inverses.

As we had predicted, we witnessed students participating with persistence and interest as the tool supported an inquiry approach to compelling and interesting problems. Consider the problem: Investigate the current worth of a debt of $450,000 resulting from a loan to George Washington's army by Jacob DeHaven in 1777 and never repaid.[6] We saw students engage this problem with extraordinary levels of energy and commitment. Since the software allowed multiple representations of both the problem and attempts at its solution, students were able to carry out independent investigations and subsequently share and compare their methods. This sequence allows students to weigh the merits of alternative approaches and thereby receive instruction from fellow classmates. Students not only learned the ideas, but also developed confidence in their ability to solve mathematical problems.

These three qualities of *using multiple representations*, *building for student-centeredness*, and *supporting inquiry* were all in the original conception. The result was invigorating. Different configurations of students would participate and excel. The best-prepared students who entered with flexible minds and curiosity continued to have strong achievement. However, those who wanted to pass based solely on diligence to task and regurgitation struggled, pleading for algorithmic solutions or criticizing us for failing to teach "correctly." Many students who were typically uninvolved or unsuccessful emerged as some of the best on-the-spot problem solvers and inventive thinkers.

Surprises and Revelations

In design, surprises are the influences that sneak up on you, and when you recognize them, there is a realization that they were lurking around the edges of intentional design for quite a while, persistent but shy. For me, a major surprise and delight was the effect of legitimating the visual in mathematics and where our initial steps in that direction led us. The problem-solving movement had recognized the value of drawing a diagram or finding a geometric proof. But now, with the graphics capability of the high-speed computer and the emergence of mathematical theories such as chaos and fractals, the visual has been brought further into parity in mathematics.

In our software, we supported visual thinking in our graphing window, permitting students to transform functions through direct mouse actions. Designing for translating and stretching of functions was straightforward, but other graphing resources were more challenging. Our stretch tool required us to identify the role of a line of invariance, which we named the *anchor line*. We designed it to be moved from the axes, thereby producing miserable algebraic symbolism but permitting strategically critical visual actions. Others in the mathematics community faulted us for allowing students this freedom, but as we witnessed a teacher demonstrate to a class the set of all solutions to a problem by moving the anchor line off the axis and stretching the function; we realized there was more to the visual intelligence which was being developed than we initially imagined. Our current redesigns for sampling and creating sequences of slope triangles, tangents, bars, and graphs promise to move us further forward in this realm of *analytic visual thinking*. Shape Shifter will bring these ideas to children at an even younger age.

As we examined other software over the years, we saw how subtle differences in design made a big difference in what students learn. Nearly all software for teaching functions includes a graph and table capability with various treatments of algebraic manipulation and calculation. However, few actually support the genuine distinctions among the representations, allowing each to promote independent kinds of thinking. In most functions software, the symbolic, either as spreadsheet notation or as algebraic description, mediates access to the visual; to see or act visually on a function, you first have to input symbolism.

The implicit reliance on symbolic activity that is built into these technologies leaves them in a serious dilemma. They reduce mathematics to one dominant form of expression, symbolic manipulation, but then build in capabilities for the computer to carry out those manipulations. One is left wondering what students in this environment are to do. In contrast, an environment that genuinely supports investigation in multiple representations requires the student to contrast and compare these representations, and powerful mathematical inquiry results. These observations led us to propose a theory of multiple representations that requires a set of representations be varied enough to produce different insights into a problem, but closely enough related to permit interesting comparison and contrast. When such conditions are met, one has created a feedback system in which students learn to act with conviction and persuasion, and to control the interactions. Designing with intentional attention to this issue rather than just including multiple representations required new awareness on our part.

For example, understanding inverses of functions in Function Probe is experienced differently in each representation. If one has a button to calculate compound interest on \$100 at 4 percent interest for x years, the button is built as "? a^x 1.04 = * 100 =." On the calculator, its inverse is input as "? ÷ 100 = $(\log_a x)$ 1.04 =." This requires the student to undo the previous procedures, reversing the order and replacing multiplication with division and exponentiation with taking a logarithm. In the table, the action for generating an inverse function requires one to switch the x and y columns, thus needing to interpolate geometric means to produce interpolated arithmetic means to get a desired prediction. Graphically, when the function $y = 100 (1.04)^x$ is reflected about the line $y = x$, it produces $y = \log_{1.04} (x/100)$.

Learning to use and coordinate feedback in pursuit of understanding is a critical concept that merits more attention and careful research. To date, new technologies boast of their increased capabilities to add representations, but unless those representations can be actively juxtaposed and their interrelationships explicitly verbalized and justified, these additions may cause more confusion than insight. This is an arena for research that remains largely uncharted, but is of great significance in establishing what it means to understand mathematics in these new environments.

Another response to the question of what mathematics is with these new technologies has to do with the relationships among mathematics, context, experience, and action. This territory provided more surprises for us. When I began my work with computers, teaching mathematics by putting the contextual problem first was rare. It was generally believed that one should present the content, and then word problems should be appended to the end of the activity. Mathematics educators have virtually reversed that order in the new curricula. This shift places activity at the forefront of mathematical enterprise and has transformative effects. Mathematics is no longer a promissory note saying "Learn this strange and unmotivated activity now and we promise you will see a need or a use for it later." Exploration and inquiry are now grounded in familiar or compelling situations. And different, overlapping populations of students thrive.

Our early attempts at the inclusion of context were tentative, text-based, and narrowly restricted to perfect or near-perfect mathematical description. Later endeavors broadened the connections of mathematics beyond science and economics to social science and other fields. This pull toward interdisciplinary inquiry and complexity is fraught with excitement and challenge. First, it demands knowledge on the part of the teacher (or researcher) that is not typically available. Second, it is all too easy to undertake interdisciplinary inquiry superficially. Because each discipline has its own methodologies, standards of evidence, procedures, and forms of argumentation, an amalgamation of these can result in doing justice to none of the disciplines. Finally, investigating complex phenomena challenges the structures of schooling, such as standardization across the years, prescribed progressions, brief class periods, and articulation among the grades and subject matter.

Even within mathematics, statistics and functions have been kept in relative isolation from each other since the late 1800s. These subjects developed different trajectories, statistics aiming for increasing control of variability and mathematics preferring the generalization of class, idealized form, and building of structure. With the increase in investigations involving motion and data, these artificial separations are being challenged. There is great value in merging these endeavors, but doing so requires very careful instructional design.

Thus, for those of us involved in the use of computers in education, the past decade opened numerous possibilities. As opposed to the dispersal of established routines to be memorized and regurgitated for the test, new ways of thinking and solving problems have emerged. Problems are given *in situ* using rich sources of data and measurement, visual intelligence has been rescued as a part of mathematical talent, and finally, students have been provided opportunities for exploration within mathematical systems with multiple sources of feedback.

Worries and Concerns

A fundamental question that must be constantly asked in an educational system using advanced technology is, Are the tools getting smarter or are the people using them getting smarter? Without returning to the conservative position that mathematics is all disciplined individual mental activity and that therefore any tools are merely crutches, we must insist on asking ourselves the question, If technologies are solving equations, factoring polynomials, producing the roots, graphing the functions, doing the calculations, and so on, what mathematics is the user doing?

In one classroom, students worked on movement down an inclined plane. They used sine and cosine functions repeatedly in their inquiry. But when interviewed, it became apparent that for most of the students, sine and cosine functions were keys to push on a calculator, and the students had no idea of the connection of these functions to the geometry of the situation, the triangles of the inclined plane.[7] Students did not view sine as a ratio of the sides of a right triangle. The mathematical actions were all carried out within black boxes by the push of a button, so what mathematics was being learned?

While the inclusion of situation is generally a positive advance, a concern lies in how such activity is characterized. Most recently, educators claim that users are mapping the mathematical models onto the world. Relieved of the drudgery of calculation, learners are freed to concentrate on finding and collecting the data and evaluating the fit of the model. However, as we add temperature and pressure probes, heat and motion sensors, and so on, data collection, sampling, and smoothing are automated, and mathematics classes are devoted to the push of a button to produce data, which are then transferred to another environment and electronically analyzed, producing graph, table, and equation. What began as a single black box—about which the question asked was, Whose box is faster or holds the most memory?—is replaced by a series of black boxes, about which one asks, Who can hook together the most black boxes?

I worry that with the new technologies, the appearance of sophisticated behaviors is relatively easy to achieve with little real understanding, and in a culture in which outward appearance is given overly high regard, pseudolearning of this sort needs to be actively avoided. Avoiding this trap requires a reexamination and reconceptualization of the very nature of knowledge and expertise. There will be active forces who will resist this reconceptualization, as a threat to their own claims to power which depend on the continuation of traditional views.

I will discuss three means of avoiding pseudolearning that require active involvement of designers of new technologies and users who select these technologies in the schools. The first method concerns how mathematics relates to the world, the second concerns how mathematics is done and described, and the third concerns the design approach required to support the first two. Subsequently, I discuss some roots of the resistance to making these changes.

Most people believe that mathematical knowledge underlies phenomena and awaits our discovery. However, constructivist views challenge this approach and suggest instead that knowledge is the result of an interaction between human need, experience, culture, physiology, and the phenomena under investigation. One cannot remove the human element from the investigation, nor is it desirable to do so. Mathematical laws are set within theory, definition of the problem, choice of approach, forms of evaluation, and decisions on technologies. From a broader perspective, they are set within cultural practices that define who can and should pursue mathematics, how these people are trained and financially supported, who is credited with the results, what solutions are legitimized and promoted, and how such knowledge is used.

Accepting such a revised view of knowledge means that it is insufficient to treat mathematical modeling simplistically as a mapping of the mathematics onto the world. We must engage our students in understanding the genesis of mathematical ideas, because herein lie their original purposes. Functions are not models of the world. They evolved as means for describing curves produced by mechanical devices and geometric conditions; ways of creating, interpolating, and extrapolating tables for navigation and finance, and models for describing trajectories of motion. They evolved within intense debate of the relationship between human science and religion, between the role of physical experimentation and the discourses to be used to describe it; the desire for regulatory power over communities using systems of taxation and means of war, and social provision of community systems of health, transportation, and utilities. Since the world is not given to us, but made by us as we act on it and gain experience, modeling is a complex activity of mind, involves multiple perspectives, and is always a contingent activity. When we describe a model as only a black box into which we feed agreed-upon data and check implied outputs, we oversimplify and make invisible these rich and varied connections between mathematics and human experience.

When mathematics is cast as mere algorithm and procedure, its relationship to human action is obscured. Yet this connection between mathematics and human action is a key to bridging mathematics and culture. Such a bridge could allow mathematical modeling of issues related to judgment, negotiation, and decision making even at the simplest unit of analysis, the concept. Each concept in mathematics is actually a miniature cognitive tool and, in this sense, we have found the term *scheme* to be useful in mathematics learning. The notion of scheme revitalizes concepts' links to human activity, uncovers those roots, and provides experience of those roots as an essential part of the learning process. Schemes remind us that concepts result as humans find a means of acting successfully to resolve a perturbation and then routinize such actions into operations, concepts, and habits. Unfortunately, schemes can also be used to reinforce a view of mathematics as a solitary activity, and so the use of this term must be diligently monitored to recognize the role of others.

Focusing on action reminds us that we should take care not to create technologies that neglect or diminish the value of sense and of body. To understand concepts, we must experience their basis in actions directly through the use of hammers, balances, weights, compasses, and rulers. If we use our technologies only to invite our students into virtual realities and simulations, we risk losing their understanding and commitment to everyday living. Doing so poses a grave danger, particularly to children whose bodies must mature not only in physical strength but also in perceptiveness and sensory-motor acuity. Simulation is a powerful learning tool, but it is not equivalent to or better than hands-on experimentation. It can extend but should not replace these activities.

I am not simply casting this involvement with physical tools as an issue of developmental stages from concrete referent to abstraction. Our nearly exclusive focus on language in modern society (as spin or public opinion) allows us to develop a great schism between our words and our actions, and the loss of embodiment affects us at all levels. Certainly children suffer if they are not encouraged to integrate the physical and the mental, but adults too may suffer from this increasing disjunction. Not only is there danger of general physical deterioration, but a loss of connection to one's surroundings, alienation from one's emotions, lack of awareness of bodily changes, and disregard for environment. To cast mathematics solely as the manipulation of symbols is to pass mathematics under a steamroller—flattening, homogenizing, and blurring the very distinctions that make it interesting. Abstraction is not a spiraling away from context; it is the identification of likeness in things that appear on the surface unlike.

Thus, if my worries are that modeling will be treated simplistically and action and physical connections to the environment will deteriorate, then what design principles for new technologies can help us avoid these outcomes? Tools with canned routines delivered to the user provide little or no opportunity to experience the felt need for an idea and to see how the construct, the mathematical idea, relieves or fulfills the need. Concepts are themselves tools for thought, but when one does not know what spawned their development, their more elegant uses are unlikely to be realized. We need to design learner-centered tools, in contrast to expert-centered tools.[8] The former are tools whose sophisticated use is learned gradually by the student through the construction of procedures, through the coordination of carefully designed representations that create contrast and comparison, and through attention to the creation of record and means of exchange. We need to ask, What can I do with the software? rather than, What can this software do? Most graphing calculators and many pieces of software for mathematics are expert tools; their effectiveness in introductory learning environments is limited. In order to design more effective tools for learning, we need careful research and evaluation, and we need to learn to describe distinctions in use and identify the qualities of environments that are effective for learning rather than for creating the appearance of expert performance. Learner-centered tools will also vary by experience of the user with the ideas, becoming more sophisticated and expert at the later stages.

The use of these tools must include questions about why concepts were created, what and whose purposes they serve, and how they are currently used. Asking such questions about mathematics reveals its discriminatory history and this too must become a serious item of discussion and critique.

Resistances

When I first solicited support from a national agency to design new technology for mathematics education, I spoke to a man who told me that any proposal must catapult ten years into the future and be visionary in its plans. His question to me was, "I'm sure you've had the experience of cooking in a kitchen designed by a man?" My response was quick: "Probably, but more to the point, I work in a university designed predominantly by men." Though he didn't fund the work, leaving me to find funding elsewhere, the story brings to mind a fundamental issue—equity.

We are facing a serious and possibly catastrophic bifurcation in our society. We still are seeing a small number of predominantly white men designing the new technologies, and if the designers are homogeneous of race, gender, or class, the designs will of necessity not produce equitable outcomes. We have seen ample evidence in other fields, such as in literature and music, that diverse participation enriches the product created. Clearly design is as expressive and as intimate an activity as these. Thus, even though many members of the dominant culture hold unquestionable commitments to equity, they will not succeed without diverse representation among their membership. Being reared into dominance is a priori to acquire a lens and that will influence any design process. Thus, equitable outcomes from technological innovations without diversity in gender, age, class, and ethnicity, are impossible.

Since knowledge of mathematical thinking and reasoning continues to be essential in the education of programmers and designers, designing new technologies for the purpose of changing the patterns of participation requires aggressive and critical interventions. If mathematics and science education in the country continues to be a set-aside primarily for the wealthy, the Anglos, or the males,[9] we will not see the diversity of inventiveness and originality we need in our new technologies. If mathematics and science remain the playground of only a small segment of our majority (soon to be minority) population, dangers also accrue. We can see some of that now in our economy's addiction to the production of computer games of war, destruction, and violence, while but few resources are devoted to educational software, or games that offer imaginative alternatives to violence.

There are disturbing indicators of the directions our country's attitudes about mathematics and science may take if we do not reverse these trends. First of all, there is a pervasive anti-intellectualism in the country, promoted by a segment of the population that seeks instant gratification in all things, including instant learning. If learning becomes a form of media blitz and not the careful creation of opportunities for lifelong learning and gains in empowerment of communities, we will see the increasing deterioration of the American mind. In contrast, learning necessarily requires persistence and determination, and it also creates its own form of reinforcing feedback. Habits of mind are deeply satisfying, as our curiosity becomes more easily aroused and our confidence in using new technologies to improve learning opportunities increases.

Not only must we aggressively address past inequalities, but we must be watchful for evidence of using our new technologies as a wedge to filter out underrepresented groups. In many supposedly liberal upper-middle-class communities, movements to detrack mathematics and science are attacked for their threat to the status quo. Thinly veiled in the language of "meeting the needs of the exceptional student" is the worry, "How can I as a parent be sure my child gets the same share of the economic resources and opportunities that I did?" Certainly, this is an understandable goal, but if it necessitates denying access to others, discrimination results. Privileged access to advanced technologies to prepare some children better than the crowd decelerates the process of change, threatening our primary means to increased democratic debate and equitable education.

Thus, close attention must be paid to who is using these new technologies and what they are using them for. What are the long-term impacts in a society when many of our sons spend more time plastered to a video game than engaging in interpersonal contact and physical exertion? What happens in a culture where instead of gaining control of oneself though self-awareness and mutual respect and tolerance, we allow youngsters to prefer virtual environments where perfect control can be achieved? We see virtual reality already being used as a setting for pornography—a place where violence against women, against children, against society can be practiced virtually without restriction. What happens when it is clear that communicating over e-mail allows us more unfettered discussion because we can walk away from the participants by switching off the machine? Does this fulfill our need for interconnection or provide us only a false sense of community?

Not to grapple with these questions represents a form of neglect of our children's well-being. In designing our new technologies, it is not sufficient to treat equity solely as an issue of access. It involves deeper issues of the design of society, the portrayal and legitimization of knowledge, ways of growing up for our children, and giving back to the next generations.

Looking to the Future

What would I wish to see the future bring? Fundamentally, I would like to see a revolution in what people think knowledge is. There is a deep schism between knowledge and responsibility. To heal this schism, education must teach students how to contribute to the betterment of the world and communicate the expectation that they do so. I would like to see new technologies that contribute to healing this wound.

Such technologies would involve early and repeated involvement of students in modeling and design. We must nurture our students' creativity and inventiveness as well as develop their capability to find their way around in the rich environment of information. New technological developments will allow problems to be informed by remote data and expertise via the Internet. Video sequences will be easily available and tools for data collection from video will allow close connections between event and mathematical analysis. Both of these activities, modeling and design, would be seen as contingent activities in which evaluation is inexorably linked to the goals of improvement of the culture and the environment. Cooperation, competition, and collaboration would be built into educational materials as opportunities for intellectual growth. And there would be stronger recognition that communication and education are essential components of any knowledge system, especially in a democratic society.

There is a fundamental question in all of this: Should new technologies lead toward the de-schooling of American society or toward the transformation of the traditional schools? There is ample evidence of movement in both directions. Home schooling in this country is on the increase as schools fail to meet parental perceptions of their children's needs. Schools continue to teach an antiquated curriculum using methods that leave children bored, unmotivated, and out of date. At the same time, reform movements are moving toward increasing use of constructivist approaches that invigorate schools and increase expectations of students. However, the schools are slow to obtain and use technological resources effectively.

If schools are to be transformed from compulsory attendance institutions to resources for human growth, they will have to drastically alter their views of the role of new technologies. This change in perspective must start with superintendents and school boards and include school administrators, teachers, parents, and aides. This means changes in physical layout, time distribution, curriculum and pedagogy, and professional development. With computers and the Internet permitting access to appropriate materials and sources of expertise outside the school setting, schools will not be repositories of knowledge but centers for the development and exchange of ideas.

It is my opinion that the issue of professional development

among educators is ultimately the critical one. If we do not change the preparation and professional education of teachers to focus on improving and enriching teachers' and administrators' knowledge of subject matter and its relationships to all forms of technology, educational institutions will become increasingly and intolerably obsolete. In this country, education across diverse communities is critical to the vitality of our democratic ideals and strengthening of our democratic practices. Thus, we must renew our efforts and our commitment to seek solutions within these institutions, while continuing to use the new technologies to pressure schools into seeing and accepting the critical need to move in these exciting and challenging directions.

Notes

1. Two unpublished dissertations and a number of publications resulted from data gathered in this project. For the dissertations (both from the Department of Education, Cornell University, Ithaca, NY), see Rizzuti, J. (1991). *Students' conceptualizations of mathematical functions: The effects of a pedagogical approach involving multiple representations;* and Piliero, S. (1994). *An investigation of teacher knowledge, beliefs and practices in the implementation of a problem-based curriculum using multi-representational software in a technology-rich classroom.* As the software and its use were transferred to a new educational setting that combined algebra, trigonometry, and physics, five additional unpublished dissertations were undertaken at the Cornell Department of Education. See Afamasaga-Fuata'i, K. (1992). *Students' strategies for solving contextual problems on quadratic functions;* Borba, M. (1993). *Students' understanding of transformations of functions using multi-representational software;* Smith, E. (1993). *Practice in a radical constructivist setting: The role of virtues and activities in mathematical knowing;* Doerr, H. (1994). *Building computational models: An effective approach to constructing student understanding;* and Haarer, S. (in progress). *Creating narrative accounts of problem-solving with integrated software tools.*

2. Confrey, J. (in progress). Shape Shifter [Computer software]. Ithaca, NY: Cornell Research Foundation.

3. I will use both "we" and "I" in this chapter. The work reported on here was performed collaboratively by a team including Forrest Carroll (the lead programmer), numerous other programmers, some graduate students, Erick Smith (a research associate), and Alan Maloney (my husband and coauthor of new multimedia precalculus materials). I directed the projects. However, the opinions in the chapter are my own reflections, informed by the work itself and by the many conversations on these issues, among this group and with others, held during the past decade.

4. See the doctoral dissertation by J. Rizzuti cited in note 1.

5. Confrey, J., & Smith, E. (1994). Exponential functions, rates of change, and the multiplicative unit. *Educational Studies in Mathematics*, 26, 135–164.

6. Belkin, L. (1990). 213 years after loan, Uncle Sam is dunned. *New York Times*, May 27, pp. 1, 22.

7. See the doctoral dissertation by H. Doerr cited in note 1.

8. Confrey, J. (1990). Student conceptions, representations and the design of software for Mathematics Education. In Bowden, B. (Ed.), *Design for learning*. Cupertino, CA: External Research Division, Apple Computer, pp. 55–60.

9. Moses, B. (1994, February). *Equity through meetings*. Speech presented at Hobart and William Smith College, Geneva, NY.

9

Reflections on
Computer-Supported Writing

D. Midian Kurland

Since the inception of the program, ACOT classrooms have had a constructivist bent. It is not surprising, then, that much of the software used in ACOT classrooms is of the tool variety, especially writing tools. It was this interest in computer-supported writing that first brought me in contact with ACOT. My own interest in computer-supported writing began almost twenty years ago. As a graduate student in 1977, I began using an arcane programming editor called TECO running over a terminal connected to a DEC PDP-10 computer to do all my writing. As primitive and clumsy as this system was, TECO, coupled with an equally arcane text-formatting program called NROFF, enabled me to experience an ease of writing unlike anything I had previously encountered with a typewriter or paper and pen. As a developmental psychologist, I watched how the computer changed the way I wrote and began to wonder whether computer-supported writing might have a similar effect on the writing experience of children. This chapter is a opportunity for me to reflect back on my attempts over the past decade to develop computer-based writing tools for children and their teachers. Along the way, ACOT played an important role by helping me sort out the relative importance of good tools and good teaching. But before getting to that part of the story, let me begin by recounting my early attempts at developing new kinds of writing tools for children.

Benefits from having students as young as kindergarten do their writing with a typewriter have been well documented as far back as the 1930s.[1] There is good evidence that when the handwriting bottleneck is removed, students tend to write more, develop a more positive attitude toward writing, and make fewer mechanical errors. Writing from a keyboard also has the side benefit of making what is written much more legible, and thus easier to share with others. Back in the early 1980s, as the first microcomputers began to appear in schools, a number of educational psychologists and software developers began to wonder what might happen if we now gave children access to powerful computer-based writing technologies.

Bank Street Writer: Tools for Revision

In the spring of 1981, I joined the Center for Children and Technology at Bank Street College in New York to help develop one of the very first word processors for children, the Bank Street Writer.[2] Think back to 1981. At that point, the Apple II was only four years old and its keyboard was still restricted to uppercase letters. At the time, 48K was considered a lot of memory. The IBM PC did not yet exist. Bitmapped screens were a novelty. Computers were just beginning to appear in schools, driven by two diametrically opposed forces: computer-aided instruction (CAI) and Logo.[3] The CAI forces promoted computers as more efficient teaching machines that could deliver content to waiting minds in verifiable packets. The Logo forces, on the other hand, promoted the computer as a tool for liberating students from the drudgery of the prescribed, carefully metered-out curriculum. Interestingly, in neither model was there imagined much of an instructional role for the teacher. The CAI model took responsibility for designing the curriculum, presenting it to students, and assessing their mastery at the end of each unit. The Logo model encouraged self-discovery by students working alone or in peer groups on projects chosen on the basis of their interest to the participants. It was into this polarized world of educational computing that the Bank Street Writer emerged.

The Bank Street Writer was a breakthrough product in its day. It was the first word processor for the Apple II that displayed both upper and lowercase letters in a bitmapped window. Rather than relying on control keys and complex command strings, the Writer used simple on-screen menus located at the top of the screen. Directions were provided on the screen for carrying out multistep operations (such as moving a block of text). Instead of trying to make the Writer as feature rich as we could, we tried to reduce word processing to its barest essentials so that as little as possible would get between students and their writing. The Writer thus had far fewer features than did its two main rivals, WordStar and AppleWriter, but its simplicity and the clarity of its interface gave it a distinct advantage with children, or so we hoped.

In 1981, conventional wisdom said that schools, especially elementary schools, would have no interest in purchasing word processing software for students. Typing, after all, was something students did not typically encounter until high school. Despite strong evidence that writing with the assistance of a typewriter can have beneficial effects on students,[4] schools had turned a blind eye to this research. Keyboarding was for secretarial training or college-bound students in their senior year.

So here we were with a keyboard-based writing tool in 1981 that required the use of a $3,000 computer plus a printer. At first, no publisher would touch the program. One leading publisher of educational titles told us they had recently conducted a market study of the types of programs teachers were interested in purchasing for their classrooms. Of the sixteen categories of programs surveyed, word processing finished dead last. Eventually, however, two publishers, Scholastic and Broderbund, decided to take a chance on the Writer and published it for the school and home markets respectively. The rest, as they say, is history. The Writer went on to become a huge success in homes and schools, ushering in the era of computer-as-tool in schools.

The Writer was the first commercially successful example of a computer-based writing tool designed specifically for the classroom rather than the office.[5] Its design was driven by what in hindsight was a rather naive theory of writing that went something like this: writing is easy, it's rewriting that's hard. Students don't engage in much spontaneous editing, and teachers rarely require it, because of the mechanical overhead. Therefore, if we make editing easy, students will write better and with more pleasure.

The design team for the Writer consisted of a large group of educators and writers from Bank Street College in New York and Intentional Education in Boston. During the design team meetings, it became clear that we were not just making a better typewriter, but were creating a tool that in subtle and not-so-subtle ways was promoting a particular theory of writing. For example, at one early design meeting, someone on the design team argued that the proper way to write is to write out a complete draft, then go back and edit as a discrete step. Students should not be encouraged to fiddle with their text as they write. Therefore, composing and editing should not be intermingled. To discourage this style of writing, this designer suggested that we design the Writer to penalize students for editing as they compose. The way to do this, he proposed, was to create separate modes for composing and editing. In write mode all students would be allowed to do is type and use the delete key to erase the last character or two. In edit mode, students could move the cursor anywhere in the text and highlight chunks of text to copy, move or delete. To further reinforce the difference between composing and editing, he proposed that we program in an irritating delay when switching back and forth between write mode and edit mode to further discourage students from casually editing while writing.

Happily, the rest of the design team rejected the idea of building in a penalty for switching between modes. We did, however, keep the idea of separate write and edit modes—this seemed to correspond to the way writing was traditionally taught. As it turned out, however, not being able to move the cursor around while in write mode was tremendously unpopular with users. This was one of the first things we changed in the next version of the program. Since for most of us the main point of having students write with a computer was to encourage revision, we biased the feature set in this direction. For example, we chose the on-screen names for our menu commands (edit, move, copy, delete, print draft, print final) to encourage editing and revision. This sounds routine now, but remember—this was years before the Macintosh arrived to make commands such as these seem as obvious as the on/off switch.

So, did putting this word processor out into thousands of classrooms lead to dramatic improvement in student writing? Obviously not. Instead, the Writer was assimilated into then-current classroom practices as both teachers and students struggled to come to grips with what difference word processors make in how writing is taught and how writing is done.

In the early days, many schools used the Writer to teach about word processing rather than as a tool for their students to use to *do* writing. I recall one review of the Writer from a district newsletter in 1982 in which the reviewer only discussed the interactive tutorial (how to enter text, manipulate blocks of text, and save and retrieve files) that came on the back of the program disk. Nowhere in the review was there mention that there was a fully functional word processor on the other side of the disk! Teaching about word processing rather than teaching writing with a word processor was understandable in the early days of educational computing. Unfortunately, this style of use is still not uncommon today. For example, in some classrooms, students write and edit their work with pen and paper. Then, once the teacher certifies that their writing is acceptable, the students are allowed to "publish" their work by typing their finished papers into the computer and printing out an attractive final version.

The problem back in 1981 and the problem with many classrooms today is that the Writer and other word processors that followed are too often used by students to do the same assignments that they would have been given were a word processor not available. In short, few schools have modified their curriculum to take advantage of the new possibilities offered by word processors and other electronic writing tools.

Throughout the 1980s, the Bank Street team continued to refine the Writer's design and port it to run on all the popular computers and networks of the time (IBM PC, Commodore 64, Atari 800, Corvus). We also added various "teacher features" (for example, frozen text, *non*-automatic spell checker, student data disk management) in an effort to encourage the use of the program in classrooms in ways more in alignment with our ideas of why to use word processing with students in the first place.

ForComment: Tools for Review and Comment

One thing the Writer did not support in any direct fashion was group writing or structured review and editing. This was an area I explored while developing another writing tool called ForComment.[6] ForComment is a group review tool. It enables an author to send around a text to a group of reviewers in series or in parallel. Each reviewer can comment on, or revise, any section of the text. When all the review copies are returned to the author (on disk or over the network), ForComment collates all the comments and revisions into a single master copy in which the individual contributions of each reviewer are clearly marked. The author can swap suggested revisions in and out of the text. Reviewers can see each other's comments and can add comments to comments or revisions. In short, the program provides extensive support for the important comment and review stage of the writing process.

ForComment was designed to support the social context of text refinement and change negotiation. In the program we tried to simulate the red pen and yellow sticky note review cycle. While we were technically successful in providing a tool that supported the review process, users found it awkward to use fundamentally different tools for editing and revising than they used for initial composition and final polishing. We heard the same complaint from users about other helper applications, such as grammar checkers, page layout programs, and outliners. In other words, it was not enough to supply individual programs to support each discrete stage of the writing process; the individual tools need to be integrated into a more coherent system.

Wordbench: Tools to Support Process Writing

In 1986, the Bank Street Team—with funding from the Rockefeller Foundation—began work on a completely new suite of integrated writing tools. The program that resulted, Wordbench,[7] was both more comprehensive with regard to its coverage of all phases of the writing process, and more explicit in presenting a particular theory of writing instruction through its design. The program itself consisted of a collection of writing tools including an outliner, a simple database for taking notes, a bibliography tool, various prewriting tools, a full-featured word processor, and text analysis and publishing tools.

Wordbench was designed around the idea of writing *projects*. Unlike traditional word processors that store each written product as a discrete file, Wordbench creates project folders. Each project folder can contain several prewriting activities, one outline, one set of notes, a list of references, and one or more documents with all their drafts. This collection of writing products is linked together in ways we thought would be useful when writing. For example, the note cards include a field for outline heading. While a student is taking notes, he or she can pop up the outliner and link the note to a specific outline heading. This enables the outline to be used to sort the notes in the database. Later, if the student reorganizes the outline, their collection of note cards can be resorted to stay in alignment. When ready to begin writing, a student can have the program paste the outline into the word processor, which automatically converts outline headings into section headings (in accordance with the settings in the program style sheet). The text of the notes associated with each outline heading is then pasted into the document as a paragraph under the corresponding section heading. In other words, by doing a good outline and taking careful notes, a student is rewarded by having the program create a rough first draft.

Wordbench was well received by a small group of teachers who were already committed to process writing as popularized by the work of the Bay Area Writing Project, the National Writing Project, Donald Graves, Lucy Calkins, and a host of other writing researchers and practitioners. Our design goal in Wordbench was to support each of the classic writing stages (prewriting, drafting, sharing, revising, editing, publishing) without requiring that each be followed in a prescribed order. In other words, a student should be able to start writing, then take some notes, then do an outline, then take some more notes, then brainstorm about what angle to take, then start a new draft, and so on. Other programs being developed around the same time, most notably IBM's Writing to Write, approached the writing process as a formula to be followed in lockstep fashion regardless of the demands of the writing project. In either case, both Wordbench and Writing to Write presented teachers with tools that came with a clear point of view about how they should be used.

In Wordbench we tried to provide scaffolding for a particular style of writing. The idea behind scaffolding is that novice writers benefit from certain explicit supports in areas where expert writers implicitly know what to do. Over time, these supports can be relaxed or withdrawn as the novice becomes more experienced. Scaffolding approaches were also tried by a number of other influential writing programs, most notably QUILL, WANDA, and CSILE. Each of these programs tried in its own way to design in supports for good writing practice. Interestingly, each of these writing environments evolved out of research programs concerned with the social context of writing and writing instruction. Clearly it was time to acknowledge that there are limits to how much pedagogy or theory can be designed into the tools themselves—equal attention has to be paid to writing instruction and the context in which writing happens in the classroom.

ACOT Writing Institute

By the end of the 1980s, I was growing frustrated with designing writing tools only to see them used in classrooms in ways that failed to exploit all the features we had worked so hard to design in. At first, I had attributed this problem to external factors such as the lack of enough computers in classrooms or inadequate technical support to keep networks running or insufficient time for training teachers or students in the use of computers and electronic writing tools. My desire to see what would happen when all these logistical hurdles were removed attracted me to ACOT. In 1990, I arranged with the ACOT staff to conduct an investigation of computer-supported writing in technology-rich classrooms. The project we put together was called the ACOT Writing Institute.

I designed the ACOT Writing Institute along with Charles Fisher and Keith Yocam, in collaboration with several teachers from the ACOT sites in Cupertino, Memphis, and Nashville. All of the participants in the institute met for a two-day workshop early in the school year to discuss writing theory and to plan activities for the year. We then continued to meet regularly throughout the rest of the year by communicating over the America Online network. Through weekly group on-line chat sessions and ongoing discussions in an electronic forum, the Institute members raised questions and voiced concerns as we explored how computers can be used to teach writing more effectively.

At first I was curious about what effect all those computers in the ACOT classrooms would have on solving some of the problems I had observed in other settings. For the first time in my experience,

I was able to observe classrooms in which all the usual technology bottlenecks seemingly had been removed. I say seemingly because it was apparent right from the start that providing lots of computers and good software tools was just the beginning.

The ACOT teachers in the Writing Institute were by then savvy enough with computers to understand that computers by themselves do not, and cannot, teach writing (or anything else for that matter). Teaching is what teachers do. The role of technology is to facilitate the teaching process, not supplant it. What the ACOT teachers were interested in learning was how to apply the computer in the teaching of the writing process, and, more important, just what teaching the writing process really means. ACOT teachers start out not unlike most other classroom teachers. They come with varying amounts of training and experience and must contend with the same pressures as any other teacher—too little time to prepare, too many students to look after, too many conflicting demands from parents, administrators, and, as ACOT teachers, from the ACOT staff and research associates such as myself. I was interested in really seeing process writing in all its richness put into practice with the aid of a wide assortment of writing technologies. The teachers, on the other hand, were more skeptical of all the rhetoric surrounding process writing and more concerned with finding good writing assignments than trying out new writing tools. I recall clearly a meeting in which one of teachers said that while she had been making students do prewriting activities for most writing projects, whenever students were given the opportunity to produce a piece of writing completely on their own, they never engaged in any of the prewriting exercises the teachers were working so diligently to teach. If prewriting was so important, she asked, how come children never do it on their own?

Process writing was a hot topic back in 1990. As it has come to be generally understood, process writing differs from traditional methods of writing instruction in many important respects.[8-12] In particular, process writing begins by viewing writing as a complex cognitive process embedded in a social context. Accordingly, the role of the writing teacher is to create discourse communities in which authentic tasks are undertaken by students with the dual purpose of learning to write and writing to learn.[13] Process writing is more than simply marching students in lockstep through the writing stages—prewriting, drafting, revising, editing, publishing. It presumes that these stages or processes are important only when the student is engaged in a meaningful writing task for a real audience with whom the student wishes to communicate. That is, it is the context in which the writing occurs that determines the relevance of the stages. Clearly, computers are not required for a teacher to embrace this pedagogical approach. For the Writing Institute, then, the two key issues were:

- In what ways can or should computers be employed with students within a process writing framework?

- In what ways might access to particular types of writing software encourage and support a process writing orientation in a classroom?

The Writing Institute teachers helped me appreciate the full life cycle of a piece of school writing. Most writing begins with an assignment initiated by the teacher in accordance with a lesson plan that is itself designed to address the set of learning outcomes specified by the district for that particular grade. Students respond to assignments by producing one or a series of written products (notes, outlines, drafts, and so on) that are turned in to the teacher or, in some cases, edited first by peer reviewers. The peer reviewers or the teacher annotate the work, write observations, or record marks in a grade book or journal, then hand the work back to the author for revision, filing, placement in a portfolio, or publishing. Over the course of the year, the teachers in the Writing Institute sampled various word processors, outliners, planning tools, idea generators, grammar checkers, and various and sundry other electronic writing tools. By the end of the year, there was uniform agreement that technology still has a long way to go before it really can be said to be suited to real classroom needs. In particular, the teachers observed that:

- Most software programs are complicated and idiosyncratic in their operation, making it difficult to use more than one piece of software at a time.

- Integrating material across different software packages is difficult and awkward, thus artificially reinforcing the notion that the writing process is composed of a fixed sequence of discrete stages.

- The more students become adept at selecting and using appropriate software for various writing tasks, the more difficult becomes the teacher's job of monitoring what all the students are doing.

- Many writing tools (grammar checkers, spelling checkers, on-line style guides) were designed for accomplished adult writers, and thus provide too much or the wrong kind of information to be of benefit to novice writers.

- Because of their adult orientation, some writing tools supplant learning rather than support it (as with spelling checkers that automatically replace a misspelled word with the correct spelling instead of asking the student to type in the correction, thereby reinforcing the correct spelling).

- Most tools help the student write. However, each new tool creates products that are in many cases difficult for the teacher to review or assess.

- Even if all these problems with the technology itself could be resolved, there would still be serious impediments to writing in the classroom stemming from the way schools organize time, compartmentalize subject material, and assess student competency.

More and better technology is important, but restructuring schools and modifying approaches to assessment need to progress hand-in-hand with advances in technology before real and lasting change is likely to occur. On balance, the teachers were cautiously optimistic about computer-supported writing. However, no one went so far as to toss out all the pencils and writing pads—even though there were more than enough computers around to make this a viable option.

TextBrowser: Tools for the Teacher

The Writing Institute ended as a project in 1992, but I continued my involvement in ACOT in another capacity. Even before starting the Writing Institute, I had begun work on a prototype for a new kind of networked writing environment designed around the needs of the teacher rather than of the students. There is an increasing array of great writing tools for students. However, as my experience with the ACOT Writing Institute had shown, there is a real lack of tools that support the teachers' role in the writing process. So with research assistance from ACOT I continued to work on this new writing support system for the teacher that I called TextBrowser.[14]

The TextBrowser prototype provides teachers with a suite of tools for systematically marking up, annotating, and grading students' electronic writing products produced from a wide assortment of writing tools. TextBrowser also provides flexible holistic assessment forms that encourage and help teachers capture much richer information about the documents they review than is possible with traditional paper-and-pencil methods. All the tools in TextBrowser are customizable by the teacher. The idea is that assessment means being able to respond to each student's work and track development in accordance with what it is the teacher believes is important. Therefore, teachers can configure the text annotation tools in TextBrowser to reflect what they feel is important about their students' writing.

To help the teacher keep track of *where* each text came from, TextBrowser maintains a database of the teacher's writing assignments. Each student text that comes into TextBrowser is automatically linked to this database. Among other uses, this enables the teacher to sort texts by type (for example, all the book reports) or specific assignment (for example, all the essays on TV violence).

In order to know *whose* text the teacher is looking at, TextBrowser maintains a student information database used to establish a link between each text and its author.

In order to keep track of *what* the teacher has seen and the comments, corrections, or grades made to each text, TextBrowser maintains a complete database archive of every text reviewed linked with all the annotations made to each text. TextBrowser uses this archive to help students and teachers create portfolios of student work. Portfolios can then undergo further analysis by the teacher or student. In addition, entire texts or portions of texts can be extracted from the archive as a whole or from just the portfolio pieces to serve as the basis for subsequent lessons or reports (for example, "Show me all the paragraphs from Billy Smith's work over the past two weeks in which I indicated there was something I wanted to discuss in our next writing conference").

TextBrowser also uses its archive to automatically assemble and maintain a hyper grade book. On the surface, the TextBrowser grade book looks like most other electronic grade book programs; it lists students and assignments with corresponding grades or status indicators, and calculates averages, end of term grades, and other student, group, and class statistics. However, because it is an integral part of TextBrowser, teachers can interrogate the grade book to find out more about any student or assignment, or to investigate where any particular grade came from. For instance, when clicked on a student's grade for a particular assignment, the program will reach into the underlying archive and retrieve information on the markups applied to the paper in question, or can display the holistic assessment form filled out by the teacher for this paper, or, if the teacher so desires, the grade book can even bring the original work back on the screen with or without the markups and annotations previously applied to it.

TextBrowser also includes a lesson and report editor that helps teachers put together reports or language arts activities drawing upon students' own work for their content (for example, "Create a lesson on use of the passive voice using as examples paragraphs from my students' essays or short stories").

In summary, TextBrowser provides a three-pronged approach to supporting the use of electronic writing tools in the classroom. First, TextBrowser helps teachers look at and comment on student texts in ways that are responsive to the teacher's own sense of what is important, as well as school- or district-mandated requirements. Second, in addition to tracking grades and assignments, TextBrowser uses the comments teachers put in each student document to maintain detailed records of the problems and successes each student is experiencing. And third, by archiving all the work students produce, TextBrowser makes it practical to go back and systematically review student work, create portfolios of their most illustrative writing, and produce language arts lessons based on the students' own work.

Work inspired by TextBrowser and its many components is still ongoing. As the prototype progressed, it exposed a number of weaknesses in the electronic environments found in schools, including ACOT classrooms. Besides the technical hurdles—fast, reliable networks, high-capacity databases, format-independent document viewers, and so on—perhaps the biggest challenge facing any tool designer for teachers is adequately taking into consideration where teachers do their lesson planning and where they review student work. Much of the planning that goes into running a smooth class-room is done, and much of the time spent assessing student work is spent, outside the classroom and often outside the school. Teachers work in the teachers' lounge, while on duty in the cafeteria, on the subway home, and at the kitchen table late at night. As long as tools require that teachers be at a specific workstation to plan assignments or review student work, they are unlikely to become widely used in the ways intended. Teachers are fundamentally mobile workers. Any technology that ties the teacher to a specific time and place for work is inherently limiting. Looking ahead, our next hurdle is ubiquitous access—anytime, anywhere computing in which information follows the teacher rather than the other way around.

Final Thoughts

ACOT began some ten years ago with the naive question: What happens when teachers and students are provided with all the com-puters and printers and other electronic gear they need? Back then, it seemed reasonable to imagine that lots of technology in and of it-self might cause dramatic changes to occur in the classroom. As I re-flect back on my career as a developer of writing tools, I see that I too began with the naive notion that an age-appropriate word processor in and of itself would dramatically change the way writing happens in the classroom. From there, I progressed to working on programs that addressed aspects of the writing process that were not well supported by traditional word processors. This in turn led me to design programs that more tightly integrated tools for supporting all phases of the writing process. Finally, I turned my attention to the needs of teachers and began to develop a system for knitting together curriculum planning, student work, and teacher comments into a co-herent whole. Along the way, the ACOT Writing Institute helped me develop a deeper appreciation for the role of the teacher in the writing process and the efficacy of using networks to create more au-thentic contexts in which writing can happen.

So where to next in this saga of computer-supported writing? As

ACOT enters its second decade, the technical landscape has certainly changed. There are many more computers in classrooms and homes and many more writing tools to choose from. In addition to text, students can now pepper their compositions with images, sounds, digital video clips, and links to other documents. This has made writing more fun for some, but we are just beginning to appreciate the importance now of teaching media literacy and developing students' critical faculties in all media, not just text. With networks and integrated mail systems, student writing can now be more easily shared with multiple audiences within and beyond the school. With the recent explosion in interest in the World Wide Web, students have even greater electronic publishing outlets for their writing. The emergence of OpenDoc, Java, and other component document architectures is opening the door to far more personalized, integrated, and collaborative writing environments than we have yet seen. As these and other new writing tools and systems emerge, ACOT teachers and students will be there as enthusiastic skeptics to kick the tires and try them out. However, amidst all these technical advances, it is as important as ever to not lose sight of why we have children write, how we have them work, and in what ways we assess their progress so that they become ever more accomplished in their writing. For me, the ultimate lesson from ACOT is that technology can never be more than one rather small part of the story.

Notes

1. Wood, B. D., & Freeman, F. N. (1932). *An experimental study of the educational influences of the typewriter in the elementary school classroom*. New York: Macmillan.

2. The Bank Street Writer was the brain child of Richard R. Ruopp, then president of Bank Street College. Many people contributed to the Writer's early success, most notably Gene Kusmiak, Charles Olson, Frank Smith, and Peter Dublin.

3. Kurland, D. M., & Kurland, L. C. (1987). Computer applications in education: A historical overview. In J. F. Traub (Ed.), *Annual review of computer science* (pp. 317–358). Palo Alto, CA: Annual Reviews.

4. See Wood & Freeman, cited in note 1.

5. The Bank Street Writer was not, however, the first word processor designed for children. Writer's Assistant, a Pascal-based editor developed at the University of California, San Diego, predated the Writer. This editor was eventually incorporated into another educational writing program, QUILL, which was being developed at BBN Corporation around the same time as the Writer.

6. Mark U. Edwards, James A. Levine, and I designed ForComment. It was originally published by Broderbund Software for the IBM PC. Eventually it was purchased by Computer Associates and is still available today in versions for Novell (DOS) and DEC VMS.

7. Wordbench was published by Addison-Wesley. It was a critical success but a commercial failure and is no longer available from the publisher.

8. Calkins, L. (1986). *The art of teaching writing*. Portsmouth, NH: Heinemann Educational Books.

9. Flower, L. S., & Hayes, J. R. (1981). A cognitive process theory of writing. *College Composition and Communication, 32*, 365–387.

10. Freedman, S. W., Dyson, A. H., Flower, L., & Chafe, W. (1987). *Research in writing: Past, present, and future*. Berkeley: Center for the Study of Writing, University of California.

11. Graves, D. H. (1983). *Writing: Teachers and children at work*. Portsmouth, NH: Heinemann Educational Books.

12. Langer, J. A., & Applebee, A. N. (1987). *How writing shapes thinking: A study of teaching and learning*. Urbana, IL: National Council of Teachers of English.

13. Hull, G. A. (1989). Research on writing: Building a cognitive and social understanding of composing. In L. B. Resnick & L. E. Klopfer (Eds.), *Toward the thinking curriculum: Current cognitive research* (pp. 104–128). Washington, DC: Association of Supervision and Curriculum Development.

14. The TextBrowser prototype was created with support from Education Development Center, Inc., and Apple Computer.

10

Redefining Computer Appropriation

A Five-Year Study of ACOT Students

Robert J. Tierney

Much has been written about ACOT teachers and the technology used in their classrooms. While this is valuable information, I contend that the real strength of ACOT lies in the vision of technology that the students themselves have discovered and appropriated. The teachers, staff, and researchers at ACOT support and influence student development, but the most significant changes have actually occurred on the margins of classrooms, in conjunction with what students have realized for themselves. What happens to the students in ACOT has not been limited to gaining proficiency in the mechanics of computer use; the entire learning process has been enhanced as students' access to multimedia tools and other technologies has increased. As the students have recognized the potentials of multimedia, their individual perceptions and innovations have moved to center stage. This shift has involved more than the showiness of the projects. Students' conceptions of and acquisition of knowledge as well as their understandings of how media might be employed have become more flexible and dynamic. Furthermore, technology has become woven into the fabric of who they were and what they do both individually and within their classrooms, schools, and wider communities. Technology has played an important role in how these students view themselves, the roles they assume in their various communities, and the cultural practices they have come to value.

Over a six year period, I was involved in a longitudinal study of computer literacy acquisition.[1] In my research, I was specifically interested in literacy acquisition that emerges from the experiences of students with high computer access. My goal was to explore student development in a manner that was observational, open-ended, and not constrained by predetermined views of outcomes, and so I have focused on development rather than on a single set of measures or comparisons with equivalent groups. The study involved two sets of students who attended ACOT classrooms for the entire four years of their high school experience. The extended duration of this investigation allowed my colleagues and me to achieve a developmental perspective, and it enabled us to assess shifts in student learning across time.

From a rather unique exploration of students' appropriation of computer literacy, we gleaned strong evidence that the circumstances of ACOT had a major, significant, positive, and sustained impact upon student learning and ways of knowing. Indeed, I feel that the data warrants some rather bold claims about the impact of computer appropriation upon students involved in ACOT. These students discovered *genres of power* in new texts, new ways of negotiating meaning, and new ways of knowing that allowed them to develop and test a variety of approaches and hypotheses. This phenomenon is at the core of ACOT and is what makes attempts at systemic reform and efforts to replicate the success of ACOT worthwhile. If we ignore the magnitude of the shifts in perspective that occurred, or if we fail to consider the nature of computer appropriation, then we will trivialize the significance of ACOT.

Computer Appropriation in an ACOT Studio Setting

In their review of research on media and learning, Clark and Salomon[2] suggest that one of the drawbacks to studies of the impact of media is that very few situations provide for the sustained daily engagement that would allow for a reasonable assessment of the impact of technology. ACOT affords students as much access to computers as students in regular classrooms have to books and pen and paper. Students are able to interact with a community of learners in various subject areas within a context that enables them to explore and learn with a range of multimedia software, databases, and word processing software. At the ACOT site in Columbus, we were involved with students who have had access to state-of-the-art software and hardware, as well as technical support. We were therefore able to look at the impact of computers on a cohort of students over the course of four years, during which time, students had more than four hours per day of access to a computer at school and free access at home. The ACOT site permitted the level of investment that Clark and Salomon called for, and therefore provided a unique opportunity to study the impact of computer media upon learning.

Participants in ACOT's Columbus site are selected by lottery each year from over a hundred applicants. Class sizes are kept to thirty and students represent a cross-section in terms of ability and background. The students came from primarily working class homes of a variety of racial and cultural heritages. Students selected for the case studies were drawn from the first two cohorts of students to complete the ACOT high school program. From these two classes, students of varying abilities were identified for inclusion in this study and agreed to participate.

The physical arrangement of the high school classrooms was largely self-contained. Most of the class periods were taught in one of three or four rooms involving team-teaching situations (for example, science and math; English and history). Within each classroom, every student had a variety of workspaces that afforded opportunities for individual or group use of computers, printers, and other media equipment, and access to a range of software.

Observations and interviews served as the cornerstone for our investigation into computer literacy acquisition. General interviews were used in hopes of providing details of the students' attitudes, expectations, perceptions of learning experiences, engagement of thinking, and learning outcomes. Within twenty-four hours of each lesson, classroom observers debriefed individual students. Records of classroom and student activities were transcribed from both videotapes and running records.

In conjunction with our open-ended orientation, we struggled with ways to discern and account for patterns in the data. The difficulty of so doing was compounded by the masses of data we had collected from each year. For some students, we accumulated over seventy-five thousand words across the four years. To cope with the enormity of data and as a way of identifying themes, we developed a coding system using FileMaker to help organize the data. First, each student's comment was coded in terms of learning activities, such as process (planning, drafting, revising, sharing, and so on), type of activity (seventeen types were included), nature of support (peer, teacher, and so on), mode (computer or noncomputer), and overall effect.

Our second pass—colloquially referred to as "the wall"—consisted of displays of all the data on the walls of our offices. It was at this point that we began to discern the types of shifts. Themes were identified by examination of these data across different years and by various procedures that we used to achieve alternative perspectives on the data. The multiyear nature of the data allowed us to examine developmental issues for each individual. As data were reorganized by years, we were able to see differences from one year to the next.

The use of TEX, a HyperCard application, afforded frequency counts for each word by year. For example, the frequency of each and every word for each student provided a comparative distribution of the number of times students used different words, such as graphics, friends, interface, and so on. These collagelike distributions provided a take on the data that served as a cross-check on some of the trends that were originally identified by other means. While these counts were seen as complementary to our other analyses, it should be obvious that such counts have limitations: they represent what was said, not what was felt, thought, or done; and decontextualized words sometimes render interpretation problematic. However, what was apparent in both the interviews and the word counts was that students were appropriating technology on its own terms. It was not until we listened closely to what students were saying and began rethinking the data in terms of the symbol systems actually used that we realized that our adopted lens was restricting our view of what was occurring.

Initially, we had unwittingly adopted the view of technology as merely an adjunct to learning. With the introduction of desktop publishing, scanning capabilities, and hypermedia, some major shifts occurred in how students represented and approached the integration of ideas from various sources. To capture these dimensions, we found it useful to characterize the shifts that occurred according to: the students' ways of representing ideas and thinking about issues symbolically; students' approaches to developing projects and problem solving; certain social dimensions of students' learning, including their collaborations and nature of support; and students' ongoing goals and attitudes. To this end, we labeled each shift as pertaining to one or more of the following: view of text, process, self-evaluation, learning goals, task demands, and social concerns. In addition, these comments were examined across time and in terms of whether they pertained to a student's expectation, perception, or outcome.

Some Findings

During the first year of the project, most students approached texts in a rather limited fashion. They would proceed with little regard to integrating graphics or other media, layout would be largely predetermined and conventionalized, text would be rather linear and non-layered, and audience was considered somewhat as an afterthought. In accordance with this tendency, computers were perceived as tools

for expediting revision to ensure accuracy. Audience served the function of offering general reactions and correcting errors. The computer-
generated copy was for presentation rather than involvement.

These tendencies can be seen in students' comments during year
one and in word counts conducted across the four years for the two
cohorts of students. Students often made remarks in which the role
of the computer was diminished. For example, one student stated:
"It helps you to just write down, or type out what you're thinking
about, and then lets you get the rough idea out, and then you can
just go back and change or add to it." Another referred to "accuracy
and neatness" as the major advantages of using the computer. Very
few students mentioned graphics and the use of other media; nor
did students discuss alternate formats or layouts for presenting ideas
in a multilayered fashion.

At the end of year two, all students reported an improvement in
their ability to write as a result of using the computer. They felt that
their final products looked better and were easier to revise. The computer was now thought of as a tool for efficiency. But by years three
and four, student involvement with multimedia became more prevalent, especially via HyperCard. And, in turn, major shifts occurred.
Accompanying the shift to multimedia was the unearthing of a new,
more powerful set of genres and text forms. With these texts, students seemed less verbocentric. They were more likely to include
graphics and appeared to display a greater willingness to experiment.
There was also a shift in their approach to developing ideas.

These new genres and possibilities brought to the surface a desire to develop electronic texts with multifaceted appeals and different relationships to both the ideas themselves and the possible
readers' responses. Their developing understandings of technology
altered how students used symbol systems (that is, graphics and
print) to explore, represent, and share ideas. The students moved
beyond the incorporation of text and graphics to consciously stretch
the capabilities of the software to create a form that mirrored the
dynamics of their ideas and the messages they wished to convey.

Students realized the possibility of developing texts that, to use their words, were "dynamic rather than static." Their approaches to ideas became less verbocentric, less linear and unidimensional. In conjunction with being able to explore the integrated use of various graphics (animation, video segments, scanned images or various ways to graphically depict data), they began to utilize diverse media as a way of achieving different perspectives on issues as they explored physics, history, and other subjects.

Some students were not engaged in using multimedia technology extensively, yet their shift to graphics was still notable in terms of the possibilities that they saw and the thinking that they did. Whereas, in years one and two, texts were largely devoid of graphics except to enhance the look of a page, in years three and four, graphics had become an integral symbol system for exploring and sharing ideas. The students were exploring ways to integrate images with written text to achieve different takes and twists. They found themselves free to develop texts that were nonlinear and multilayered. They embedded buttons in their texts and graphics that, if clicked upon, accessed other layers of information. By year four, students would experiment with graphics, sound, animation, and text so that their projects were integrated, aesthetically pleasing, and engaged the attention of fellow students and others. As the students stated:

"A lot of times I'll work with graphics and experimenting. I'll create new graphics or new drawings like I did like that and then figure out new ways to put it in there so it catches the person's eye and they want to read more or try to get away with—a picture is worth a thousand words. Try to—I work experimentally a lot with that. Trying to make it so my report only has to be a picture."

"I thought it would be kind of hard to get the graphics and text together at first. And especially when we were doing Hyper-Card. To get the graphics so they would look good. So they didn't just look like a stack. I wanted it to look like a computer program and not a HyperCard stack. It wasn't as hard as I thought it was either. Just putting your ideas down and just doing it a little differently than you first expected to."

"The things that we created weren't really something that could be done on a page. They could be printed out but they still wouldn't be the same, clicking on a button. It wasn't something you could look at; it was something you had to become involved with. . . . I think it makes it more nonlinear sometimes. . . . Like they'll be showing a process on a computer screen."

"I tried to find some graphics that would appeal. I tried to figure out how to do animation so it wouldn't be too boring. I tried to make it as fresh as I could."

Their strategies had shifted toward using the computer to crisscross their explorations of a topic or issue as they enlisted various media in search of different but complementary perspectives. For example, one student described how his process of developing projects had evolved throughout the years. He labeled each year: ninth grade as the year to work on writing; tenth grade as the scripting year; eleventh grade as working with graphics; and the twelfth grade as "combining it all together in one big media project."

Technology appears to have increased the likelihood of students' being able to pursue multiple lines of thought and entertain different perspectives. Ideas were no longer treated as unidimensional and sequential; the technology allowed students to embed ideas within other ideas, as well as pursue other forms of multilayering and interconnecting ideas. Students began spending a great deal of time considering layout, that is, how the issues that they were wrestling with might be explored across an array of still pictures, video segments, text segments, and sound clips. It was apparent that students in the high-access classroom had begun exploring texts in very complex ways. These tendencies are also apparent in the terms used by students in assessing their own learning. In year one, words such as type, read, and write were among the most frequent terms used when they assessed their learning. By year four, words such as graphic, layout, multimedia, project, show, and see had become much more prevalent.

Literacy is a social act. Oftentimes, what is read, written, dramatized, or symbolized is intended for others; usually it has involved others in the selection and formation of ideas, and at the very least it involves a negotiation with oneself amidst a community of co-learners. These social dimensions are not an offshoot of what is involved in literacy experience, they are integral. Students' engagement with computers is no different. Whereas computers may be viewed as isolating students and minimizing interaction with others, data from our case studies suggest this is not the case. All of the current case-study students both were engaged in and viewed their experiences with computers as involving complex social dimensions. Students interacted and collaborated with others in a variety of ways, including joint construction of projects, cooperative ventures involving differential expertise, coauthoring, parallel development of similar work, and side-by-side consultation and group sharings. In these processes, students assumed a range of roles such as demonstrator, partner, helper, sounding board, advisor, mediator, supervisor, and decision maker. In other words, the social facets of computer literacy in ACOT were pervasive, dynamic, and complex. Students were engaged in literacy that was socially transforming for themselves, their friends, and sometimes their families. In high school, students' views of themselves as learners often decline together with their appreciation of the relevance of their experience. ACOT seems to have afforded students an experience that is different in direction and kind—especially in relation to community building.

Students were well aware of the extent to which ACOT encouraged students to work together. They often noted the social dimension of the program in regard to both the bonuses of cooperation and the effect interaction had on their relationships. As one said, "Well, one thing, especially when the class is new, it helps build confidence and friendship among the people, because no one knows what they're doing. But there'll be a few people who catch on quicker and people will be asking them 'how do you do this' or they'll be offering help—the ones who have learned it faster. So it's one way to meet people."

Students often found themselves cast in the role of experts advising others on software use, and this interaction with others enhanced their own pursuits. Their expertise was also accessed in the wider community. For example, one student asserted: "My friends in ACOT, they're in it so they understand what it's all about. I have a lot of friends who aren't in it. And they think it's neat too. That I can do some stuff. Sometimes I work with them on projects using the computer, like I just got done working on a newspaper where I worked with a lot of people I knew. Sometimes I'll offer suggestions like—'I could show you how to do that on the computer a lot easier'—things like that. It's kind of just the sharing of ideas." Similar sentiments were expressed by other students who valued the exchange of ideas and the support, as well as the efficiency in completing tasks.

Students in ACOT constantly worked together in groups. Sometimes they worked with friends, other times with assigned partners. The groups generally worked by meeting and discussing an idea or topic and then dividing up the work. They would go their separate ways and then come back together to compile their findings into an integrated whole. During the compilation process they often sat together as a stack was created and took turns controlling the mouse. Finally, they presented their work together as a group.

Working together in groups gave students opportunities to interact, provide assistance, and share ideas. The sharing of ideas was emphasized by many students as being important to the success of a project. This was, one student asserted: "Because they all chip in and work together and you are basically doing the same amount of work but you've got so much more put into it."

Having spent four years together, the students knew each other very well and were comfortable using each other for support, as well as for academic help. "Most of the time we divide the work together because outside of school we don't really get to do things together so each person has different tasks and then when we go back to school when we have time to work in class we'll get together and then kind of tell each other what we have. Or ask for ideas or help." The fact that everyone had different ideas sometimes caused difficulties, but students felt that in the long run projects were improved by cooperative efforts.

The classrooms assumed the feel of studios and think-tanks where artists and scientists work together on various projects. The shift toward a dynamic multimedia studio for learning was supported by the collaborations among students and teachers in the classrooms. As one student stated: "I think it increases your ability to communicate and to take criticism, because you just get used to it after a while. People are always saying 'Hey, try it this way. That might work out better.' And you just kind of look at it, 'OK, I'll try it like that.'"

The social dynamics became pervasive as students were engaged in their own projects and projects for others. They worked with and for others and technology was seen as an important part of the process.

On another level, ACOT is a project involving working relationships with various groups—researchers, computer hackers, and businesses. This involves the students in diverse discourses, as one student noted: "I think ACOT definitely helps just because they come into contact with so many more people, so many more different types of people. You've got the students for most of the day but you're communicating with business executives and you meet people in educational fields. Just so many types of people. That's one thing that will be helpful."

The longitudinal data suggested that over the course of their involvement in ACOT students shifted from cautious optimism about themselves to what might be viewed as a connoisseurship of their computer-based learning experiences and respect for their own capabilities. Their involvement with computers was not seen as superfluous, but rather as integral to and having the potential to socially transform their lives. The comments of the students support an appreciation of the meaningfulness of their learning experiences, including an attitude toward computers as a tool that afforded them ways of achieving their ends. That is not to say that they might not be able to achieve these ends by other means, but that computers had become a vehicle for achieving a range of goals, both immediate and long term. Students improved their ability to solve problems and communicate ideas effectively, use alternative symbol systems, establish goals for themselves, and perceive strengths and weaknesses of their work. They also recognized the long-term advantages of newly acquired skills for their career aspirations and achievement of personal goals. At the same time, their experiences were also individualized. All of these students have different goals and dispositions that define to some extent what they gained, as well as where they saw themselves headed.

While these observations and interviews of the students are not comprehensive, they suggest that students engaged in a range of different forms of collaborations for a variety of different purposes. Moreover, these collaborations are an integral dimension of their learning. It would seem that if we are to come to grips with understanding computer literacy, then we need to understand its dynamics, especially the social dimensions.

Discussion

The ACOT site was a platform where the envelope was pushed in lots of ways: how student learning was defined, what was entailed in teaching and learning with technology, how technology might be enlisted in classrooms governed by constructivist learning tenets, how students might work together in such environments, how technology might be appropriated by teachers and students, and how systemic change occurs. The longitudinal study at the Columbus site explored some of these issues.

Students in both cohorts became independent and collaborative problem solvers, theorists, communicators, record keepers, and learners with the computers. They developed a repertoire of abilities with which they could explore possibilities that would be too cumbersome or difficult to attain without the technology. Furthermore, their ways of thinking shifted to align with options afforded by multilayered texts. While they had the capability of achieving independent agendas, their approach to learning was collaborative. The studio environment at ACOT contributed to their visions of the future and to their sense of authority.

Certainly, the complex nature of computer appropriation and the differences that exist across individuals and groups over time should not be dismissed. For example, different literacies are apt to be appropriated in different ways and variations are apt to exist in the social dimensions associated with different literacies. While our general findings apply across students, individuals vary in expertise, experience using particular software applications, and the ways in which expertise developed over time. Various factors appear to contribute to these differences including motivation, goals, exposure, and interests.

As should be apparent from our observation and debriefing procedures, we approached our data without a rigidly fixed agenda. One of the advantages of so doing was that we did not establish boundaries of our study *a priori*. If we had done so, we would not have uncovered what we uncovered. However, rather than clone ACOT, we would encourage sites to emerge in accordance with local situations and stress the need for the investment of energy, resources, and time befitting the vision. The kind of computer appropriation that we witnessed is not something that one can prepackage.

It is essential that the vision of technology that emerged not be slighted. Sometimes new media predispose students to superficially engage in activities that have doubtful value. This was not what occurred with multimedia at ACOT. The software and teaching goals afforded generative—rather than tightly constrained and predictable—pursuits. Indeed, the media prompted the pursuit of ways of knowing aligned with complex knowledge acquisition. This involved multilayered explorations, including extensive use of resources as well as more in-depth pursuit of topics. It promoted an appreciation of the perspectives that different media provide. In some ways, students became critics of text as vehicles for communication and management as they began to view knowledge in terms of the media used in accessing and presenting ideas.

In closing, the results from our research shed some light on the integration of technology in education and might guide others in this arena. In many ways, the ACOT research provides possibilities for a major shift in education toward constructivist views of knowledge, use of multiple symbol systems, and use of integrated technologies in the context of generative learning tasks. Furthermore, it represents a study of community development in which technology became woven into the fabric of everyday teaching and learning and extended students' sense of community beyond school boundaries.

Notes

1. This chapter is based on a multiyear research project carried out at the Columbus ACOT site. Additional information on the study can be found in Tierney, R. J. (1989). *The influence of immediate computer access on students' thinking.* ACOT Report Number 3. Cupertino, CA: Apple Computer; and Tierney, R. J., Kieffer, R. D., Stowell, L., Desai, L. E., Whalin, K., & Moss, A. G. (1992). *Computer acquisition: A longitudinal study of the influence of high computer access on students' thinking, learning, and interactions.* ACOT Report Number 16. Cupertino, CA: Apple Computer. Related studies: Galindo, R., Tierney, R. J., & Stowell, L. (1989). Multimedia and multilayers in multiple texts. In S. McCormick & J. Zutell (Eds.), *Cognitive and*

social perspectives for literacy research and instruction (pp. 311–322). Chicago: National Reading Conference; Sidorenko, E. B., Tierney, R. J., & Kaune, C. (1990). *Emergent video: The integration of student-mediated video technology into a high computer access classroom.* Paper presented at the International Reading Association, Orlando, Florida.

2. Clark, R. E., & Salomon, G. (1986). Media in teaching. In M. C. Wittrock (Ed.), *Handbook of research on teaching* (3rd ed.). New York: Macmillan, pp. 464–478.

11

Does Technology Work in Schools?

Why Evaluation Cannot Tell the Full Story

Eva L. Baker, Joan L. Herman, Maryl Gearhart

Digital technologies are a new phenomenon in schools. Beginning with the introduction of a few personal computers scarcely more than a decade ago, we now have an impressive array of digital devices in some schools and at least one or two computers in practically all schools. While it is still early in the game, and the numbers and kinds of technologies in schools continue to change rapidly, what can we say about when, where, and how technology influences learning in classrooms? In the past two decades, we have had numerous opportunities to study students and teachers interacting with technologies in their schools and classrooms. In this chapter, we reflect on our general work in the evaluation of technology and the design of educational technology interventions. In the process, we offer strategies and suggestions that we believe may be useful for future implementations of technology.

We begin with personal background information that contributed to the productivity of the authors' long-time partnership, partly because we believe our personal predispositions have played a role in our strategies. We then describe our connection to ACOT and highlight the processes and outcomes of our evaluation efforts. We conclude, based on our experiences with ACOT as well as other technology projects, with our own take on the seemingly perpetual issues in design, use, and evaluation of technology in schools. Thus, the chapter moves outward, from reflections on our individual predilections and aptitudes, to our collaboration, to our work with ACOT, and finally to our perspectives on the study of technology's role in schools.

Personal Takes and the Framing of Technology Assessments

There exists a code in education that loosely guides the role of evaluators. One of its precepts is that evaluators should be neutral in their observation and reporting of the outcomes of interventions. Like jury selection, however, reality suggests that perhaps the best we can do is to achieve a balance of biases rather than prolong the illusion of impartiality. Most evaluators attempt to be truly impartial. But our predispositions inevitably play out in our choice of projects, in our expectations, and in our evaluation designs and actions. Educational technology is a case in point. In this particular domain, the authors, although conscientiously striving for impartiality, actually represent a balance of biases. This mix colored our selection of evaluation goals, methods, and project strategies. It also deeply influenced the sense we made from ACOT and our prognostications about the success of future technology-based interventions.

One of us is drawn to technology, a gadgeteer, dealing in technology superlatives: newest, fastest, smallest, most powerful, most flexible, most functional. She had the first personal computer in her institution, the first Mac, the first cellular phone, the first home fax in her group—you get the idea. She happily anticipates cranial memory implants, the sooner the better. She harbors fond memories of the early 1980s, when one slight cost of learning about intelligent tutoring and expert systems was repeated challenges and insults by artificial intelligence researchers—apparently a preferred style. Minor pain was worth the pleasure of their puckish language—the simultaneity of their impenetrable nouns (augmented transition what?), sensory verbs (concatenate, cascade), their winsome metaphors (flavors), and the grand literacy of software names

(Sherlock and Proust). Next most fun was getting closer to military applications of technology, for instance SIMNET,[1] with its selective fidelity and rapid diffusion, and the almost sentient pilot associates.

A personal defect, the lack of stereoscopic vision, hurts her all the more in the realization that she will miss out on emerging 3-D experiences. She designs technological prototypes for schools because she believes that technology will ultimately solve many more educational problems than it creates. On Indian summer nights, she dreams of how technology will provide the content knowledge sorely missing in many teachers' repertoires, how multimedia will truly transform teaching and learning, how computers can equalize rather than exacerbate resource differences, how informal, recreational use of technology will merge with its systematic, institutional application to help people accomplish unforeseen goals. These dreams motivate her search for positive technology stories. She watches all *Star Trek* reruns. Lacking only a pocket protector, she is an archetype.

Another of us likes to (falsely) claim to know very little about technology. As in the rest of her life, she is not acquisitive. She is happy with whatever castoff upgrade she receives. If last year's model does the job, she is happy. She has no need for her computer to fly. She sees technology as a tool rather than as a general solution, but happily incorporates the latest technologies into her everyday life—if someone else figures out how to do it. She has supervised and developed considerable amounts of technology herself, in lots of different media and for many purposes. She values getting good information to people who need it in forms they can understand. Part of her job is in the area of research dissemination. In this work she has been mostly driven by explicit needs and audience requirements, real-life constraints. She will always choose to make something that provides a key function well rather than something with lots of surface appeal that performs imperfectly. She is interested in what technology actually does, not in endless promises of what it may be able to do in the future. She is more interested in technology as a means to solve existing problems than as a means to generate new goals. She is the money manager of the team and, while indulging her partner's need for toys, is hard-nosed about spending for everything, technology included.

She sees the world in trade-offs. Although she appreciates technological advances, their dazzle rarely obscures her vision. She understands and jokes about the language of current technology operations, for instance, server has a gender-free obsequiousness about it, but it is the reality of day-to-day activities that captures her attention. She's the one who has to deal with surge protectors that didn't, and systems that freeze, and notebooks that weigh too much to drag along on business trips. She is impatient with grand claims for education when it appears that many of the schools are too troubled to accomplish even the simplest goals. She worries about the operational strategies for moving from vision to reality. Above her desk is an autographed picture of Patrick Stewart.

Our final partner focuses first on people, the sense they make about interventions, and the value of their participation. Her favorite question is, "What are the kids learning?" Her motivation grows from her prior training as a developmental psychologist and her current experience as a better-late-than-never parent, and she prefers to watch and listen to kids than manage data files of achievement test scores. With some reluctance, she has adopted research approaches that have a stronger quantitative component to them— second-best but practical. Probably more than any of us, she focuses on the changes and on the impact of interventions on the entire person.

When we started, her computer was an Apple IIe. She isn't dazzled by technologies; her children are MIDI-fascinated musicians who started with an acoustic piano and plastic recorders, and she is pleased that they still play them. If technology is supposed to do something, she wants the evidence, and wants to be sure it is correct. If crunched numbers make no sense, she hauls out the raw data; if teachers and students use technologies, she wants to document what students understand and can do in specific subject areas. So, along with her theoretical and qualitative interests, she is fundamentally practical. But technology has helped her to cope with pulls between her work and her home life, and she is more than ready to consider new uses of newfangled hardware and software. Her e-mail often shows predawn time stamps, and she's a master of collaborative writing with faceless colleagues.

This odd trio shares values, values that enable and sustain both their educational technology studies and their relationship as well: what happens to kids is most important; educational profit motives sometimes corrupt (an assertion not particular to technology); false educational claims—in assessment, technology, and organization—come home to roost; scrupulous honesty is best, but understanding consequences of public pronouncements and actions is also important; and good methods exist to study most problems.

Collectively, we have studied technology for more than sixty years, a daunting statistic suggesting prenatal interest. We have studied its use in schools, from mainframe programmed instruction to batch programming for data analysis to the systematic design of instructional products. We have supervised its development in laser disc and CD-ROM, video, hypertext, database development, electronic reports, the creation of Web sites, compendia of assessment measures, television documentaries, educational films, games, interactive television, and satellite distance learning. We have taught about it in graduate courses, workshops, and undergraduate classes, through formal apprenticeships, and in our training of students. We have played around with mental models, video poker, HDTV, fundamental mathematics programs, and ways to teach art production, and to evaluate what people learn from broadcast television. Our former students work in the entertainment industry, government, research and development institutions, universities and businesses; many of them ply or examine technology.

In evaluation, we have looked at systems intended to serve children in schools, teachers, senior military officers, sailors operating radar, stay-at-home geriatrics, health professionals, and museum-goers. We have created or instigated technology-based achievement measures, tools to help manage school quality, systems for automatic authoring, scoring, and remote training and rating of student-developed products. We have conducted technology reviews for national agencies, military research and development commands, local school districts, private corporations, and international organizations. We do research on technology in education and give speeches about it. We have written hundreds of proposals and secured millions of dollars in research money. We are mostly happy in our work, but far too stressed. We like technology projects because of the illusion of their concreteness, but we dislike managing software development projects because of their black hole properties: before things disappear, they slow down to an imperceptible crawl. In short, this threesome has been around the technology, evaluation, and research tracks and done considerable work before and since ACOT became another opportunity to mix hope, cynicism, and scientific methods.

ACOT and Its Challenges

Our contribution to the evaluation of ACOT began in the following way: one of us attended an early ACOT advisory meeting in Cupertino in the fall of 1987. She had a vicious cold and left early. During that same quarter, she was teaching a course on technology development and evaluation at the University of California, Los Angeles. She called to find out how the meeting ended, and in the course of the conversation she invited David Dwyer to come to talk to her students about his aspirations for the project. He spent a day with the class, and collectively the group decided that students and teacher would plan and submit to ACOT an evaluation design; its purpose was to give students a real-life problem to think about with a real audience. The plan was created, and in a surprising turn, ACOT accepted it. Students who contributed most were offered research assistant jobs. Thus, ownership of the evaluation work began from the bottom up.

ACOT—Way Back When

In 1987, ACOT was focused on computer-saturated environments, one computer at school and one at home for every participating child and for every participating teacher. The project was implemented in single classrooms within schools rather than on entire school sites. It encompassed a handful of sites across the country, representing a melange of grade levels and demographic characteristics. At the outset it was not clear whether ACOT would provide participating children with a consistent, technology-rich experience as they moved up the grade levels, or whether children would have only a year of ACOT, experience a technology-intensive slice of life, and, like Dorothy, go back to the black-and-white Kansas palette of regular classrooms.

Part of the uncertainty derived from ACOT's multiple, conflicting goals. ACOT designers wanted to affect the fundamental assumptions on which education was operating and to presage new possibilities for active, effective student learning. Initially and on a continuing basis, ACOT sought to satisfy a variety of different audiences representing diverse interests and motivations: project teachers with real day-to-day concerns; school districts looking for near-term solutions and identifiable results; scientific communities looking to explore theoretic applications; the teaching community looking for future directions; developers looking for ideas for new products; future users of technology and their parents looking to prepare themselves for future success; and internal management at Apple exploring new uses of advanced technologies in schools.

To address the diverse goals of ACOT's multiple audiences required different strategies, different degrees of innovation and risk, and varying schedules and timelines. Evidence for different outcomes required a range of credible data, a circumstance that complicated the evaluation design. On the one hand, ACOT presumably could not risk a large investment that resulted in objective failure; it had to keep the door open for future developments. On the other hand, it wanted to document and publicize any early successes, with all the attendant risks of an untried strategy.

These conflicts played out in a number of ways: How could ACOT support and evaluate its impact on the fundamental re-design of classrooms if it needed to provide evidence on existing and publicly credible achievement measures such as regular standardized tests? How could ACOT undertake a fair shot at classroom restructuring (with the expectations that technology costs were going to drop) in the context of day-to-day rising budgetary pressures on school operations? What was possible within the constraints of existing school systems and staff who were accountable for traditional goals and had little experience with integrating state-of-the-art technology into instruction? ACOT had to work in a current world but design for a future environment.

Approaches to the Evaluation of ACOT

Our actual approaches to the evaluation of ACOT grew as much from our attempts to accommodate conflicting goals as from the fundamentally different technology perspectives of the authors. Our previous technology work, coupled with our ample experience in evaluating school reform projects, furthermore suggested the futility of a straight experimental-control design, even if it were preserved against the day-to-day changes and contaminations of complex school programs. Sounding highly scientific, control group designs nonetheless usually fell apart in the reality of school programs. Randomization of students was not possible; common treatments did not exist but, rather, varied across sites; staff, instructional foci, and project goals were not stable, over time; and, of course, the appropriateness of the dependent measures was problematic. One important goal for us was the development of outcome measures intended to be more attuned to the possible directions in which ACOT might go.

Second, Apple supported both strong comparisons on outcome measures and more ethnographic approaches as companion interpretative bases. Because we hoped to provide evidence of relationships among student outcomes and classroom processes, we believed that we needed to capture systematically what the ACOT program meant, as it was enacted in classrooms. Thus a good deal of our energy was invested in trying to record classroom process.

We were well aware that, in technology projects, many important consequences will emerge rather than be preordained or designed at the outset. We posited a model designed to enable technology-sensitive evaluation, a model that represented our decision to eschew off-the-shelf measures and our openness toward exploring ways in which new goals might be developed and appropriated in the course of the project.[2]

We intended to use multiple sources of information about project needs, processes, and outcomes to provide information on ACOT's progress toward the goals of its many stakeholders. The full implementation of the model was unrealized because we were stretched beyond capacity to meet the schedule of even the more conventional of our evaluation goals, and we were confronted with formidable methodological circumstances. Here are some of the challenges that we faced: the project operated in five sites in four states. Each school represented a different constellation of student background, teacher distribution, involvement of the school district, and technology orientation. Each school chose its own grade level of students to participate in ACOT. Grade levels ranged from primary to upper elementary to high school. ACOT was committed to an evolve-and-support, bottom-up approach to project development, restricting the degree to which we could develop and document a clear understanding of the intervention at any one time even in one site. Sites developed different curricular and instructional emphases. Accountability measures used in participating school districts demanded teachers' continued attention to traditional learning goals, regardless of ACOT's new visions for student learning. Despite pressure to show comparative benefits of technology matched against standard or traditional practices, we recognized that technology-based projects show strongest gains when measured by the new outcomes, new student capabilities, and the accomplishments they enable.

Our Aspirations

In the first phase of our effort in 1987, we were committed to creating an innovative evaluation design that might permit us to aggregate findings among different sites, with the recognition that our approaches would need to be robust enough to traverse the boundaries of participant background, grade level, and curricular emphasis, but still sensitive enough to respond to the multiple ways in which technology impacted each classroom. If we could develop an approach to combine data across sites, we would be able to describe the overall impact of the ACOT program. To this end, we selected two sets of preliminary student measures. The first was based on the writing measures used in the U.S. component of the International Association for the Evaluation of Educational Achievement (IEA) assessment. We also knew that a good deal of ACOT instructional activity was focused on the use of word processing and document preparation tools. The IEA assessment seemed to be appropriate, because it had been used across grade levels and would meet some of the requirements for aggregation. To address continued concern by school districts for more traditional measures, we also included a standardized, norm-referenced test. For the latter, we selected subtests from the Iowa Tests of Basic Skills, hoping that the quality of their vertical equating among grade levels would enable us to compare progress across sites implementing the program at various grade levels. We also developed common measures of teacher, student, and parent satisfaction.

Desiring to understand how ACOT operated and what outcomes might be anticipated, we also sought to integrate evaluation information from other sources. Beginning with the 1988–89 school year, ACOT supported coordinated observational studies, using the techniques of structured observation and ethnography to understand classroom practices. We hoped that these approaches might yield data systematically related to observed patterns in student achievement data.

We continued collecting and reporting data from these and other measures during the multiple years of support we received from ACOT. But although we had thought that part of our major contribution would be in the development of evaluation designs for aggregating information across complex technology innovations, that goal, as eventually realized, became less and less important to us. Perhaps it was inevitable: despite our sensitivity to the evaluation problems we faced and a variety of innovative measures, our findings across sites would be more equivocal than we hoped. We did not find sweeping evidence across sites that ACOT qua ACOT was having positive effects on the quality of instruction, on the depth and breadth of student learning, on the attitudes and aspirations of students and parents. We took these findings for granted: in an evaluation context of evolving ACOT goals and site-specific project strategies, we would have been suspicious indeed of overwhelming good news.

Our work uncovered patterns of effects that were more useful as guideposts to further inquiry than as empirical evidence of ACOT impact. Our questions are thus our ultimate contributions. Consider three examples.

By our third year, we produced evidence of positive ACOT outcomes at sites where third- or fourth-year projects were maturing— sites struggling less with the basics of hardware and software implementation and the first steps of technology training. These ACOT students, when compared to appropriate local students (if we had them) or to national norms, were more likely to show relative strength in writing and to express more positive attitudes toward school. These students did not necessarily perform better on *all* of our achievement indices, and thus we found selective impact at each site. The complexity of these student outcome findings underscored the critical importance of generating and pursuing adequately detailed evaluation questions. What we produced, in this case, were better questions about technology impact, questions that addressed issues of project maturity and project focus.

In our third year, we also collected classroom observation data at two ACOT sites. Our findings confirmed that changes in instructional practices were consistent with ACOT goals. For example, teachers were making greater use of cooperative groups and less use of traditional directive teaching, but our findings did not reveal a particular role of technology in these changes. Were teachers embracing new pedagogy because the availability of interactive technologies invited and supported student-centered work or because they were encouraged to do so by ACOT staff? We had new questions to pursue, questions that regrettably required long-term studies beyond our funded timeline.

Across sites and classrooms, we found considerable variation in instructional uses of technology across curricular areas, in uses for skill practice versus project-based student work, and in choices among the many technology options available. What could account for these differences in technology-supported practice? Teachers' content and pedagogical knowledge, we believe, provide the key explanatory variables underlying our uneven findings. ACOT technology resources could not and did not obviate the need for effective teaching. We needed additional studies to address new questions: How are patterns of technology innovation influenced by teachers' subject matter knowledge, understandings of new methods of teaching a particular subject area, and competence with nontraditional pedagogies (for example, cooperative and collaborative work and long-term projects)?

Signal Events

One of the precepts of our technology assessment model was that old measures were unlikely to assess true innovation. Part of our global strategy was to be alert for opportunities to measure serendipitous developments, that is, to be alert for emerging outcomes that had not been anticipated. In retrospect, considerable payoff accrued from this strand of our ACOT work, not so much to document the superiority of ACOT students in comparison to others on fairly standard measures, but to stimulate attention to new outcomes possible only with ACOT or other similar technology infusions.[3] The etiologies of these newer developments differed.

The ACOT project staff and some academic advisors met in 1988 to talk over the development of ACOT and its future directions. At one point in the meeting, a vision was framed for a new kind of instruction in which technology played a central role, a role supporting student-focused, project-based learning. Following this meeting, we began to develop a classroom observation instrument to assess not only the usual aspects of instruction such as who's talking and how are students grouped but also the kinds of learning episodes that were enacted, the ways in which media were incorporated, and the continuity of engagement. This instrument,[4] although originally intended to help us generate hypotheses about relationships between classroom practices and outcomes, became more valued as a peer-evaluation and feedback occasion for ACOT teachers. It has subsequently been used in other technology and teaching studies as well.

Another set of outcomes emerged from our attempt to be sensitive to site-specific goals and the contexts in which they were enacted. Focusing on the project-based, developmental orientation of ACOT, we explored portfolio assessment as a means to evaluate ACOT impact. Co-supported by the U.S. Department of Education's Office of Educational Research and Improvement, we engaged in a series of studies of student writing portfolios, coordinating an examination of the implementation and impact of portfolio assessment in ACOT classrooms with technical laboratory studies of the scorability of portfolios.[5] The results of these studies emphasize the benefit of portfolios for supporting improvement in teaching and learning, but raise clear questions about the credibility of portfolios for systematic use in accountability. Some limits to their use in this domain involve: fairness of opportunity (are all students provided similar levels of instructional support?); control of administration conditions (are portfolios produced under similar circumstances?); and various conditions under which portfolios may or may not be scorable.

In the Columbus high school classrooms, we were fascinated by ACOT students' facile uses of HyperCard. In our assessments of their writing, their performance did not appear to reflect the level of content understanding that we thought they may have developed. Consequently, we created an alternative form of assessment for the understanding of content knowledge. We developed a measure that required students to build HyperCard stacks to illustrate their understanding of important historical eras, for instance, the Depression period of American history. Our interest was not in their HyperCard facility, but rather in their use of the tool to represent their understanding of concepts. The use of such stacks was not unusual in ACOT classrooms. Our innovation was in attempting to develop metrics to allow these assessments to be scored and validated. Among the struggles we encountered was the determination of adequate scoring criteria. In the end, we used a combination of quantitative measures of types of links and nodes, a content-oriented metric, and a measure of structural similarity to experts' understanding of the same content. Among our most fascinating results was the finding that a sizable proportion of students who used HyperCard well to express their understanding of principles, themes, facts, and relationships were so-so or worse performers judged by more traditional forms of testing.[6] Subsequent development of this line of work resulted in a model and accompanying software that automatically administers and scores student representations of knowledge.

Finally, we experimented with an electronic reporting approach using HyperCard and graphics that allowed users to enter data archives and pull up a detailed story about particular elements such as school, type of goal, grade level, measure, and so on. The approach allowed direct access to elements in order of the user's priorities. To our surprise, a similar approach was recently exhibited at an international meeting.[7] These contributions, though beyond the normal conduct of the evaluation, were among our most satisfying and productive consequences of the work with ACOT.

Conclusions

Based on our broader experiences with innovation and technology, including our experiences with ACOT, we have some general musings about the fitful development of technology-based projects, and, for that matter, innovative educational reform in general. Not all of us agree with each point, but together these five observations may assist our creation of fruitful strategies for the study of technology.

Because bureaucracies need to be promised outrageous benefits to commit even marginal resources, early claims always outstrip performance. Then everyone is disappointed. Our ACOT evaluation studies, for example, produced findings that could easily be interpreted as no news or even bad news, but not by us. Our work provided empirical documentation of the school scene confirming that change is complex and slow. People need to know this.

Many innovations, technology based or not, suffer because teachers do not have a clear vision of what is expected of them and their students. Part of the difficulty resides in the particular ways teachers have come to regard their work, that is, as part of a continuous stream rather than as a deliberate set of rational acts to achieve particular ends. Successful technology use implies both change of underlying frameworks as well as the incorporation and appropriation of technology benefits into classroom practice.

New models for professional development are needed, particularly in technology-based projects. Although possibly a one-generation problem, current approaches treat teachers' ability and willingness to use technology much more gingerly than analogous attempts to introduce technology to professionals in other sectors. Hesitant to impose specific patterns or uses to encourage specific strategies, projects have encouraged teachers to develop their own understandings and uses. The results have been sensitive to principles of constructivist learning and to building ownership and support for change, but perhaps have inadvertently lengthened the learning curve and contributed to continuing dependence on step-by-step training.

Technology alone cannot improve teaching and learning. If it could, we would have documented improvements in student learning in all subject areas in all our technology-related evaluations. Technology use must be grounded firmly in curriculum goals, incorporated in sound instructional process, and deeply integrated with subject-matter content. Absent this grounding, which too often is neglected in the rush to glittery application, changes in student performance are unlikely.

Evaluation can only enlighten what is studied. Yet numerous factors obscure an evaluation's focus: conflicting needs of multiple constituents who possess vastly divergent priorities; lack of clarity about evaluation purposes; emergence of new priorities; entry of new audiences; and personal viewpoints of those who act as evaluators. Although changes in audiences, purposes, and priorities cannot always be precisely anticipated, they almost always occur. Evaluators need time to develop program sensibilities and to develop plans and methods in advance and in parallel with program implementation.

Finally, the moral of our story. Evaluations are ever-chasing the "real" story when the story line and characters keep changing. While there is no one solution to many of the dilemmas we raise, we do believe that stories about the real worlds of schools are most effective when written collaboratively and with commitment to balancing biases in the quest for impartiality.

Notes

1. Alluisi, E. A. (1991). The development of technology for collective training: SIMNET, a case history. *Human Factors, 33*(3), 343–362.

2. Baker, E. L., & O'Neil, H. F., Jr. (1987). *The evolution of the ACOT evaluation model: Sensitive technology assessment research (STAR) and STARFRAME*. Los Angeles: University of California, Center for Technology Assessment.

3. For example, see Baker, E. L., Gearhart, M., Herman, J. L., Tierney, R., & Whittaker, A. K. (1991). Stevens Creek portfolio project: Writing assessment in the technology classroom. *Portfolio News, 2*(3), 7–9; Baker, E. L., Gearhart, M., & Herman, J. L. (1994). Evaluating the Apple Classrooms of Tomorrow. In E. L. Baker & H. F. O'Neil, Jr. (Eds.), *Technology assessment in education and training.* Hillsdale, NJ: Erlbaum, pp. 173–197; Baker, E. L., Niemi, D., & Herl, H. (1994). Using hypercard technology to measure understanding. In E. L. Baker & H. F. O'Neil, Jr. (Eds.), *Technology assessment in education and training.* Hillsdale, NJ: Erlbaum, pp. 133–152; Baker, E. L., Niemi, D., Novak, J., & Herl, H. (1992). Hypertext as a strategy for teaching and assessing knowledge representation. In S. Dijkstra, H.P.M. Drammer, & J.J.G. van Merriënboer (Eds.), *Instructional models in computer-based learning environments.* Berlin: Springer-Verlag, pp. 365–384; Gearhart, M., & Herman, J. L. (1995, Winter). Portfolio assessment: Whose work is it? Issues in the use of classroom assignments for accountability. *Evaluation Comment,* 1–16; Gearhart, M., Herman, J. L., Baker, E. L., Novak, J. R., & Whittaker, A. K. (1994). A new mirror for the classroom: A technology-based tool for documenting the impact of technology on instruction. In E. L. Baker & H. F. O'Neil, Jr. (Eds.), *Technology assessment in education and training.* Hillsdale, NJ: Erlbaum, pp. 153–172; Gearhart, M., Herman, J. L., Baker, E. L., & Whittaker, A. K. (1992). *Writing portfolios at the elementary level: A study of methods for writing assessment.* CSE Technical Report No. 337. Los Angeles: University of California, National Center for Research on Evaluation, Standards, and Student Testing; Gearhart, M., Herman, J. L., Novak, J. R., & Wolf, S. A. (1995). Toward the instructional utility of large-scale writing assessment: Validation of a new narrative rubric. *Assessing Writing, 2,* 207–242; Gearhart, M., & Wolf, S. A. (1994). Engaging teachers in assessment of their students' writing: The role of subject matter knowledge. *Assessing Writing, 1*(1), 67–90; Herl, H. E., Niemi, D., & Baker, E. L. (in press). Construct validation of an approach to

modeling cognitive structure of experts' and novices' U.S. history knowledge. *Journal of Educational Research*. Herman, J. L., Gearhart, M., & Baker, E. L. (1993). Assessing writing portfolios: Issues in the validity and meaning of scores. *Educational Assessment, 1*(3), 201–224; Novak, J. R., Herman, J. L., & Gearhart, M. (in press). Providing evidence of validity for performance-based assessments: An illustration for collections of student writing. *Journal of Educational Research*; and Wolf, S. A., & Gearhart, M. (1994). Writing what you read: A framework for narrative assessment. *Language Arts, 71*(6), 425–445.

4. See Gearhart et al., A new mirror for the classroom, cited in note 3.

5. See Baker, E. L., Gearhart, M., & Herman, J. L. (1991). *The Apple Classrooms of Tomorrow: 1990 evaluation study.* Los Angeles: University of California, Center for Technology Assessment. In addition, the following sources (all cited in note 3) will be of interest here: Gearhart et al., *Writing portfolios at the elementary level;* Gearhart & Herman, Portfolio assessment; Gearhart et al., Toward the instructional utility of large-scale writing assessment; Gearhart & Wolf, Engaging teachers in assessment of their students' writing; Herman et al., Assessing writing portfolios; Novak et al., Providing evidence of validity for performance-based assessments; and Wolf & Gearhart, Writing what you read.

6. See Baker, E. L., & O'Neil, H. F., Jr. (Eds.). (1994). *Technology assessment in education and training.* Hillsdale, NJ: Erlbaum. The following references, both cited in note 3, will also be of interest here: Baker et al., Hypertext as a strategy; and Herl et al., Construct validation of an approach to modeling cognitive structure.

7. Fagan, L. P., & Hodgkinson, G. D. (1995). *Demonstration on applications of technology.* Paper presented at a symposium of the Asia-Pacific Economic Cooperation Education Forum Project on Performance Measurement Systems sponsored by the U.S. Department of Education's Office of the Undersecretary and National Center for Education Statistics, Alexandria, VA.

12

New Technologies, New Literacies, New Problems

Brian Reilly

Computers and the Internet seem to be all around us. Computers are at work, at home, at school. People buy more computers than televisions, and use them for all kinds of things. The computer is an information appliance, harder to use than a toaster or blender, but more powerful than a telephone or a television. Computers are different. They're interactive and entertaining. They're business machines, game machines, and creative tools. They're expensive and hard to use. They have to be upgraded frequently and they need software to run. Software is also expensive, hard to use, and has to be upgraded frequently. The richest person in the United States made his first fortune selling software. He hopes to make his next fortune via the Internet. The Internet is big. The President of the United States wants all classrooms connected to the Internet and the World Wide Web in the next five years. The Pope, the Dalai Lama, Elvis, Richard Nixon, and the Grateful Dead are already on the Web. Are you? The Web will be a resource for schools, a source of current information, cultural exchanges, and expert opinions. It will replace your television, telephone, post office, video rental store, and newspaper. It's the next mass medium. It's anarchy. The Internet doesn't need Oprah, Geraldo, or Sally. Everyone on the Internet hosts their own talk show.

The Internet has information about everything from everywhere and opinions from everyone. Students will use the Internet to research, create, and publish. They will exchange ideas with scientists in Moscow, students in Malaysia, and politicians in Newark. It's big, it's slow, and it's not user-friendly, but everyone wants to use it anyway. Technology can help us, and we need help.

One place we need help is in our public schools. They're crowded, underfunded, and dangerous. Students carry guns along with books. Teachers are overworked, underpaid, and underprepared to guide students into a future far different than the one they grew up in. Education, ever reforming and in need of change, is in trouble.

Computers can help students do incredible things in science and math, art, writing, and animation. Yet the same machine that can serve as a tool for exploration and self-expression in one classroom works just fine serving up isolated facts as part of drill and practice software or delivering multimedia edutainment in another classroom. Computers are expansive. They can help stretch our creative limits. Computers are great. How come everybody isn't using them?

Background

My first experience with computers in a K–12 classroom was about ten years before ACOT started, just about the time the first personal computers came into being. I was a high school student, and in a tradition that has continued in many schools, our advanced math class had the first chance to use the computer. We used a teletype, a bulky keyboard and printer combination, connected to a minicomputer at 110 baud using a telephone and a modem. There was no monitor, no disks, no mouse, no network, no manuals. There was also no computer. The computer we used was about fifteen miles from the school at Bell Labs, in Holmdel, New Jersey. We learned to program in BASIC, but we also found the games on the system and spent much of our free time playing those games. In that respect, we were no different from many students using computers in schools today; we learned about the computer, how to run the computer by programming it, and we played games more than we should have. Our machine crashed frequently, we had no backup system, storage was limited to a paper punch tape, and the user interface was a command line.

My next experience with computers in a K–12 classroom was in one of the ACOT schools. Things had changed drastically in the ten years since I graduated from high school. Students had lots of computers to use, almost one per student, with color monitors, laser printers, hard disks, and a network. They were still learning to program, now in Logo and HyperTalk instead of BASIC. And they were still interested in playing games—some of them created their own games—but they were also doing other things like word processing, music composition, and animation.

One of the ongoing goals of ACOT has been to imagine and assist schools in creating environments that help us understand what things might be like in classrooms in the near future. Initially, this was based on the premise that someday students and teachers might have easy and immediate access to computers and related technology. The early days of ACOT were interesting to many people because the ACOT classrooms were technology-intensive and, soon after their inception, emphasized a constructivist approach to learning, a combination that wasn't as common even five years ago as it is today.

ACOT was also a place where innovative uses of technology were developed and tested in classrooms. Projects explored a range of issues, from the use of wireless networks and mobile computing to simulations, multimedia composition, and more.

One of the earliest multimedia composing tools for schools was a project called StoryShow that I developed with David Dwyer in one of the ACOT schools. The concept was simple; an easy-to-use slide show tool that first and second graders could (and did) use to create reports and stories. We started in 1990, before multimedia was as closely associated with computers as it is now, and before the hardware and software were ready to support it. We learned the hard way. I sat for hours watching students work and watching the software crash. After many revisions, the software ran reliably and it really was easy enough for a first grader to use. Students captured images from a video camera, recorded their voices, wrote, drew, and painted. They shared their work with classmates and teachers, but in one of the ironies of computer-based multimedia, they couldn't take it home. Their 30-megabyte projects didn't fit on floppy disks and didn't play on their home computers.

Technology, when widely used for children's reading and writing activities, is changing the kinds of interactions children have with text as well as the kinds of texts with which they interact. New computer-based tools allow us to combine text, sound, image, and video in various ways, providing new methods for creating texts. The World Wide Web is potentially a great distribution point for these multimedia texts. Yet, as much research—including our Story-Show project—has shown, technology is not always the key element when considering how a particular hardware or software innovation actually gets used by students. The classroom is a social environment with a variety of relationships, norms, and practices that exist prior to the introduction of a new technology. How technology is used owes as much to the ongoing activities of the classroom as it does to any particular features of the technology.

What I learned from working on StoryShow was that software and hardware may allow students to do things they couldn't do before, or may make it easier to do things students were already doing, but the teacher has an essential role in determining what gets done and who does it. Even when the teacher may not be directly involved in the moment-to-moment decision making that is part of students' individual or group projects, the classroom culture created by teacher and students has a considerable influence on how technology gets used. Students may bring a range of experiences with computers and video games into the classroom from home, but the teacher's interpretation of the role of technology will influence what kinds of software are available, how it is used, and how students gain access to the software. In the end, this is more important than speed, power, or ease of use. The most important piece of hardware in the classroom isn't the multimedia computer, the video camera, or the network. It's the teacher's desk, where any innovation must pass in one form or another before it gets to students. The teacher isn't merely a gatekeeper; he or she is an orchestrator of activity and will greatly influence how technology fits into the classroom.

This lesson about the primary role of the teacher and the secondary role of technology in classrooms led me to explore the work of some innovative educators, which I describe in the next section.

Innovation

The future doesn't always jump up and surprise us all at once. Innovation may be a slow process of trying something, succeeding and failing, making changes, and trying something new. This kind of change, in schools, is measured in years, not weeks or months. Classroom innovators are often teachers who have strong beliefs about how students can learn, a passion for teaching, and some idea of how technology can help everyone involved do things a little better or a little differently. Putting new computers into a classroom is likely to lead to changes, but those changes aren't always predictable and they don't always include creative uses of technology. The innovators will find the technology and figure out how to make it work for their students—but for every classroom where students are creating Web pages or animations or videos, there are ten more where students' experiences with technology amount to identifying the parts of the computer and learning to format floppy disks in preparation for computerized typing lessons.

In this section, I describe innovative uses of technology at three California high schools. Each school is very different, but all three share some common traits. All have multimedia programs that started small and were championed by one teacher. Each program helps students use technology as a way to express ideas and create artifacts such as videos, images, and music that can be shared with others. Finally, each program provides a real connection between students and an audience beyond the classroom. In unique ways, each of these schools has evolved a multimedia culture where technology serves a larger goal of letting students express ideas, collaborate with others, and think critically and creatively.

Video Production at Bell High School

With some support from ACOT, I spent most of the 1992–93 school year at Bell High School in Los Angeles trying to understand and document how students learn to make videos. Bell High School is located in the city of Bell, in southeastern Los Angeles county, and is part of the Los Angeles Unified School District. Bell High School is a year-round school with over 4,300 students in three tracks. Ninety-six percent of the students at Bell are Latino, and 98 percent qualify for the federal student lunch program. With a drop-out rate close to 40 percent and an environment where drugs, gangs, and violence are commonplace, Bell is like many urban schools in the United States. And like many schools, it's not the kind of place where one would expect to find students using advanced video and computer technology. Yet over the past four years, Bell students have won more than a hundred awards for their work in local, state, national, and international video competitions.

Ed Murphy, an English teacher at Bell, has been using video with his students for almost twenty years. His classes are chaotic and structured at the same time. Students work in groups as they progress from idea to written script to raw footage to finished video. In one class period, different students may be doing all of these things at the same time, some in the classroom, some out. During the year I spent at Bell High School, two hundred students collaborated on 125 videos and an hour-long video yearbook using a relatively small amount of technology.

The first time I visited Ed's classroom it had six Apple IIc computers, ten video cameras, and a video editing station with two

Amiga computers that were used to create animations and special effects. The video editing station, located in a closet-sized room next to the classroom, was perpetually in use. Students used the computers to write scripts, but most of their work was done planning, writing, shooting video, and learning to work in teams. Students were so enthusiastic about creating videos that some spent forty hours a week or more working on their projects. They came after school, before school, during lunch or free periods, and they borrowed cameras at night and on weekends. They worked with fellow students, friends, and family.

The production process at Bell begins with an idea and often, a chosen genre (public service announcement, video poem, video essay, music video). Students develop their idea in a one- or two-paragraph written proposal that describes the aims of the piece and some of the key shots. When the proposal is approved by the instructor, the student writes a script describing the video in detail, including dialogue, music, camera angle, and shot information. Following a script conference with the instructor where the written ideas are brought to life through visual description, students pitch their ideas to their classmates, form a production crew, and get to work. They may shoot video for a few hours or a few weeks, then review, edit, and add effects. Not all scripts get produced, but each student writes a script and participates in a production as an actor, cameraperson, director, or editor.

Once a video is done, it's time for the final event in the video production process—the premiere. The premiere is a significant event, a ritual that helps create and maintain the video culture in the classroom. It begins with a brief introduction delivered by the student producer, often detailing the difficulties encountered during the project (actors didn't show up, shots were lost, and so on), describing the personal nature of the video (family member involved in gangs or drugs; personal experience with topic of video), providing a testimonial regarding the extensive help given by other students to help complete the project ("I really have to thank . . . "), or pointing out the swiftness of the production ("It took two days, really. One day to shoot and two hours to edit.") The lights go out, and the student's work appears on a television screen at the front of the room. Discussion about the work follows, then it is shown a second time, with more discussion.

This public showing of student work serves multiple purposes. For students, they share their work with peers and get relevant feedback from them, feedback more valuable than a grade from the teacher. As a teaching opportunity, the premiere uses student work as part of an ever-changing curriculum. Each video is a chance to advance the skills of the class, both in understanding video and in raising the group's standards of production. Each time a student expresses an idea in a new way, it gives the rest of the class a higher standard to aim for. The premiere is the culmination of a long process and marks the end of a student project. It validates student work in a way that doesn't happen regularly in schools, and helps promote the idea that video, a medium with little currency in school, is a legitimate way for students to express ideas.

This is a different kind of composition class. Ed Murphy's students don't create their videos for him. They don't spend their free time after school and on weekends videotaping, writing scripts, and editing to hand in a videotape for the teacher to view. They do it in part because video gives them access to a bigger audience. Their tapes play on the television and VCR in the classroom where their peers critique them. They play on a local cable television station and they play at home in the VCR that almost every family owns. Video is a relevant medium for these students. Like most teenagers, they watch MTV and countless other programs each week. They "read" video for many hours outside school, but in Ed Murphy's class they learn to create it and in the process come to a much different understanding of the power of this technology. Their work is a new kind of literacy, one where text, image, and sound are equal parts of the process of reading and writing.

Video as multimedia has some strong points compared with

computer-based multimedia. First, the tools are easier to use than computer authoring systems. Ed Murphy spends no class time teaching students how to operate hardware or software. He employs an apprenticeship method of instruction. Students learn by asking other students and watching them work. Everyone who wants to edit learns in a few minutes and more complicated special effects can be added by students who have mastered those skills. Students start by generating ideas and gradually move into using technology to express those ideas. Second, video levels the playing field among students. No students have sophisticated video editing systems at home, so everyone starts out with nearly the same skill level. Third, the video genres used in the classroom (public service announcement, video poem, video essay, music video) offer students a specific structure that guides their work while leaving plenty of room for creativity. A public service announcement is thirty seconds long, usually ten shots, and contains a message at the end. With computer-based multimedia, in addition to creating the content, students often have to invent a format and develop an interface. Video has an established, simple interface; play, pause, stop, and rewind. Finally, video is easy to share and can be stored inexpensively. Each student can get a couple of tapes costing a few dollars and have all the storage space needed for the class.

Animation at Rowland High School

A couple of years before Ed Murphy started working with video at Bell High School, forty miles away at Rowland High School in Rowland, California, art teacher Dave Master started an animation program with a Super-8 film camera and some lights. Eighteen years and hundreds of student-produced animated films later, Rowland Animation is a multimedia production studio within a school, serving several hundred students and community residents each year. With video cameras, computers, clay, pencil and paper, and hours and hours of hard work, students collaboratively produce animated films as a way to express themselves.

Rowland's success owes a great deal to Dave Master's beliefs about learning, teaching, and the role of technology. His method is to use animation as a way to teach students how to think, how to present information, how to work together, and how to complete a complex project. Along the way, they learn how to use video cameras and computers, but technology isn't the focus of what they do. Dave Master, former IBM Technology Teacher of the Year, likes to say that he never taught a student how to use a computer.

Over the past three years, Rowland has expanded the animation program to include students in math and science classes. These students receive some training in animation and storytelling, and spend the school year producing a film about an issue or research topic they choose. Planning the projects can take several weeks as students create storyboards and revise their scripts repeatedly until they satisfy a critical audience—their classmates. The time spent on planning is essential because their projects take months of work to finish and require collaboration among groups of three to five students.

A computer-animated explanation of the fourth dimension, an animation using clay about overpopulation, and a story about the geometric properties of rectangles told using the tale of Cinderella (in clay) were among the student productions completed in 1995. These projects, along with many others, were showcased in Rowland's annual Animation Open House, an event held each spring where students present their work to the local community as well as to professionals from the film and multimedia industries. For the Open House, students spend six weeks decorating the animation classrooms with elaborate figures, props, and mechanical devices reminiscent of Disneyland. This project alone is an incredible undertaking, all managed and run by students, and it follows immediately after the completion of animated films that may involve several hundred hours of work. The Open House is a time when student work takes center stage.

Rowland High School's animation program is impressive in many ways. Lots of students participate each year and their finished projects reflect a strong understanding of how to use animation to express ideas. Many go on to careers working on movies and television shows, but all the students who participate in this program take away a hands-on experience with media that forever changes the way they look at movies, television, and interactive media.

Multimedia Curriculum at Lincoln High School

Lincoln High School in San Jose, California, is taking an active role in creating the future of technology in schools. Lincoln is an arts magnet school with a four-year curriculum devoted to multimedia. The program was designed and implemented by Cliff Herlth, an industrial arts teacher at Lincoln (now the technology coordinator), and includes drawing, painting, animation, MIDI music composition, interactive multimedia, digital photography, and digital video production distributed over seven technology-intensive classrooms connected via a local area network. In terms of technology, Lincoln is as advanced as any public school in the United States. Guiding the use of technology is a commitment to a student-centered, project-based curriculum where advanced technology and creativity are the primary tools.

Compared to Rowland and Bell High Schools, Lincoln's program is relatively new, but it is already providing access to interesting opportunities for several hundred of Lincoln's students. During 1995, students in the digital video class worked with the San Jose Police Department and a local television station to produce public service announcements, thirty-second videos that address issues important to teenagers such as drug use, runaways, and independence. The videos were created by student teams who wrote, directed, shot, and edited each piece. Representatives from the police department and television station acted as advisors and provided guidance when needed. The finished projects continue to air on local television along with other public service announcements produced by local and national organizations.

Scott Cornfield, a homicide detective with the San Jose Police

Department, began this collaborative project as a way to give students opportunities to constructively express themselves and to work with people from the community. Computers and video equipment provide a common ground where students can express ideas while learning how to complete projects on time and get their message out to an audience that goes far beyond the classroom. Detective Cornfield's hope is to expand the program into middle and elementary schools to reach younger students and get them interested in media production before they get involved in gangs or head off on a course away from school.

Instead of upgrading existing photography lab facilities, Lincoln created a unique digital photography program. Chemicals, film, and photographic paper have been replaced by digital cameras, computers with photo editing software, and a high-resolution color printer. The change has allowed students to complete a wider range of assignments while still learning the basics of photographic composition.

Lincoln's digital photography classes provide a relatively easy way for students to work with the same advanced tools used by professionals and learn skills that take them into video, multimedia, and desktop publishing as well as on to college. In the digital photography class, students learn about photography and use computers and digital cameras in the process.

Students from Lincoln's multimedia class collaborated with NASA scientists during the summer to produce an interactive educational CD-ROM about the effects of space on the heart. NASA provided video footage and images, and students completed the project in five weeks. Using skills they developed during the school year, students digitized and compressed video, searched the Internet for graphics, created animations, and developed the interface to the content. Their work will be made available to high school science teachers through NASA's educational outreach programs.

Issues for the Future

Schools change very slowly. Most classrooms, unlike those I have just described, don't look much different today than they did fifty or a hundred years ago, and most of them won't look much different ten years from now. They may have a few more computers, or they may have newer computers, but there isn't necessarily a strong relationship between having a computer in a classroom and having students learn more, do more, or think more. What happens in the classroom is largely the responsibility of the teacher. More or better technology isn't enough.

In this section I consider some of the issues I think are essential as we look ahead to the next five or ten years. At a time when technology is more and more central to discussions about school reform and restructuring, I think it's important to focus on what we can and can't do very well with technology, and how we can provide the kinds of opportunities I've just described to more students and teachers.

Access

There are enough computers in schools in the United States to provide at least one for each classroom, but the reality is that the technology is not evenly distributed and much of it is already old. Most students use computers for a very short time each week, often in a lab, and their experiences commonly treat the computer as an object of study in the form of computer literacy. Most of the computers they use are old enough to be considered obsolete by current standards. These machines are more likely to run drill and practice software than provide access to the Internet or multimedia CD-ROMs.

The availability of computers in schools will continue to be an important issue over the next ten years. California, home of Silicon Valley, ranks near the bottom in the United States in computer-to-student ratio. California voters regularly turn down the majority of bond measures that could bring more technology into classrooms. Computer hardware has improved tremendously over the past ten years, but has not gotten significantly cheaper. The current presidential administration's goal of Internet access for every classroom in the country by the year 2000 is admirable and very optimistic, but only a small step toward effective technology use in schools.

Most classrooms ten years from now won't look like the ACOT classrooms of ten years ago. Without a drastic change in the kinds of computers that are built and their cost, the ratio of computers to students will remain too low for computers to become a ubiquitous tool that all can use. Access to the Internet may be available in most schools, but the Internet may not be what we see today. Web addresses have quickly become so common they are flashed on television screens as part of advertisements and regular programming. It seems that everybody has a Web page and e-mail address. Everybody that is, except students and teachers in most of our schools. Only 3 percent of all classrooms have access to the Internet, and by the time the other 97 percent get access, much of the Internet may become a pay-as-you-go medium that could price many people out of the system. Once a forum for the free exchange of information and software, the Internet is rapidly becoming commercialized and regulated. Universal access needs to be available on the scale and cost of the telephone system, but as long as the cost to participate is a $2,000 computer, access alone won't help. If the Internet does become an essential source for information, schools, libraries, and community centers will need to provide access for those who can't afford it at home.

Teachers and Teacher Education

Current teachers often have little support within their schools for their work with technology. When software or hardware doesn't work, and there isn't someone to help remedy the situation, learning can come to a stop. Current teachers, like the teachers who will follow them over the next ten years, are likely to have little training in the use of technology during their time as students in teacher preparation programs. Technology training once they start teaching is often limited to in-service presentations where they sit and listen to someone tell them how to use technology. Sometime in the future, training teachers to use technology won't be an issue, because they will have been using it all their lives. Until then, integrating technology into teacher education programs should be a high priority if we believe that new technologies are essential tools for participation in society.

Rather than be surprised at how few computers are in schools, we should probably be surprised at how many there are given the serious shortcomings they bring with them. As tools for learning go, most computers are expensive, large, hard to share, and very difficult to use and maintain. Six months after they've been purchased, they are replaced by models that are faster and cheaper. A year later they are no longer being produced, phased out in favor of a new line. Outfitting a room of computers with the necessary software can sometimes double the initial hardware cost. When things break down, and they inevitably do, teachers are usually on their own.

The Classroom in 2005

In an ideal world, every classroom in 2005 will enjoy the opportunities teachers and students have today in ACOT classrooms. Teachers will be supported by an administration committed to helping students learn in ways that meet their needs, using technology that helps them do so. Classrooms will be part of a learning web that reaches beyond the school to homes, community centers, museums, libraries, and other schools around the world. Students will have easy access to a wide range of resources in many forms, and will share their work with an audience that extends around the world.

The ideal classroom in nine years will remain a distant goal for most schools. Limited funds and resources, large class sizes, and technology that's too hard to use will still be with us. In nine years, teacher education programs will have graduated thousands more teachers underprepared for teaching with technology. The ACOT classrooms of 2005 should have among them at least one located in a teacher education program at a university. ACOT's current focus on providing training for teachers is a unique and effective program, but it touches only a few drops in a flood of teachers graduating with less experience using computers and other technology than the students they will be teaching.

Literacy

Among the many contributions to ideas about learning made by the Russian psychologist L. S. Vygotsky is the idea that the tools we use shape both what we do and how we come to understand the world around us. Computers, along with multimedia software and hardware, help us express our ideas as animations, video poems, slide shows, interactive movies, virtual environments, and other forms yet to be created. As we create these new texts, we are changing how we define literacy. The essential medium of expression in classrooms is no longer print. It's a hybrid of print, video, audio, and video games, but unless we provide access to the tools to compose in this medium, we will be training our students to be readers but not writers. And if all they do is read these multimedia texts, not only will they have sore eyes, they will be missing out on an important part of what it means to be literate.

The computer screen is a great place to search for text, but a poor place to read it. Reading on a computer screen is significantly slower than reading on paper as the resolution of current displays is much lower than the resolution of printed books or magazines. Search engines can help us find all kinds of texts stored on the Internet, and with the right software we can download, reformat, print, and read these texts. If we expect that students (and teachers) will someday do much of their reading with computers, we need high-resolution displays to make it possible. When the display technology to effectively support reading on computer screens does become available, how will schools pay for it? Who will fund the replacement of the thousands of monitors that don't have the resolution we need to really use the computer as the place where we interact with all forms of information?

Conclusions

Computers and related technologies will continue to get faster, smaller, more powerful, and, if we are lucky, easier to use for the immediate future. We are currently in the midst of a great transformation of all our communication technologies. As more of our information is transformed from "atoms to bits," as Nicholas Negroponte puts it, the implications for how we create, distribute, and obtain information are tremendous. The explosive growth of the Internet and World Wide Web holds out the possibility of a new mass medium, similar to and different from print, radio, and television, and encompassing all that those media do and more. Whether we consider the continued rapid growth of technology as progress depends a great deal on how we use it. Media delivery controlled by a small number of large broadcasters has given us network television. The Internet presents an alternative model of media access, but we have a long way to go in providing access to everyone.

Faster computers and larger hard drives don't mean more learning and better thinking. Technology that is becoming commonplace in businesses and homes remains rare in classrooms. The biggest problems holding back the use of technology in schools are social, not technological. Engineers will make the machines faster and smaller and cheaper, and interface designers will make them marginally easier to use, but unless we change the training and status of teachers, little will change in our classrooms. The United States will experience a significant turnover in the teaching population over the next ten years, and if the low pay and low status afforded prospective teachers isn't enough to keep people away, the working conditions may be. In California, as we hurry to wire all schools to the Internet, we have classrooms with one textbook for thirty-five students and teachers photocopying pages for everyone to share. If you think collaboration is tough with one computer in a classroom, try it with one textbook. In Silicon Valley, while we ponder the merits of ISDN, ATM, and cable modems so students can surf the World Wide Web at high speed, we rank near the bottom in teacher-to-student ratio. As we wait for technology's "next big thing" to reach our schools, we see more and more students graduating without the skills to succeed in college or work. Technology isn't the answer to the problems in our schools, but technology in the hands of students working with creative teachers can provide new and interesting ways for students to express themselves. That, at least, is a step in the right direction.

13

The Image Processing
for Teaching Project

Richard Greenberg

Until the early 1980s, images radioed back to Earth by U.S. interplanetary spacecraft were converted into photographs at a central computer facility. This procedure was expensive and slow. Moreover, the photos delivered to the scientific community contained only a fraction of the information in the original data, often hiding important features. For example, images of Jupiter's moon Io taken by the Voyager spacecraft in 1979 showed an unusually puzzling surface. Initial explanations of the photographs were unsatisfactory. Eventually, an optical navigation engineer identified the volcanic plumes that explained everything, but only after the original digital data were reprocessed in an image processing laboratory to enhance the background. The plumes were always in the data, but could only be seen when those data were processed digitally.

During the 1980s, the technology for processing digital images developed rapidly. By the end of the decade, sophisticated applications were widely available, even on microcomputers. By 1990, discovery of volcanism on Io could be replicated in seconds on a Macintosh. To a great extent, progress was driven by needs in two areas. Planetary exploration was continuing to provide very rare and expensive data from spacecraft and biomedicine was supplying image data from probes while minimizing invasion into living bodies.

What Is Digital Image Processing?

Images can be stored as arrays of numbers—as *digital* images—and computers are ideally suited for processing them in that form. Digital images of photographic quality can be manipulated relatively quickly and inexpensively on a computer. Processing can include various measurements, contrast enhancement, false coloring, animation, filtering, and, among other things, unlimited quantitative analysis. Image processing can bring out features and properties that had previously been difficult or impossible to capture. When it was introduced, it simply revolutionized the way images were perceived, analyzed, communicated, and stored. It is now an important standard tool in many areas of scientific study.

In the fields of primary and secondary education, most images currently available to students are in analog rather than digital form. Like the photographs that frustrated planetary scientists in the early years of the Voyager mission, they are mechanical or electronic representations. Even with modern multimedia systems, computers are essentially being used as devices to catalog and retrieve analog images. Multimedia systems present images to users, but generally do not allow users to modify or process them. The new digital image processing technology that developed in the 1980s allows users to explore image data in ways that are not possible with older media. The technology has advanced to the point where state-of-the-art public domain software runs on the kinds of microcomputers that are becoming widely available in schools.

This chapter describes how digital image processing tasks have been introduced into schools to provide an exciting, sophisticated, and practical tool for inquiry on a broad variety of science and mathematics topics. The story focuses on the birth, development, and maturation of the Image Processing for Teaching (IPT) project at the University of Arizona's Lunar and Planetary Laboratory. The IPT project places a new high-tech tool in secondary schools and engages students in active, authentic scientific inquiry. The project invites students and teachers to take a hands-on investigative approach to learning and, as such, is often a departure from more traditional treatments of science and mathematics in schools.

Introducing innovations in teaching and learning is not a trivial pursuit and, later in the chapter, I reflect on lessons learned as part of the IPT project about curriculum development and school implementation. Perhaps the strongest theme of this story is that greater portions of the resources available for supporting classroom learning with technology must be allocated to the hard problems of school implementation rather than technological development itself. Substantial resources are needed to demonstrate the value of an innovation to teachers and administrators, show them how to use it, create appropriate curriculum materials, and provide frequent follow-up support in schools. IPT, like many projects that introduce new technologies to schools, does not simply bring a new tool; it changes the nature of classroom work and the relationships among teachers and students.

Origins of the Image Processing for Teaching Project

I had for some time been a strong proponent of using computer technology for image processing in the space program when (in 1989) I learned that the National Science Foundation was sponsoring projects to introduce new science technologies to classrooms. It immediately struck me that image processing, for a variety of reasons, could work well in schools.

Regardless of an image's content, image processing combines high technology, information theory, and cognitive issues. Just as word processing and other computer tools were finding roles in classrooms, image processing seemed a logical tool to introduce. Moreover, the content areas to which image processing is being applied in the worlds of science could be very interesting to students and span several subject areas in the school curriculum.

It seemed to me that image processing's great potential as an educational tool came from the way it facilitates the processes of exploration and discovery in the research community. These science processes appear to be at the heart of learning. As infants we start exploring the world, having experiences, and making observations. We construct sets of rules that impose some pattern on our experiences and allow us to make useful predictions about what may happen under various circumstances. When additional experiences or observations fail to fit our schema, we are obliged to revise or reconstruct them. Scientists follow the same procedures, constructing theories based on experiments and observations, testing the theories with further experiment and observation. The real fun starts when the results do not fit, and the theory must be modified or completely replaced. Children, then, can be viewed as natural scientists.

In this sense, students have been doing science well before entering a science classroom, and, as a result, they bring with them their own scientific theories. These relatively naive theories are usually based on a limited set of observations and experiences. By doing experiments and making observations that may clash with their preconceptions, students are forced to change their views, in much the same way as professional scientists update and revise theories. This kind of learning could be useful far beyond performance on a test.

I also thought that visual learners might find image processing a more attractive entrée into science and mathematics than traditional language-based methods. People are physiologically structured to learn visually. From the standpoint of information theory, images are by far the fastest and most efficient way to deliver information to the human brain. Consider this for speed and efficiency. The typical field of view of the human eye contains roughly one hundred million bits of information and is revised and reanalyzed several times per second. This figure is obtained by taking a typical image that you see, dividing it into tiny picture elements or *pixels*, assigning values to each pixel expressing its brightness and spectral characteristics, and then determining how many numbers are needed to encode the information. In contrast, the written or spoken words that one can absorb in a fraction of a second could be encoded with only a few hundred bits. Formally, a picture is worth about a million words.

Traditional teaching methods in science and mathematics have generally failed to inspire many students, especially those from diverse linguistic and cultural backgrounds, and we suspected that learning through image manipulation might be a particularly significant opportunity for these students. Some tasks might use familiar images from students' experiences or environments to motivate learners. At the very least I thought that learning through image manipulation would complement language-based instruction for all students.

I presented these ideas to my colleague Robert Strom, who directs the NASA Regional Planetary Imagery Facility at the University of Arizona. Professor Strom is an experienced teacher of undergraduates and has had considerable experience with outreach programs for teachers and students. We assembled a group of teachers to advise us and together we developed a plan for the Image Processing for Teaching project.

We proposed that cohorts of teachers learn image processing during intensive summer workshops and develop ways to use it in their classrooms. Each teacher would return to school with a computer to try the activities that had been developed by participants in the workshop.

The original plan contained two interesting flaws. First, we originally planned to use image processing to teach planetary science (our field) in schools. NSF reviewers astutely pointed out that it could be used equally effectively in other, more common school subjects: biology, earth science, physics, and so on. We took that advice and IPT has covered a variety of areas in science, mathematics, and technology ever since. Second, because we knew of some image processing software that was available, we had proposed to use DOS computers. Besides, as scientists with decades of number-crunching experience with computers, we were intimately familiar with DOS machines. Shortly after the IPT project was funded, professor Strom spotted an unusual demonstration of image processing software at an American Astronomical Society meeting. When I arrived at the meeting, he came breathlessly running over to me and dragged me to a display of NIH Image software running on a Macintosh computer. It was immediately obvious to us that this was the system for IPT.

Why was this system so appropriate? NIH Image is a real research tool, designed for, and now a standard of, the biomedical research community. Adopting it for IPT would give secondary school students experience with a tool actually in use by professionals in the field. At the same time—in contrast to the parametric line commands still common in most DOS- or Windows-based processors—NIH Image is easy to use. Moreover, NIH Image, developed and maintained by a generous genius named Wayne Rasband at the National Institutes of Health, is in the public domain. Schools with Macintoshes[1] could have sophisticated image processing systems for zero cost.

At this point, everything seemed to be in place. Now we could try the idea in the field and see if it would work with students and teachers.

The IPT Experiment

To explore the potential of digital image processing as a medium for learning, the project began with an experimental phase. We worked with eighty experienced, exemplary teachers on the techniques and technology of image processing. Participants attended a four-week workshop and explored a wide variety of scientific content by processing numerous data sets. As experts on practical education issues and the implementation of image processing in specific school contexts, teachers were full-fledged members of the project team. Together, we developed curriculum activities for students in different grades, subject areas, locations, and kinds of schools. Subsequently, the units were tested in teachers' home schools. They reported and compared results from these trials and participated in an extended evaluation process.

Even early in the project, large data sets as well as the NIH Image software were distributed on CD-ROMs we produced ourselves. This method was simply cheaper and faster than using the very large number of floppy disks that would have been required. While CD-ROM technology has achieved a certain mystique, in effect it really just produces fast, high-capacity, read-only floppies.

We began the IPT project as an experiment. It seemed plausible that image processing could be an effective and exciting way to attract students to science with broad new possibilities for exploration and discovery. On the other hand, we recognized that not all good ideas come to fruition in practice.

In the experimental phase, exciting things happened with IPT in the classroom. Students found image manipulation to be attractive and fun, often leading to exploration of new science content and appreciation of the underlying mathematics. Students became aware of and practiced the investigative processes of science. Evaluation of the IPT project yielded a number of interesting results, some of which were unexpected.

Underrepresented Groups

In many cases, students who might not have been expected to do well in conventional science classes were enthusiastic and persistent participants. Students from ethnic minority groups, including those with limited English proficiency, females, and students with identified learning disabilities generally did well in the program. With image processing, it appears that some traditional obstacles in learning science and mathematics are largely eliminated, resulting in participation for a broader range of students.

Mathematics

While our original expectation was that IPT would have an impact on teaching science, we have been impressed with its tendency to motivate and enrich mathematics learning. Our participating teachers, especially those in tune with recent standards of the National Council of Teachers of Mathematics, realized this immediately. To motivate students, many of our teachers introduce image processing with images of cars, rockets, or the students themselves, but regardless of the content of an image, its manipulation is a rich environment for exploring mathematics. Students become familiar with coordinate systems, numerical arrays, scale, histograms, lookup tables, and so on. Some teachers use the gray scale map to teach concepts of slope (contrast) and intercept (brightness). More advanced students delve, often more deeply than we anticipated, into the technical details of the software and quantitative analysis.

Student Attitudes

At many of our participating schools, image processing under the guidance of our expert teachers appears to have influenced the attitudes and self-esteem of at-risk youth. Some individuals, once viewed as being on paths leading to academic failure, are now doing extra work in image processing, taking leadership roles in training classmates, and becoming serious students. The appeal of images and the opportunity to become an expert seem to build self-esteem to a degree we had not foreseen.

Effects on Teachers

We have found that teachers' perceptions of subject matter, pedagogy, and their own professional roles have been profoundly affected by participation in the project. Many have reported seeing closer connections between what can happen in their classrooms and the work of scientific researchers. Initially, we expected that the most effective IPT teachers would be those with the strongest scientific and technical backgrounds. In fact, we find that other characteristics are at least as important for effective integration of image processing into schoolwork. Our most successful teachers often are enthusiastic, energetic people with sophisticated pedagogical repertoires. They also seem to have the administrative acumen and flexibility to introduce and sustain a major innovation in their classrooms. Teachers must be willing to allow surprising discoveries and original problem solving to occur in their classes.

Middle School Success

Our project includes teachers from the upper elementary grades through high school. While we anticipated that IPT would be effective in high schools, it is proving to have substantial impact in middle schools as well. We think that there are at least two reasons for this. First, the science curriculum is not rigidly defined for middle schools, so teachers can incorporate innovations relatively easily. Second, younger students appear to be more open to exploration and discovery. In contrast, advanced high school classes can be bound to a traditional curriculum, with students who are already highly invested in the status quo. In many cases, school systems may discourage potentially creative scientists before they reach the upper grade levels.

Scientific and Technical Contributions
by Students and Teachers

Equipped with state-of-the-art technology, IPT teachers and their students have had an impact on the research community. They have, for example, introduced image processing to tree-ring research, influenced the continuing development of software at NIH, developed new techniques for 3-D imaging, and contributed original research papers at NASA's Lunar and Planetary Science Conference. Students and teachers have been responsible for generating innovative data sets beyond those provided by the IPT project. This professional interchange among teachers, students, and researchers has provided the basis for some of our most successful curriculum activities.

Dissemination

Just as the experimental phase of the project began to demonstrate the usefulness of image processing in education, availability of appropriate hardware in schools began to mushroom. Many schools were receiving funding for technology enhancements from bond issues or grants. At the same time, Macintosh hardware for IPT systems became more affordable through a series of price reductions. In some cases, decisions to buy specific hardware have been driven by interest in the IPT program.

We began to receive requests to design and run schoolwide or districtwide in-service courses in IPT and to distribute curriculum materials for the program. In 1992, we designed the current dissemination phase of IPT. The centerpiece of our strategy was the creation of a nonprofit Center for Image Processing in Education. The Center, in a strong supportive relationship with the University of Arizona, conducts teacher education, provides follow-up and outreach services, and develops and distributes materials for image processing in schools. The Center's activities are guided by results of ongoing evaluation of all components of the project.

Teacher Education

The four-week workshop format of the experimental phase was not practical for working with large numbers of teachers. Based on our earlier experiences, we developed in-service workshops of three to five days duration. This shorter, more manageable format also corresponded to the amount of in-service training typically allocated in well-planned school-district technology programs. Workshops are designed for groups of up to eighteen teachers. No previous experience with computers is required. We introduce the computer operating system, theoretical background on image processing, use of NIH Image software, available digital image data sets and sources, and IPT curriculum materials. Over two thousand teachers have participated in this teacher education program. We encourage school-based follow-up activities to reinforce technical issues and encourage teachers during the earliest stages of integrating technology into their teaching.

Follow-Up and Outreach Programs

A strong program of follow-up support is perhaps the most critical, but most widely neglected, component of technology implementation in schools. We have found that teachers benefit from follow-up support in technical, pedagogical, and scientific areas. We maintain contact with teachers, in part, through a toll-free phone line and via the Internet. An annual IPT conference and a newsletter also provide forums for technical information, updates, and exchange of experiences with school implementation.

Materials Development

As part of the experimental program, our team of scientists and teachers developed extensive curricular units for IPT. These activities are designed to lead teachers and students into active inquiry and discovery, taking advantage of the power of technology to access vast new data sets. We are continuing to develop materials that align more closely with emerging national standards for science educators. At the same time, we strive to retain elements of exploration and personal discovery that have been the hallmark of IPT activities. By design, our materials allow teachers to learn image processing doing the same kinds of activities that their students might do in their classes.

Our curriculum materials development is guided by a set of principles, based on both the original premises of the IPT project and on what we have learned during the past five years. Our best materials have some or all of the following characteristics.

IPT materials are curriculum based. We have found that for widespread use, materials must be recognizable by teachers as supporting valued curricular objectives and fitting realistic scheduling constraints, while at the same time allowing open-ended exploration, discovery, and analysis.

The materials should include appropriate image data sets needed for the curriculum activities. We also strongly encourage use of student-generated data. Such data can come from in-school laboratory experiences, Internet exploration, or distributed measurement projects—among other sources. The following examples provide a sense of the possibilities for activities using either archived image data of data generated by students.

Several widely used IPT curriculum units involve analysis of GOES weather satellite imagery of hurricane systems and diurnal surface temperature variations.[2] A CD-ROM distributed by the IPT project contains time-sequence data sets for these phenomena as well as supplemental image data for further exploration. Students on the Tohono O'odham reservation in Arizona extended this activity by using the Internet. They obtained same-hour satellite data for correlation with local weather conditions. Using these data obtained by students, the IPT activity was expanded to a three-month project in weather prediction and satellite data interpretation. IPT materials also contain images to be used with mitosis and cell structure activities. However, students can generate their own images on wet-lab days by using video cameras (now available in many school laboratories) to record microscopic images, which they can then digitize for subsequent analysis with image processing.

IPT materials and activities use the unique capabilities of image processing. Most activities depend on image enhancement and other analysis features that would be difficult or impossible with other image media. The activities build on image processing as a state-of-the-art research tool to provide authentic project-based experiences that allow students to explore the complexities recorded in image data.

Wherever possible, materials and activities support emerging national standards in science, mathematics, and technology education. Curriculum activities in IPT materials are keyed to the existing mathematics standards supported by the National Council of Teachers of

Mathematics, and the project is in the process of keying its materials to the recently finalized science standards put forth by the National Research Council.

IPT curriculum activities minimize routine instructions and encourage exploration and discovery. In developing IPT activities, there is always a narrow path to be followed in providing enough guidance to direct students into personal exploration and discovery while avoiding being overly prescriptive. Similarly, while we emphasize visual learning, materials should also enhance literacy acquisition and vocabulary building. Learning to achieve the appropriate balance has not been trivial. The best activities provide just enough structure to guide students, but lead to open-ended learning.

IPT curriculum development assumes an active role for both teachers and students. Activities are intended to be done by small groups of students working together to explore and solve problems. The guidance of teachers in this discovery process is crucial.

IPT materials are relevant to the real world. Many are based on current issues and recent data from scientific research. Others represent practical applications or potential career opportunities in which image processing plays an increasingly larger role. Still others relate to the daily lives of students, including sports, medical issues, and images of friends and family. IPT teachers who work with diverse populations have emphasized the value of incorporating culturally meaningful imagery to excite and motivate students.

IPT materials are complementary to, but distinct from, simulation software. It is important to clarify the distinction. IPT provides a tool for analyzing messy, real-world data in all their complexity, allowing scientists and students alike to grapple with the underlying principles and laws that govern nature. In contrast, simulation software allows a student to model an artificial world, assuming that the software already incorporates the correct laws of motion or behavior.

IPT materials include built-in assessments of students' learning. Image processing leads to creation of concrete products that allow teachers to track the process of exploration and discovery. Some materials ask students to generate written reports, quantitative solutions, or digital image products.

Conclusion

The images used in IPT are not just pretty pictures. They are original data from recent research in a wide variety of disciplines and practical applications. The data are in digital form, not the analog form generally accessed through educational multimedia systems. IPT teachers and their students manipulate the original data bits as they carry out image processing activities. The vast amount of data involved in complex images creates the continuing possibility of real scientific discovery. When students engage in image processing, they participate in a new kind of educational experience that often diverges from traditional science education.

However, the story of the IPT project is not about a new technology. The history of image processing will be written elsewhere. This story is about how a new technology can be exploited and disseminated as a meaningful tool for learning. While the technical aspects are challenging, the task of developing and integrating the programmatic components to support teachers and students in the real world of schools is an equal if not greater challenge. We believe that concentrating our limited resources on the educational applications, not squandering them on technological development, is one key to success. Ultimately, the experiences of teachers and students will determine the role of technological tools in schools.

Notes

1. To take advantage of this opportunity to use NIH Image, the IPT project needed Macintosh computers. Apple Computer, Inc., and the ACOT project generously responded to our request by donating an initial complement of color Macintoshes.

2. See for example, the "Storm that Ate South Carolina" in *IPT 2.1 CD-ROM and Sourcebook,* 1995, Tucson, AZ: Center for Image Processing in Education.

Part III

Engaging Teachers on the Road Ahead

The initial decade of the use of digital technologies in schools reaffirmed the critical importance of teachers in creating and orchestrating productive learning events for students. As the decade began, some educators feared that the expansion of technology would reduce teachers' roles in classrooms, but by the end of the decade this fear was shown to be unfounded. On the contrary, when technology was used to support inquiry-oriented, collaborative projects, teachers were critical contributors to the development and completion of thoughtful, sustained activities. While teachers continued to have a role in presentation and interpretation of content, much more of their effort was invested in organizational and interactive structures designed to increase students' responsibility for their own learning. As students became more active in classroom learning activities, teachers' roles expanded to include facilitation and coaching skills.

The introduction of digital technology constitutes a major change in the classroom learning environment, and like all educational changes, both teachers and students require time and support to accommodate the new tools and activities. Teachers require new knowledge and skills to use these new tools appropriately. During the last decade, studies of professional development among teachers, including those who were implementing technology, initially favored long-term programs in working classrooms over single-occasion information sessions at a remote site. By the end of the decade, policy analysts were advocating that in order for innovative programs to be successful, training and staff-development components should constitute approximately 30 to 40 percent of the total effort.

Part Three provides four perspectives on the professional development of teachers in the first decade of the ACOT project. In Chapter Fourteen, Jane David presents key lessons learned about integrating technology into instruction. David identifies core elements of an expanding network of teacher development centers, reflects on the operation of public-private partnerships in education, and draws implications for educational reform. In Chapter Fifteen, Robert Carpenter describes ACOT's first decade from the perspective of classroom teachers at an ACOT site. He characterizes the decade in three phases and concludes with reflections on professional development. In Chapter Sixteen, Keith Yocam examines the ACOT experience from the perspective of the project staff who were responsible for professional development activities. Finally, in Chapter Seventeen, Judith Sandholtz and Cathy Ringstaff describe how ACOT teachers' beliefs about teaching and learning changed. Sandholtz and Ringstaff provide useful insights into structures for supporting teachers during the change process, and they reflect on their own use of technology to study technology.

The ACOT project, like many projects before it, is attempting to share its hard-won lessons about the importance of teachers in the school change process. The ACOT Teacher Development Centers represent a coordinated effort to affect classrooms beyond those participating directly in the project. A portion of each of the chapters in Part Three describes aspects of the design and implementation of these centers, inviting comparisons among the various perspectives.

14

Developing and Spreading Accomplished Teaching

Policy Lessons from a Unique Partnership

Jane L. David

In the ten years since I first visited ACOT classrooms around the country, I have witnessed the evolution of a unique public-private partnership that has tackled the biggest challenges facing education reform efforts. ACOT's history parallels that of recent education reform themes—introducing an innovation from the outside, discovering that teacher knowledge and school structure are major influences on implementation, and then confronting the fact that most models of professional development for individual and for organizational change are seriously inadequate.

ACOT's initial approach rested on the assumption that access to technology in itself was sufficient for teachers and students to realize its potential. It also began as something foreign to school systems—a research and development effort designed to generate new knowledge. Since then, ACOT has evolved into a multiyear professional development experience for teachers, and now, with support from the National Science Foundation, into a model for sharing that accomplished practice with hundreds of teachers beyond ACOT.

In retrospect, it is hardly surprising that ensuring access to technology was insufficient to change practice. Teachers used technology to support what they already knew how to do, and what fit into the constraints of traditional classrooms, schedules, and curricula. On the other hand, people's worst fears were not realized, either.

Computers did not replace teachers, nor did they decrease interaction among students. In fact, the opposite has occurred. Teachers are the key to whether technology is used appropriately and effectively, and technology increases conversation, sharing, and learning among students and between students and teachers.

From my perspective, as one who studies school reform efforts and the role of policy in supporting such efforts, ACOT's ten-year history generates three important sets of lessons. The first are lessons about integrating technology into instruction, that is, the kinds of experiences and support teachers need in order to learn to use technology in ways that support new practices. The second are lessons about spreading accomplished teaching practices, which grow out of ACOT's recent evolution into teacher development centers. The third are lessons about public-private partnerships derived from the unusual ACOT partnership involving a large corporation, a set of schools and their districts, universities, research organizations, and, most recently, the National Science Foundation.

By presenting new ways of thinking about professional learning, research and development, and replication, these lessons transcend issues of integrating technology into instruction. They speak to the broader issues of reforming the whole educational enterprise in order to ensure teaching for understanding for all children.

Integrating Technology into Instruction

One overarching lesson from the original ACOT classrooms is this: to help teachers incorporate technology in ways that support powerful instruction requires an array of professional development experiences quite different from traditional workshops and how-to training sessions. Rather than focusing on technology per se, these requisite experiences must focus on changing pedagogical beliefs and practices, with technology as a tool when appropriate.

The crucial role of technology is to provide an impetus and an occasion for thinking differently about instructional practices.

Open-ended and always changing, technology puts students in a more active role, forcing new relationships between teachers and students. Moreover, powerful, versatile, and exciting technology can be a tempting invitation to take on the task of rethinking classroom organization and traditional teaching practices.[1]

Over a period of several years, ACOT staff and teachers began to create a different conception of training and assistance, a conception that goes beyond teaching teachers about hardware and software operations and applications. ACOT staff began to construct an array of professional development experiences for teachers. These experiences included workshops and institutes that introduced teachers to the latest technologies, but they also included on-site, classroom-based assistance as well as opportunities to reflect on and to discuss beliefs about teaching and learning. In addition, ACOT staff encouraged teachers to take on more professional activities, including research collaboration, writing, and presentations at professional conferences.

At Apple and in the classroom, ACOT staff came to understand that the very kinds of instruction desired for students had to be incorporated into learning environments for teachers. Classroom teachers and ACOT staff faced the same dilemmas: how to create environments that support learning by doing, how much structure and direction to provide, and how to balance learning to use technology with developing new pedagogical strategies.

ACOT teachers began to change their practices, incorporating not only technology and project-based instruction but also new organizational arrangements, including teacher teams, different schedules and physical arrangements in classrooms, and different groupings of students. (See Dwyer for a more detailed description of how teaching practices changed.)[2] In so doing, teachers encountered a host of barriers. Some were constraints internal to their school; others were external.

By virtue of its experimental nature, ACOT involved only a few classrooms in each school. Consequently, where schedules and physical space were changed to accommodate their needs, ACOT teachers faced the same dilemmas that confront any school within a school. For example, to learn new ways of teaching in which technology is appropriately integrated requires additional time to learn, plan, work with colleagues, develop curricula, write, prepare and give presentations, and attend institutes and conferences. Teachers especially need time to reflect on their experiences and to discuss them with colleagues. Where schedules were changed significantly for ACOT teachers, some of their peers resented the special treatment, and others discounted their accomplishments, attributing them to these exceptional circumstances.

An early lesson was the critical role principals play in either minimizing or exacerbating the differences between ACOT and non-ACOT teachers. Where the principal saw ACOT as a model of innovation to be shared and learned from, friction was minimal and ACOT expanded as more teachers became interested. Where the principal reinforced the view that ACOT teachers had special privileges and equipment, the spread of ideas was limited. ACOT teachers overcame some antipathy by reaching out to their colleagues with offers of workshops and explicit invitations to their classrooms.

As with other reform efforts, ACOT teachers' progress was helped or hindered by local and state factors as well. Progress in changing classroom practices was hampered in each site by required district or state testing that was aligned with traditional instruction and skills-based curriculum. This mismatch between testing and new practices has stimulated teachers' interest in using new forms of assessment. Progress was enhanced when district support resulted in sound choices for site leaders, and flexibility for nontraditional roles and schedules.

Spreading Accomplished Practice

Clearly, ACOT could not make the same substantial investment in technology and in support to more than a handful of schools. How then could these lessons—about creating accomplished teaching in a small number of classrooms—be translated from a few schools to many? This question is *the* major challenge facing all of education reform: How do we bring about significant changes in teaching and learning in large numbers of schools, not just a few with the benefit of substantial investment and assistance?

ACOT's response was to develop a strategy that would capitalize on the expertise of experienced ACOT teachers and embody the lessons about integrating technology into instruction. To transform the ACOT sites into ACOT Teacher Development Centers, representatives of all the ACOT partners devised a strategy based on the underlying principles and essential elements of their own learning experiences and drawing heavily on Faye Wilmore's pilot teacher development efforts at the Nashville site.[3] In 1992, the ACOT partnership was awarded a three-year grant from the National Science Foundation to implement this strategy in three ACOT sites.[4]

The centers are organized to provide three sets of experiences for participants: a week-long practicum during the school year in the ACOT classrooms, a three- to four-week long summer institute with students, and follow-up support in participants' home schools. However, the hallmark of the teacher development strategy is not the details of its structure and organization but the principles of teacher learning they are built on. Because ACOT classrooms were not something to be replicated, this strategy is quite different from traditional program dissemination. The goal was to create structured experiences in which participating teachers could learn from the expertise of ACOT teachers and apply the results to their own relatively low-technology classrooms.

The underlying principles for the ACOT Teacher Development Centers are embodied in the experiences that participants have during the practicum and summer institute, and in the overall structure of the program. For example, at each center participants work with a coordinator whose activities model the constructivist approach of ACOT teachers. Participants actively use technology for composition, communication, and knowledge construction, as they are expected to do in their home schools. Instead of the notion of scattering seeds—as the literal meaning of dissemination suggests—experiences at the ACOT site are designed to *plant* seeds. The program structure is designed to help create fertile soil at the home school. These elements continue to be refined as lessons are learned from each round of participants.

Participants' experiences at the Teacher Development Centers include the following key elements.

Structured observations of accomplished practice. Through week-long classroom observations, videos, demonstrations, and conferences with teachers, teams from participating schools are exposed to examples of accomplished teaching in technology-rich settings. The ACOT coordinator guides the observations and provides additional context to enhance understanding. For example, coordinators often initiate discussions about the fact that technology is not always in use. The overall experience at the centers is designed to maximize participants' exposure to accomplished practice in real classrooms without disrupting teachers or students.

Reflection on and discussion of teaching and learning. Interwoven throughout the practicum and the summer institute are opportunities for participants to reflect on their experiences, both in groups and individually through computer journals. Participants also hold discussions among themselves in structured and unstructured settings. They compare beliefs about teaching and learning that underlie accomplished practice, talk about the dilemmas teachers confront in balancing didactic and constructivist pedagogies, and analyze ways to determine when technology is an appropriate tool. Reading and discussing relevant research are part of this process as well.

Hands-on, collaborative learning. In month-long summer institutes, participating teachers have extended time to learn alongside students and accomplished teachers how to use computers, camcorders, and telecommunications equipment as tools to support learning for understanding. In contrast to the school-year practicum, where the benefit comes from watching a real school situation in action, the summer institute provides far more hands-on time to learn to use technology tools, with assistance from accomplished ACOT teachers and students.

Curriculum project development. To provide concrete goals and a structure for learning to use new tools, participants are asked to create projects of their choice that incorporate the technology they have available in their own classrooms, tied to ambitious learning goals for students. In this way, learning to use specific hardware and software is embedded in the development of usable projects. The development process is collaborative and iterative, with opportunities for assistance and feedback from ACOT staff and students. Teachers are also asked to prepare implementation plans for incorporating what they have learned when they return to their home schools.

Participants' experiences at the centers are enhanced by several key elements of the program structure.

Teacher teams and principal participation. Criteria for selection are designed to ensure that participating teachers have support to incorporate what they learn in their home schools. Teachers must attend in teams of at least two so there will be peer support. Principals of schools sending teams must make a commitment to support schoolwide instructional change and integration of technology and to help participating teachers share their knowledge with their colleagues. In addition, these principals must attend the practicum or the institute for at least one full day, and must ensure that teachers have access to at least one computer—with printer and appropriate software—in their home classrooms immediately upon their return from the center.

Commitment to share with colleagues. Teachers participate with the understanding that they carry an obligation to share their knowledge with their peers at their school site. They are encouraged to view themselves as agents of change at their home sites, with technology as a tool for changing practice. On their return, teachers share their knowledge through school-based workshops for colleagues, invitations to observe their classrooms, and efforts to acquire technology for the school.

Follow-up support. Even with commitment at the home site and peer support, participants need access to follow-up guidance and assistance. The ACOT coordinator visits each participant's classroom twice to provide support including technical troubleshooting, feedback on instruction and integration of technology, and assistance with grant-writing, purchasing decisions, and ways to continue professional growth. Plans are under way to augment the support with telecommunications access.

Support for accomplished teachers. Accomplished ACOT teachers need support and continuing opportunities to further their own learning. They risk overload from taking on additional responsibilities during the school year and the summer and, in the process, their opportunities for continued learning and for keeping abreast of newer technologies can fall by the wayside.

Iterative expansion plans. The centers are designed to propagate themselves. Schools that send several teams to the centers and support sharing knowledge have the potential to become Teacher Development Centers themselves. Over a period of several years, each center can spawn additional centers that, over many years, will allow the program to expand geometrically. In addition, teachers are forming their own networks across schools, and these networks have the potential to create long-lasting professional communities.

Participating teachers are generally enthusiastic about their experiences at the ACOT Teacher Development Centers. They value the practicum experience because they are observing real school activities, and they value the summer institute experience because it provides extended time for hands-on learning and working collaboratively with teachers and students. Ideally, all participants would have the opportunity to attend both the practicum and the summer institute as well as have more intensive and longer-term follow-up support.

Most teachers report a range of changes in their attitudes and beliefs about teaching and learning and in classroom practices and uses of technology. Many take the initiative to acquire more technology for their classrooms and schools and take on new roles as leaders and trainers in their home schools.[5]

But not all teachers change and continue to develop as a result of their ACOT experience, and not all schools offer leadership and support for their continued development and sharing accomplished practice within the school. Of those who do, only a few schools have the potential to become the next round of Teacher Development Centers.

Even if it takes several years to create a few more development centers, it is a process with far greater potential for lasting influence on large numbers of teachers than any known alternatives. The approach embodies sound principles of learning for teachers and for students. Moreover, it rests on building, nurturing, and spreading the expertise of classroom teachers, without removing them from the classroom, which is the only conceivable strategy for building systemwide capacity.

Public-Private Partnerships

A third set of lessons emerges from the unusual partnership represented by ACOT. The ACOT partnership—Apple Computer, schools and districts, universities, researchers, and most recently the National Science Foundation—is unique among public-private partnerships in its focus on teaching and learning, its adaptability to new knowledge and changing circumstances, and its longevity.[6]

Rarely do business partnerships with schools focus directly on the challenge of transforming teaching and learning in the classroom or building on the knowledge and experience of teachers. Equally rare are business partnerships created for the express purpose of learning about teaching and learning and directing that knowledge toward strengthening teaching. Rarer still are corporate partnerships that survive over a decade and continue to evolve.

What has allowed this partnership to flourish when so many others remain superficial and short-lived? I see six principles that characterize this partnership and, together, set it apart from other attempts to forge public-private collaborations.

Personal commitment. The ACOT partnership is built on individuals inside Apple Computer and inside districts and schools who have a personal commitment to the improvement of public education and who share the belief that technology can play an important role in stimulating and supporting change.

Trust, not self-interest. Building a relationship of trust began when Apple Computer made it very clear that ACOT classrooms were laboratories for research and development about learning with technology and not opportunities for sales and marketing. This distinction is crucial and has been maintained since its inception.

Quid pro quo. Like a good marriage, each partner gives and receives. Teachers receive considerable technology, a host of development opportunities, and attention. In exchange, they are obligated to experiment with new technologies and new forms of instruction, be open to close scrutiny by researchers and Apple staff, and host visitors from around the world. And the districts carry an obligation to support these teachers. On the other side, Apple Computer has access to real classrooms in which to learn about how its technology can be used and its impact on students and teachers can be enhanced. All partners must see the arrangement as mutually beneficial.

Continuous renegotiation. Even with commitment, trust, and mutual benefit, key people come and go and organizational leadership changes. Relationships have to be renegotiated and commitments reestablished inside each partner organization and between partners on an ongoing basis. But the principles and direction remain constant.

Ongoing learning and adaptation. One hallmark of the partnership is constantly putting assumptions about technology and about learning to the test in real schools and classrooms. Throughout ACOT's history, ideas have been continually revised and adapted as unexpected findings emerge and new knowledge is generated.

Continuing evolution. Each phase leads to a new set of challenges. After creating technology-rich, student-centered learning environments, the partnership took on the challenge of how to spread accomplished practice. As the Teacher Development Center model evolves, the partners are taking on the new challenge of working with universities to redefine the role of student teachers.

Not that the process was always smooth. Poor communication, misunderstandings, and shifts in priorities among all the partner organizations have been inevitable parts of the endeavor. But the results speak for themselves. ACOT is a unique public-private venture that has persisted for over a decade and that continues to have a major influence on those directly involved, as well as a growing influence on a much larger audience of educators, researchers, and policy makers.

Implications for Education Reform

The goal of reforming public education is to guarantee that all students have the skills and knowledge to be productive citizens and lifelong learners. Teaching for meaning and understanding embedded in content is necessary to achieve this goal. Such teaching provides opportunities for students to construct knowledge through working individually and collaboratively on extended and challenging tasks, engaging in discussion, testing out ideas, and making connections across subject areas. In spite of this exciting new vision of learning for understanding, and the whole grand policy vision of systemic reform, strategies for transforming established practice remain unchanged and grounded in the very model of learning deemed undesirable for students.[7-8]

If current efforts to reform public education are to succeed, it is essential to move beyond reliance on traditional one-shot models of professional development, validation of successful practices for replication, and sending in experts to help. These strategies presume that the essence of building professional capacity is presenting educators with the information they need to do a better job, rather than creating opportunities for educators to learn through engagement in intellectually challenging activities, as they are expected to do with students.

Such strategies cannot meet the broad and deep challenge of transforming the system through building professional capacity.[9] Strategies must instead be based on the need for educators to have opportunities to learn new beliefs, practices, and content through active engagement in their construction. And they must be built on the expertise that exists and can be enhanced among practicing educators.

At present, accomplished teachers tend to be marginalized, described as rare and unusual. And they are constantly fighting against constraints imposed by school structures and external regulations and demands. When they are noticed, they are likely to be either removed from the classroom or made objects of study by researchers who extract a set of characteristics isolated from their context for others to imitate. This is a process analogous to teaching facts isolated from the context that gives them meaning. Instead, accomplished teachers should be valued and nurtured, and their strengths exploited for the benefit of their less-accomplished peers.

The challenge for policy makers and education leaders is to create situations that develop and nurture accomplished teaching practices and that spread these practices by creating conditions for educators to learn from each other. ACOT has met this challenge head on. The ACOT Teacher Development Centers exemplify a very different strategy for enhancing the teaching profession by seeking to: create accomplished practice through serious investment in classroom-based teacher development; maintain and learn from these best practice environments over a period of several years; and spread accomplished practices from teacher to teacher based on underlying principles rather than the imitation of specific programs. ACOT not only demonstrates such a strategy in the context of technology, but also demonstrates that valuable lessons can be gleaned in a technology-rich environment and applied to classrooms with minimal technology.

The ACOT Teacher Development Center strategy is not a panacea. Like all serious education reform efforts, ACOT faces challenges and resource constraints that limit its effectiveness. Some examples include: how to provide the time both for accomplished teachers to take on additional responsibilities and for novice teachers to learn; how to create analogs for administrators, especially site principals, given the critical role they play in supporting accomplished practice and teacher development; and how to ensure access to appropriate technology for all teachers and students.

As the pressure mounts for new forms of assessment, more challenging curricula, more varied teaching strategies, and powerful uses of technology, the need for both research and development and new strategies to develop and spread accomplished practice could not be greater. ACOT demonstrates that research and development inside school systems is possible and can form the basis for a new conception of professional learning and development.

However, the success of research and development activities rests on whether they are used to generate usable knowledge. As long as the whole research and development enterprise is hamstrung by the strong tendency of policy makers and educators to judge each effort on whether it can be reproduced in multiple settings, usable knowledge will not result. Policy makers and education leaders must break away from the dominant paradigms of decontextualized approved practices and dissemination-as-replication. Classroom research and development efforts like ACOT will succeed only when they are designed to produce lessons in the form of principles that will manifest themselves differently in different contexts.

Although ACOT participants are accomplished with a range of technologies and pedagogies, they represent a tiny fraction of the teaching force. It is hard to provide challenging instruction; it is harder still to incorporate technology—yet the results, when the investment in support and time to learn have occurred, are exciting learning environments for children and adults alike. In the case of ACOT, the impetus came from an external agent and external support—Apple Computer. In principle, other private as well as public agencies can play this role, as the National Science Foundation is doing, and as other federal or state or even local agencies could and should do.

Notes

1. David, J. L. (1991). Restructuring and technology: Partners in change. *Phi Delta Kappan, 73*(1), 37–82.

2. Dwyer, D. (1994). Apple classrooms of tomorrow: What we've learned. *Educational Leadership, 51*(7), 4–10.

3. Yocam, K., Wilmore, F., & Dwyer, D. (1992). *Situated teacher development: ACOT's two-year pilot project.* Paper presented at the annual meeting of the Society for Technology and Teacher Education, Houston.

4. Chapters Sixteen and Seventeen provide alternative perspectives on some of the design features of the ACOT Teacher Development Centers.

5. For more detail on how participants changed, see Ringstaff, C., Marsh, J., & Yocam, K. (1995). *ACOT teacher development center annual progress report: Year two.* Cupertino, CA: Apple Computer for the National Science Foundation.

6. David, J. L. (1992). *Partnerships for change.* ACOT Report No. 12. Cupertino, CA: Apple Computer.

7. Corcoran, T. C. (1994). *Transforming professional development for teachers: A guide for state policymakers.* Washington, DC: National Governors' Association.

8. David, J. L. (1993). *Systemic reform: Creating the capacity for change.* Draft paper. New Brunswick, NJ: Consortium for Policy Research in Education, Rutgers University.

9. Little, J. W. (1993). Teachers' professional development in a climate of educational reform. *Educational Evaluation and Policy Analysis, 15*(2), 129–151.

15

In the Midst of Change

Robert A. Carpenter

West High School in Columbus, Ohio, is the original high school ACOT site. Since the inception of the project, we[1] have spent approximately 200,000 hours developing and implementing educational experiences that incorporate digital technologies as learning tools for ourselves and our students. Our site operates as a school-within-a-school, providing a four-year program for students admitted as ninth graders. Each ACOT class has about 30 students, and with four grade levels per year, we serve approximately 120 students annually. Total enrollment at West High is about 1,200 students. Typically, about 15 percent of West graduates enter college. Although students who enter the ACOT program have about the same distribution of scores on academic predictors as the entire group of ninth-grade students, 90 percent of ACOT students typically go on to college.[2] What follows is our collective view of the evolution of the program at our school, with comments on our roles as initiators of and reactors to the personal, professional, educational, and organizational changes that unfolded. As we construct this chapter, we are acutely aware that our program continues to evolve.

One striking characteristic of the Columbus ACOT teaching staff has been its continuity. Not only has our group worked together for a long time but we also have become good friends. This was obvious when we met to generate the content for this chapter.

In traditional ACOT fashion, we sat around a table with a tape recorder running while we revisited ten years of teaching and program development. As we shared memories and experiences, it became clear that during the years since the beginning of the partnership between ACOT and the Columbus Public Schools there have been three distinct periods of development. In our view, the first phase—from 1985 to 1988—consisted of planning, recruiting staff, recruiting students, and initial teaching. During the second phase, 1988 to 1992, classrooms were remodeled to accommodate more students, additional staff members were selected, and new technologies were added. During this phase, ACOT was growing and developing relatively quickly. The third phase, in which we are still engaged, focuses on sharing lessons learned in ACOT with teachers and administrators from our local district, as well as with significant numbers of educators from many parts of the United States.

In the Beginning

During the fall of 1985, four teachers, a technology supervisor, and a media specialist met to plan a small research project within our school. The teachers represented four core subject-matter areas: mathematics, science, social studies, and language arts. This group met many times during the 1985–86 school year to plan for the implementation of an educational vision that had been created collaboratively. The initial question focused on changes that might occur in teaching and learning processes when students and teachers had almost constant access to technology both at home and at school.

The ACOT project at that time consisted of four sites scattered around the country, each with a locally determined focus for research and development. Our site at Columbus was the only high school site, as well as the only site to begin work with Macintosh computers.

The initial complement of equipment included thirty Macintosh 512s (without internal hard drives), one laser printer, and five Image-Writers. During the second year, one of us was trained to upgrade Mac 512s to Mac Plus machines. There was no educational software available for these machines, so we had to rely on MacWrite, Mac-Paint, and MacDraw. Later, we added Excel, Microsoft Works, and PageMaker—in their earliest versions. We had to develop new instructional strategies in order to apply these business programs to the teaching and learning process.

During these early years, MacJanet, a Canadian company specializing in networking products, used our location as a beta test site for their software. Our first network connected two Macintosh 512 computers, each with a 20-megabyte external hard drive. Early in the first full-classroom implementation, an entire class attempted to log on to the network at the same time to access printers. It took forty-five minutes to accomplish the task. We've come a long way since then.

In the first year, there were thirty students in one classroom with two teams of two teachers each. One team combined mathematics and science; the other, social studies and language arts. All four teachers also taught additional classes outside the ACOT program every day. During the first year, students had high levels of ownership of the program and of their personal workstations. Many students had family pictures and other personal items on or near their workstations. In fact, a memorable incident during the first year resulted from a student placing a cigarette in the mouth of a plastic Gumby figure that was attached to the top of a computer. The student who owned the Gumby station felt that her private space had been violated and she and the trespasser came close to blows. This feeling of personal ownership seemed to diminish during the second and subsequent years as workstations became more specialized and students began to share them.

Staff development during the first couple of years began with people from Apple's Pittsburgh office coming to teach us how to use

Macintosh computers. After the first semester, most teachers were up-to-speed on the technology. From that point, teachers and students learned together as new technologies and software became available. Most of the staff and many students participated in a summer community technology training effort called SummerTech. In this program, we learned new technology skills in a wonderfully supportive atmosphere and met like-minded people who were also learning to use technology more effectively.

During this early phase of the Columbus ACOT program, university-based researchers were collecting data in our classrooms almost constantly. Unfortunately, these researchers were not able to share any findings with us until after the research was completed. It was frustrating for those of us who were desperate for information about how we were doing and how we might improve our teaching. One finding that did prove to be encouraging pointed out that, unlike the drill and practice exercises of conventional computer-assisted learning systems, we were using computers as learning tools.

Two highlights of the early years were the publication of *Harvest* and the implementation of hands-on robotics projects. *Harvest* was a semiannual publication featuring high-quality examples of students' writing and art, and results of students' ethnographic investigations. It was a departure from student publications of the time. A page layout program was used to compose the work, and the final product was produced on a laser printer.

Our site was frequently approached to beta test many educational products. In one such experience, we acquired materials for constructing robotics devices. These materials included motors, axles, pulleys, relays, lights, and building blocks. The robotic devices could be controlled through interfaces that were provided for Apple IIe and Macintosh computers. During the second year, students built a twenty-foot by thirty-foot scale model of part of the downtown section of Columbus. The model included elevators, stoplights, and numerous other moving parts created using the robotics materials and controlled by software running on the computers. Students visited the actual buildings and consulted scale drawings provided by the architects. A color printer was borrowed to create exterior designs that matched the elements and colors of the real buildings. Students also authored and pressed their own laser video disc to provide an interactive multimedia representation of what they had learned about their hometown.

Looking back at this time in ACOT, several lessons become clear. First, we could have reduced our stress levels by working fewer hours per week. The teaching staff regularly logged eighty-hour weeks for most of that first year. Second, students could have been given more responsibility for their own learning. These lessons were applied to later iterations of the ACOT vision. Third, we were fortunate to have school administrators who understood that while we were developing effective educational uses of technology, we needed considerable latitude on numerous written and unwritten expectations about our classrooms. Finally, with free rein to try new ideas, we had to be willing to take risks, to proceed when we didn't know exactly what the outcome would be.

The first period of the ACOT program in Columbus can be encapsulated by a statement that was posted above one of our desks. It read: "What have you done today that no one else in the world has done?" This challenge was given to the students and staff during this initial phase of ACOT at West High School.

Bigger and Better

During the second period, 1988 to 1992, the ACOT program added more staff and more students. The staff now consisted of two teachers each in math, science, social studies, and language arts. We continued to be organized primarily as math-science and language arts–social studies teams. As a consequence of this teaming, the rooms themselves started to have a focus. The language arts–social studies rooms developed more resources for publishing, while the math-science rooms emphasized projection and connectivity capabilities. We also had a project coordinator on staff who taught technology and computer applications classes.

By this time, all grade levels from nine through twelve were represented, and students actually entered ACOT as freshmen and remained in the program until they graduated four years later. One consequence of larger populations and more rooms was the loss of ownership of workstations by the students. They had to learn to share or schedule time at a particular workstation. This changed the way students conceptualized their use of time and technology.

In this second period, ACOT at West High School had evolved into a college preparatory program. Our students, who in most cases would not have considered college to be an option before entering the program, began to show strong interest in continuing their education. The program prepared them not only to attend colleges but also to get college scholarships, sometimes as computer laboratory assistants.

Our program continually tried to take advantage of new technologies as they became available. New models of computers were added to ACOT classrooms, including Macintosh SEs, IICxs, and portables. MIDI workstations were added, as well as color scanners and more sophisticated image processing tools. It seemed that data storage space, which had always been a problem, was solved—if only temporarily—by the introduction of Syquest cartridge drives. It seemed like we were always adding RAM or CD-ROM drives or something to the machines.

In response to the infusion of new technologies, a class was developed to teach students how to use specific machines and applications. Like other courses in the program, this computer applications class was designed on an authentic project-based model. Students learned to use desktop publishing software as they produced a newspaper for the local Kiwanis Club. They produced videos and entered national contests. One major project focused on foreign language and culture. Students authored and produced their own color interactive multimedia laser disc, often extending their technology skills outside of scheduled classes.

This period witnessed tremendous growth in project-based learning at ACOT. Many large projects were designed and completed. Some of these thematic projects included content from all of the traditional content disciplines. Teachers and students became more adept in the design and implementation of cooperative and collaborative learning strategies. Teachers broadened their understanding of other disciplines and made more authentic natural connections in their teaching. One example of interdisciplinary work included a project based on Roman civilization, in which students grouped themselves around a common interest such as science, culture, family life, athletics, food, clothing, or politics. Each group was required to produce a product that demonstrated their learning. They also had to agree on the amount of work each member of the group had contributed to the final product. Another example involved a traveling exhibit featuring artifacts from China that stopped in Columbus. The Son of Heaven exhibit inspired another large project. Students researched the topic and used a specially pressed laser disc to prepare multimedia presentations. They also converted their classroom into a Chinese experience including clothing, music, and food.

Alternative assessment became an important part of project-based learning at our site. As students found new ways to demonstrate their learning, new forms of assessment were required to capture the richness of the experience and the scope of the learning that was taking place. Portfolios were used in some classes. Assessment on the projects included input from teachers, students, classmates, and outside observers. Students were also rated on their participation in projects.

Staff development during this period consisted of a major focused retreat once a year and then local customized training throughout the year. During this time the staff was encouraged to try to envision what teaching and learning could look like if the power, speed, portability, and flexibility of technology were to be increased. Curriculum meetings were held once a week in which all of the ACOT staff at West High met to discuss projects, problems, assessment, and future directions. Once a month, teachers who shared particular students got together for collaborative curriculum development and integration.

Our technical training was often conducted by people who were developing new products. Since they invariably wanted the ACOT program to act as a test site, they were usually generous with their time and attentive to our needs. Teachers attended conferences and workshops as presenters and then were able to attend other presentations after they had completed their own. Still, much of the new learning that went on occurred late at night in the homes of both students and teachers. Everybody at ACOT was a learner and a teacher.

Some highlights from this period include an appearance on *Good Morning America*, teachers and students testifying before Congress, and receiving a superior rating at a national History Day competition. Columbus ACOT students also became presenters at local, state, and national educational conferences.

With the new technologies in our program, students became very resourceful in finding ways to repurpose these tools for their own goals. A few of these uses were not quite what we had anticipated or intended. When scanners were introduced, for example, one of the students found a way to scan his report card and alter the grades before taking it home to his mother. An objective assessment would have given high marks for applying technology as a tool to solve a problem, but low marks for trying to report false grades to parents.

Until 1990, the Columbus ACOT site remained open to researchers who wanted to study various aspects of our work. They were required to share their research proposals with the school district and Apple Computer. However, most proposals went forth largely unquestioned on our part, and we attempted to work cooperatively with researchers. Most researchers were considerate of ACOT teachers and students. However, two incidents brought conflict to this relationship and after 1990 we changed the way researchers were permitted to work at the Columbus site. In one instance, a researcher seemed oblivious to the numerous pressures on teachers and students, especially near the end of a school year. We were asked to fit a large student survey, with very fast turn-around, into the last six weeks of school. This caused a lot of resentment among our staff, but we cooperated as much as we could.

In the second incident, a teacher allowed an observer in her class for an extended period of time. The commitment was substantial; many evenings and weekends were spent preparing lessons in the manner required for the research. The roles that each would play were part of an informal agreement between the teacher and researcher but not set out in a formal contract. In partial return, the teacher was to receive several credit hours toward a graduate degree. When the research was complete, the teacher, expecting to receive the credit hours, was informed that she needed to submit a written paper and pay university tuition. In the end, the paper was submitted and the fee was waived.

After these incidents, the relationship between teachers at the Columbus ACOT site and potential researchers changed dramatically. There were many more questions asked and written understandings were required before research was undertaken. Even in a setting with an explicit expectation that participation in research is valuable and part of the everyday experience, the relationship between teachers and researchers is a delicate one at best.

Spreading the Word

We mark the beginning of the third period of development in 1992, when the Columbus Public Schools with three ACOT partners were awarded a National Science Foundation grant to implement professional development centers to support teachers in using technology in their classrooms. Based partly on research from the previous six years, our work with teachers took place in real operating classrooms, with support for participants as they reflected on and revisited their own instructional practices. A coordinator was added to the staff at each of the three new centers. With the existing ACOT staff at each site, the coordinator planned, developed, and implemented training and support activities. (See Chapters Fourteen, Sixteen, and Seventeen for additional information on Teacher Development Centers.)

At the West High Teacher Development Center, teams of participating teachers take part in a five-day practicum and/or a four-week Summer Leadership Institute. During the five-day practicum, participants complete several learning experiences. They observe ACOT teachers modeling a variety of teaching strategies, observe students working in collaborative groups with technology, and learn about a variety of instructional tools, strategies, and assessment techniques. They reflect on and discuss principles of instruction and learning, and they use a wide variety of technologies as tools to support learning through composition, collaboration, simulation, and guided practice. They also begin to develop a project that they can use in their own classrooms. While the practicum is an introductory experience, the Summer Leadership Institute enables participants to have similar in-depth experiences, but for a longer period of time. At the Institute, our students and students from the participating teachers' schools explore various technologies and develop technology-supported projects.

Our site had been host to thousands of visitors, but having a team of teachers at the Teacher Development Center for an extended period of time was a new experience. We became teacher trainers. With the coordinator of the Teacher Development Center and a local university faculty member, we developed a variety of materials and procedures to work with other teachers. We developed presentations on collaboration, alternative assessment, curriculum development, new technologies, and site-based restructuring.

As the Columbus ACOT team took on the role of teacher trainers, our high school students also became partners in the process. Several students volunteered their time in the afternoon to work with groups of teachers on specific technologies. Participating teachers were impressed with the ability of our students to work with adults. One student used this experience to win a major scholarship established by a local business for students who are actively involved with innovative community projects.

During the first year of the West High Teacher Development Center, our biggest problem was not having enough space. There wasn't a training room for participants. Space was needed to explore software and hardware, hang coats, meet for group instruction, and have a cup of coffee. Initially, discussions took place in the hallways, often while students changed classes. During the second year, a room was designated as a training room, and a pattern for the practicums was developed. ACOT teachers were actively involved with practicum participants, answering their questions during observations, spending the afternoon working individually with participants, and giving presentations on specific topics such as alternative assessment, multimedia, and developing collaborative work groups.

The impact of these experiences on participants was significant. One teacher who was part of the first Summer Institute initiated and won several grants, including a GTE Pioneering Partners grant, enabling her to bring telecommunications into her classroom. As telecommunications has broadened its appeal to teachers and learners, she has become a valuable resource to her school and school district. Closer to home, a fifth-grade teacher in our district had a phone line installed in her room, and students began to develop collaborative projects with other fifth graders in a neighboring district. Because of their experiences at the Center, several teachers have enrolled in master's and doctoral programs in instructional design and technology.

Our ACOT programs at West High School have served as a resource for the Columbus Public Schools as plans are implemented to restructure the teaching and learning model being used throughout the district. The situated model of professional development established at the Teacher Development Center was a primary stimulus for the district's application to the National Science Foundation for an urban systemic initiative grant. The superintendent has also created a strategic plan for the district, incorporating many of the lessons learned in ACOT over the past ten years. In another development, the State of Ohio is undertaking the SchoolNet project, which will wire each classroom in the state for voice, video, and data transmission. We expect that the ACOT Teacher Development Center will participate in training and support for teachers as they integrate this technology into project-based teaching and learning.

Similarly, participants from outside the Columbus Public Schools have been instrumental in helping their districts create professional development opportunities based on the ACOT model. As their districts develop technology plans, local teachers become valuable resources when deciding how technology will support teaching and learning.

The third period of development at the Columbus ACOT site was also marked by changes in our classroom work. Before this period, student projects were interdisciplinary but student work groups tended to stay within grade levels. We now began to develop projects that not only crossed curricular boundaries but also engaged teams of students who differed in age and grade level. For example, a project based on the popular novel *Jurassic Park* involved both sophomores and seniors and dealt with genetics, fractals, exponential growth, and literature. This project used a range of technologies including laser discs, HyperCard, QuickTime movies, and presentation software. Technology and computer application classes were offered to help students develop basic processes and technological skills. These classes focused on using a variety of technologies to accomplish authentic projects. Besides the Jurassic Park project, students and teachers also developed a video yearbook and several Excel spreadsheet applications for the West High School Alumni Association.

Recently, students completed an extended video history of West

High School. Students spent time in local libraries and completed video interviews of alumni of all ages. Proceeds from the sale of this video were used to establish a scholarship fund for West High School students. All of these projects were real-life problem-solving situations that required the use of technology.

In concluding, we take pride in our students, their work, and the contributions they have made to the dialogue about teaching and learning. At the Columbus site, ten years of ACOT have provided many challenges requiring us to apply new strategies for teaching and learning. One constant in our program has been the inevitability of change. As soon as the target seems to be clear, it moves— and students, parents, administrators, and staff all have to rethink their work in order to hit the new target. Another constant has been an unwavering belief by a small group of committed people in an educational vision. Just as it was impossible for us to anticipate where we would be after these ten years, it is equally difficult to predict the future of our, or perhaps any, educational program. We can only hope that teachers and students in other schools can enjoy the kind of exciting, energizing experience that ACOT teachers and administrators at Columbus West High School have had in pursuing their educational dreams.

Notes

1. To develop this chapter, many of the teachers who participated at the Columbus ACOT site got together and talked about our work during the past decade. I composed the chapter based on these discussions, and often use "we" to remind the reader that approximately a dozen of my colleagues contributed in one way or another to the content.

2. A bibliography of program descriptions and research reports from the Columbus ACOT site is available through Apple's StartingLine materials distribution program and on the Internet at http://www.info.apple.com/education.

16

Conversation

An Essential Element of Teacher Development

Keith Yocam

S oon after I began working on the ACOT project in 1985, I read
Garrison Keillor's *Lake Wobegon U.S.A.* You might wonder what
Keillor's book has to do with technology and education. Well, noth-
ing specifically, but it helped to prepare me for my first visit to Blue
Earth, Minnesota, site of one of the two original ACOT classrooms.

It wasn't long after my arrival in Blue Earth that I was sitting in
a rocking chair on the front porch of the ACOT teacher's home
wondering what this ACOT project was all about. There I was,
rocking, some two-and-a-half hours south of Minneapolis, in a
small, rural town on the prairie, surrounded by endless vegetable
fields whose yield would soon be canned under the watchful eye of
a fifty-foot plastic statue of the Jolly Green Giant, having a conversation about technology and education. Keillor's insights into
front-porch etiquette and rural communities in Minnesota proved
to be more helpful than I had anticipated.

Who Are These ACOT Teachers?

I had been hired to provide technical assistance to teachers and coordinators at the ACOT sites. "Pretty simple, just train them to use
the computers—as experts in curriculum and instruction, the teachers will do the rest," I was told. That's it, that's all! Fresh from the
classroom myself, I had been wrestling with this very challenge of

finding appropriate instructional uses for computers for the last six of my eleven years as an elementary teacher. But I did not think of myself as an expert in curriculum and instruction. I, like most of my previous colleagues, let the state and district curriculum guides and testing programs direct that part of my work. And after all, there really didn't seem to be any need for me to be an expert in curriculum. Weren't those the people who were called coordinators and resource specialists that worked at the district office?

Because of their exceptional knowledge about curriculum and instruction, I was pretty interested in getting to know these people who were selected as ACOT teachers and coordinators. So there I was rocking and thinking that these teachers are just like most of the teachers I had been working with just several months earlier. In fact, even though there were nearly two thousand miles between this rural Minnesota school and the suburban schools where I had worked in Southern California, there were many things that were profoundly similar.

I came to the ACOT project with an expectation that the sites had been selected because they were exemplars of technology-using classrooms. However, the teachers at Blue Earth and the other ACOT sites were no better or worse in terms of their practice—how they taught, what they knew about curriculum, and what they knew about technology—than most of the other teachers I had worked with. As a result, I decided that the best way to work with my new colleagues was the same way I had worked with other teachers in my district and students in my classes—get to know them, get to know their strengths and weaknesses, and if I couldn't help them personally, find other resources that could help them.

Professional Development Among ACOT Teachers

In 1985, ACOT began with the assumption that computers might change classrooms. To speed up the time frame of this imagined technological evolution of the classroom, ACOT designers decided to saturate classrooms with computers in an attempt to know about a future when computers might be pervasive in schools and homes and constantly accessible.

The challenge seemed simple enough back then. With students and teachers having immediate access to computers, it was nothing more than teaching them how to use the technology and introducing them to the best available examples of educational software. Though my own inclination for using software was to encourage word processors, graphics, and LOGO, the teachers—especially at the elementary level—were drawn more to drill and practice software for skill development and reinforcement. Nearly all the ACOT teachers who were part of the project in its first years seemed to be most interested in using computers to raise student test scores. To this end, the teachers and I spent many hours searching for and reviewing software that would *teach* the next objective prescribed in the district's curriculum guide. You can imagine the task of trying to identify software to teach each of the scores of skills that were identified in the guides and for which teachers were held accountable. For teachers, the challenge of finding software that taught the curriculum objectives was compounded by the task of trying to manage the use of a variety of software packages to meet the needs of thirty or so students. Though some interesting examples of problem-solving and productivity software were being developed, their use was relegated to special times in the classroom schedule, usually after students had finished daily skill-and-drill sessions.

Unlike the elementary school sites, what was happening at ACOT's only high school site in Columbus, Ohio, was different. These secondary school classrooms were using Macintosh computers, which ten years ago weren't considered to be computers for education, and only business productivity software was available for them. Teachers liked the idea of using Macs, but they initially thought that the lack of content- and skill-oriented software was unfortunate and asked for a few Apple II computers like those at the elementary school sites.

In retrospect, they were fortunate not to have Apple IIs. Their thinking about using computers wasn't constrained by trying to find specific educational software to prepare students for tests. There wasn't any. Observing these secondary teachers as they designed student activities using business-oriented productivity tools was an important factor in ACOT's shift to using technology to support more constructivist learning opportunities for students. Over time, ACOT's design changed from computer saturation, which supported the existing knowledge transfer approach to learning, to the current emphasis on routine access, where technologies are used to support collaborative, project-based knowledge construction. This shift placed me in the position of supporting not only uses of technology but also fundamental changes in teaching and learning in which new technology uses would be embedded.

It's one thing to help a teacher learn how to use a computer and software. It's quite another to help teachers broaden their repertoires of teaching strategies to include constructivist approaches that incorporate the use of technology. It seems far easier to help a teacher who is already practicing constructivist methods learn to use technology to enhance student learning than it is to help a teacher who has a lot of knowledge about technology but limited knowledge of constructivist pedagogy. Though we may not have fully appreciated it at the time, this shift in ACOT's design created an enormous and exciting challenge for everyone in the project.

In the mid 1980s—and today, for that matter—I found that most teachers teach didactically during most of their teaching day. To help teachers change their strategies to ones that differ from what they learned in teacher preparation programs, what they use in their classrooms, and how the community expects them to teach, is a tall order. Add to this the need to help teachers use tools that for many seem mysterious and even intimidating, and you indeed have a challenge.

At first, we worked with teachers in a variety of ways to help them explore the potentials of using technology. We tried traditional approaches such as workshops either after school or, in some cases, for entire school days. For several years, we also conducted week-long summer institutes at Apple. As one colleague described it, we tried all the "spray and pray" approaches.

Teachers were enthusiastic about learning to use new technologies and thinking about how they would integrate them into their curricula. But on follow-up visits to classrooms, I didn't see that much had changed from my last visit in terms of teaching strategies incorporating technology. In fact, when I asked teachers if the previous workshop had been useful and what had happened as a result, they would often say it had been helpful and offer an example or two of what they had done or were planning to do. What usually followed was a conversation about what they were going to do next and some brainstorming about how they might involve technology.

Probably our finest hour with designing and implementing a fairly traditional approach to staff development occurred during the last week-long summer workshop, where we introduced constructivism to ACOT teachers. The workshop was designed to provide teachers with a grounding in its major themes by involving them in a project-based learning experience. They had opportunities to use a variety of technologies to create units of study that subsequently could be implemented in their own classrooms.

Though the workshop involved some directed teaching, it was designed so that session leaders were modeling facilitation, guiding teachers through activities that engaged them in learning about knowledge construction. When teachers returned to their classrooms, we hoped that they would use technology more often for knowledge building and less often for delivery of instruction. But on follow-up visits to classrooms, I still did not see that teaching strategies had changed much or that teachers were implementing the units they had designed during the workshop. It is interesting that to this day the ACOT teachers who attended this workshop still talk about its impact on them and often ask for a repeat of the experience.

Over time, visitors to the sites reported dramatic changes in the ACOT classrooms. Most often they would talk about interesting conversations they'd had with students and how deeply engaged the students were in their work. They often mentioned how teachers' roles were different and how technology was being used in support of the new roles. To me, there was a difference between what I was observing and what others reported. I saw ACOT teachers as not having changed much where others thought they had radically shifted their practice. For me, it was probably a case of standing too close to see what was going on. But the differences in perceptions led us to some productive reflection on the teachers and their practice. Using data from teachers' audio journals, weekly project reports from the sites, and teacher interviews, we identified a series of stages that teachers went through as they integrated the use of computers into their practice.[1]

There was also another phenomenon at work. When I met with ACOT teachers, they would describe what they were doing in their classrooms and what they anticipated they would do next. When I visited their classrooms, what I observed was often very different from what had been described. There seemed to be a gap between teachers' espoused beliefs about their practice and their practice in action. What I came to realize is that change occurs differently for each teacher. This gap seemed to be different for each teacher and though we would have liked for everyone to move at the same rate, that wasn't happening. The stages we identified helped to guide our work with individual teachers. The differences we were seeing between beliefs and actions helped us understand that to challenge their professional beliefs about practice, teachers need sustained support. Helping them to articulate their visions, and providing assistance to get there, was what made change happen.

As I look back, our essential contribution to staff development was that we, the ACOT staff, were helping teachers to do something that they rarely—if ever—had an opportunity to do. We were engaging them in ongoing conversations and reflection about their practice and how they might change and enhance it with technology. These conversations almost always ended with additional support that would help teachers make changes in how they used computers in their teaching. One topic would lead to another, giving rise to conversations about what they envisioned they could change next.

As we continued to look at both the data on instruction and student outcomes, we began to see that, indeed, ACOT classrooms were becoming very different kinds of environments for learning. One of the high school teachers described students and teachers as becoming a "community of learners." Though this was not a new term to education, it was something I had not actually seen in any school at the time. What was emerging was a view of ACOT classrooms as places where both teachers and students were learning, places where expertise was distributed among the learners, where teachers and students actually changed roles when technology was involved.

As the idea of a learning community began to take hold, the classrooms became an even more challenging place for teachers. They often described what was happening to them as if they were beginning teachers again. The technology seemed to cause teachers to see themselves as learners again, possibly seeing the challenges of learning from a student's perspective. It seemed to level the playing field by providing opportunities for teachers to talk with their students about mutual learning goals and seek students' assistance to learn about new hardware and software. The teachers started talking about their students more as individuals with varied goals and less as a collective where every student worked on the same page toward the same objective.

As time went on, more visitors provided us with their thoughts and questions about the project. Most often they wanted to know what kinds of staff development approaches we employed that helped teachers to create the ACOT learning environments and use constructivist teaching strategies. They would ask if we had written anything that could help them to create similar kinds of technology-enhanced learning environments. They were surprised that we hadn't and would strongly suggest that we write a *recipe* book for teacher development that would deliver the same results.

What we knew was that when we introduced technology to the ACOT teachers, the old ways of doing staff development didn't work well. When we thought about what did work, it always seemed to involve the teachers in conversations about change and reflection on their practice. Sometimes these conversations took place at meetings or workshops, but they weren't episodic. They were ongoing. A conversation might start at a workshop, but would continue during site visits, over e-mail, by phone, and even during real-time, on-line group meetings using telecommunications. It seemed that these conversations had greater impact on teachers' changing what went on in their classrooms than the traditional staff development approaches that we tried. A conversation that began at a meeting or workshop often became grist for a different conversation with each teacher. Over time, a common terminology about change and technology emerged that would engage the teachers in talking about standards, assessment, tasks, situations, interactions, and tools.[2]

We felt that describing the methodology we used with the teachers did not fit well into a recipe. We were practicing a constructivist approach to staff development and wanted to capture the process we used. We knew that the significant changes that resulted from the conversations we had with teachers were achieved because the conversations were personal and meaningful to them. So we asked ourselves, How do we capture this process that includes conversation and reflection in such a way that it can be useful to others?

ACOT Teacher Development Center Model

Believing that new teaching skills require new models of staff development, I convened a group of teachers and administrators from three of our partner districts, along with researchers and ACOT staff, to have a conversation about our approach.[3] This conversation took shape over a year, building from the staff development work that was under way at that time at the Nashville site. Our design was informed by the latest thinking about staff development, peer coaching, and cognitive apprenticeship.

About midway into the conversation, we agreed that existing ACOT sites might be good settings in which to engage teachers in reflection and conversation about changes in teaching, learning, and technology. The sites were provocative enough to elicit invariably some kind of comment from visitors about student learning, teacher roles, and the effects of technology. The challenge for us was to design a staff development program that capitalized on ACOT's experience in supporting teachers to think and talk about how they might change what goes on in their classrooms. Our group identified six guiding principles that had been effective in our staff development activities up to that time:

- Staff development activities were to be situated in contexts of practice so that attendees could see new teaching strategies modeled during routine school days.

- Participating teachers would attend in teams of two to four members from the same school. This principle was intended to reduce the isolation that many teachers feel during the change process.

- A constructivist learning approach, like that used in ACOT classrooms, would be used with participating teachers. Center coordinators would model the facilitative role of an ACOT teacher, and attendees would use technology regularly during their learning activities.

- The coordinator would engage participating teachers in an ongoing conversation and reflection about their practice, their students, theories of learning, assessment, technology, and how they might begin to change their classrooms.

- Participant teachers would develop a unit, lesson, or other learning task that used technology, and implement it on returning to their home classroom.

- The coordinator would provide follow-up support by visiting participating teachers' classrooms to continue the conversation and assist with both technology and implementation of the unit the teachers had developed.

The model proposed three kinds of experiences: one-week practicums during the school year, four-week summer leadership institutes, and follow-up support visits. Participant teachers could attend both the one-week and four-week sessions, and all participants were provided with some kind of follow-up support. In 1992, the ACOT Teacher Development Center project was awarded a three-year grant to develop and study this model.[4]

We believed that the strength of the model relied not only on the guiding principles, but also on flexible implementation. While the principles provided a firm pedagogical foundation, each site required somewhat different schedules and support arrangements. It was important to us to be responsive to the specific needs and challenges of different teachers, schools, and school systems. As attendance at the ACOT Teacher Development Centers expanded to include teachers from different districts and states, the guiding principles and flexibility during implementation proved to be increasingly important. Unlike a structured workshop, experiences at the centers put participating teachers in charge of what they wanted to learn and the skills they wanted to develop. Whenever possible, we tried to engage participants in the process of change in ways that were meaningful to them. For example, participating teachers could choose to build on their technical skills, regardless of their current skill level, and design a unit or lesson around their new skills. At all times, however, participants were systematically drawn into continuing conversations about what they would like their classrooms to become.

Interestingly, many participants came to the program thinking that on the first day they would learn word processing, on the second day HyperCard, and so on. The experience was anything but that. Participants were almost immediately engaged in conversation about who they were as teachers and asked to begin thinking about what they would like to change with regard to their practice. You can imagine that many teachers were taken somewhat aback by this approach, accustomed as they were to traditional staff development structures. They were used to being told what they would be doing, when they were doing it, what they had done, and why it was relevant to their classrooms. In the ACOT experience, they were in charge of determining what was relevant to their personal and professional growth and what they needed to support change in their current school's context. Staff members at the centers became very skillful at guiding participants through this personal professional development experience.

Outcomes of the new model are promising. What is important about this approach is that if you want things to change in the classroom, you have to work at the level of the individual teacher. For me, the most important outcome was identified in an evaluation study at the Nashville Center. Data from that site revealed a significant change in both the personal and professional efficacy of participating teachers.[5] Teachers were beginning to restructure their classrooms, change their practice, and look at their students differently. In a sense, these teachers became learners again. They saw their students as individuals and seemed to have an empathy for them as they encountered the challenges of learning. It was as if the playing field had been leveled and everyone on it, students and teachers, was there to grow and learn.

This kind of personal change wasn't just for veteran teachers, it was evident in first-year teachers as well. I recall a conversation in a summer institute with a first-year kindergarten teacher. She described what her kindergarten students were doing as a result of her staff development experience. In the past, she felt constrained by an age-specific curriculum and only thought of her students' abilities within that context. After working in the summer institute with kindergartners and first graders, she changed her expectations about what her students could do and become when they had opportunities to go beyond the expectations set by state and district guidelines.

Similarly, a twenty-year veteran, after a year and a half in the project, pulled me aside to tell me about a recent personal observation. She described a conversation she had had with her classroom aide while her students were taking a state-mandated standardized test. Standing next to her aide at the back of the room, she turned to the aide and said, "There's something very wrong here." Her aide, looking somewhat bewildered, said, "No, all the students are sitting quietly and taking the test." The observation that she wanted to share with me was that "all the students sitting quietly" was in fact what was wrong. For the twenty years prior to her participation in the program, one of her main goals was to keep her students quiet and working on something. In the past year and a half, she had realized that her classroom had changed; students were not only talking to each other, they were talking to her. She pointed out that she was learning more about the students and their needs by allowing them to be active in the classroom. She looked at me and said, "Now I know my students at a more personal level, and I find that it makes a tremendous difference both in my teaching and in their learning."

For me, this is real evidence of real teacher change. Each realization is going to be different for each teacher as they start to challenge their beliefs about their practices and to see their professional actions in a different light. Only when each individual teacher can have the opportunity to reflect on and learn about teaching will there be meaningful reform in classroom practice giving rise to new opportunities for student-centered learning.[6]

What Might be Done?

The question then can be asked, How do you provide all teachers with this kind of experience? One way is for each district to take staff development seriously, to adopt the idea of creating a community or culture of learners where teacher learning is expected and encouraged. Schools, districts, and universities could benefit from developing opportunities for teachers to engage in professional discourse and ongoing reflection. It needs to be as much a part of the daily operation of schools as collecting attendance data.

Providing new learning contexts and models that interest teachers, that excite their curiosity, and challenge them to think about and talk about change have been the bases for our work with teachers. And to this end, the ACOT project has been as much about teacher development as it has been about technology. Part of what we have been building in ACOT are ways to help educators make personal and professional transformations. Reform-minded school districts might want to think seriously about how they might profit by providing similar opportunities for their teachers.

Change is personal. The ways in which the education community has gone about encouraging change in the past have not looked at the individual teacher, for the most part. Teachers and schools will only change when districts and ultimately the community practice what they preach. Districts say they want teachers to reflect, but they don't give them the time to do it. They want teachers to use technology, but they don't give them the tools or support to do it. In many cases, even when tools are provided, those tools are outdated. If we want student outcomes that will be more applicable for twenty-first-century jobs, we must stop relying on nineteenth-century pedagogy and equipment.

To address these issues, more time and resources are needed to support classroom practitioners. Teachers need to see change as part of their professional charge and feel supported in taking risks that result in change. They need to have more professional tools and feel supported in learning to integrate new tools into their classrooms.

They need to understand how they can guide and help each student become successful and better prepared for their future. That doesn't happen in a one-hour workshop or during a couple of days allocated to staff development. That happens when teachers become active learners with regard to their own professional development. That happens when teachers can talk about who they are and where they are going. That happens when all of the stakeholders of education become engaged in the conversation.

Have you ever walked into a classroom and thought to yourself that this is a place where you would like your child to be learning— or better yet that you wished you had been in a classroom like this when you were a student? Many visitors to ACOT classrooms have shared these kinds of thoughts with us. And many of them quickly observe that the reasons for ACOT's appeal are closely connected to the teachers in these classrooms, who have worked diligently to develop rich and active learning contexts. ACOT teachers were able to do this in part because of more effective support systems. It takes only a short conversation with any ACOT teacher to know that they are empowered professionals who work hard and care for their students.

Since that day sitting on the front porch in Blue Earth, I have spent more than nine years in my own conversation and reflection about teaching, learning, and technology.[7] Back then, had I been asked about staff development's importance to building a better education system and its need to be meaningfully based on individual teachers' vision, I'm not sure what responses I would have given. Today, I believe that too many people nod their heads and acknowledge that staff development is essential without appreciating what the statement really means. Perhaps some of what we have been learning in ACOT can influence the creation of new learning communities and the support systems that are essential to their development.

As we become more global in our thinking and our work, there will be increased pressure to educate students for a world where change is ongoing, where technology is used for communications, inquiry, and problem solving, and where successful people are involved in continuous learning opportunities. If these are the outcomes that we would like for students, and I believe they are, then our teachers must model their application and guide their development. And that requires that *all teachers* have opportunities to learn, reflect, and discuss; to have an invitation to participate in the conversation.

Notes

1. Dwyer, D. C., Ringstaff, C., & Sandholtz, J. H. (1991). Changes in teachers' beliefs and practices in technology-rich classrooms. *Educational Leadership, 48*(8), 45–52.

2. Ringstaff, C., Kelley, L., & Dwyer, D. C. (1993). *Breaking the mold of instruction with technology: Formative case studies of the unit of study process.* Unpublished report prepared for the National Center on Education and the Economy, Washington, DC.

3. For additional perspectives on ACOT Teacher Development Centers, see Chapters Fourteen, Fifteen, and Seventeen.

4. Ringstaff, C., & Yocam, K. (1994). *Creating an alternative context for teacher development: The ACOT Teacher Development Centers.* ACOT Research Report No. 18. Cupertino, CA: Apple Computer. This report provides a full description of the model.

5. Marsh, J. E., & Sherwood, R. D. (1991). *An evaluation of the outreach program of the Teacher Development Center of the Nashville Apple Classrooms of Tomorrow.* Cupertino, CA: Apple Computer.

6. Ringstaff, C., Marsh, J., & Yocam, K. (1995). *ACOT teacher development center annual progress report: Year two.* Cupertino, CA: Apple Computer for the National Science Foundation.

7. I have been fortunate to have had many partners—teachers, administrators, researchers, and colleagues—with whom to share these conversations and reflections. In particular, I want to thank Cathy Ringstaff and Joanne Koltnow for being reflective colleagues who helped me revisit the past and put it into perspective.

17

Teacher Change in Technology-Rich Classrooms

Judith Haymore Sandholtz, Cathy Ringstaff

*If I had my druthers, I don't think I would ever look
at a computer again. One of my students got into
the network and lost lots of information because he
doesn't know what he is doing. It's a typical situation,
and it's caused a major problem because now the
computers are down. There are so many variables
like this that we deal with on a day-to-day basis
that I didn't anticipate being part of this program.
I'm anxious for the weekend so I don't have to do
anything with computers.*
> —John Erickson, High School Teacher

We knew just how he felt. As a teacher in the ACOT project,
John Erickson[1] found himself working in a totally new classroom setting. The ACOT project brought changes in the physical
environment, teacher roles, and student behaviors as well as a
plethora of technical problems. Although he brought years of teaching experience to his job, John felt like a novice again. As researchers studying teachers' experiences in ACOT classrooms, we found
ourselves working in a totally new research setting. This setting involved massive quantities of text data, a new relational database
program, and a host of technical difficulties. In developing a text-
retrieval and analysis system for use on personal computers, we

definitely were treading new territory. We knew firsthand the frustrations that plagued neophyte technology users.

As former teachers, we knew how John felt on another level. Teaching presents ever-changing challenges. As the context changes, so do the demands. Experienced teachers quickly become novices when the classroom environment shifts dramatically, transforming tried-and-true strategies into ineffective approaches. We vividly remembered challenges such as trying to teach consumer survival skills to an eager group of refugees without the aid of a common language, or to devise methods to be used in a summer camp for emotionally disturbed children. We learned about teaching by immersing ourselves in as many different teaching experiences as possible. Like John, we encountered the emotional highs and lows that accompany new and diverse teaching environments.

We joined the ACOT project shortly after its inception, specifically to help in compiling and analyzing a database containing teachers' narrative descriptions of their experiences. We had mounds of qualitative data. From the beginning of the project, teachers had submitted weekly reports via electronic mail, corresponded among sites, and twice a month reflected about their experiences on audiotapes. Even with a group of indexers, it took years for the data entry to catch up with the incoming information. After six years, the data included over twenty thousand episodes and had to be divided into two databases. The narratives provided rich descriptions on events at the sites as well as teachers' personal observations and feelings about those events. Moreover, having longitudinal data provided unique insights into teachers' experiences in technology-rich classrooms.

In many ways, our experiences as researchers paralleled those of the teachers we were studying. The teachers were using technology to enhance student learning; we were using technology to study technology. All of us, in attempting to employ technology in new ways, had to confront our beliefs, deal with management issues, grapple with technical problems, analyze our strategies, and alter our approaches. In this chapter, we focus on three main issues related to our experience in studying ACOT teachers: changes in the teachers' concerns over time, the ongoing need for support and professional development opportunities, and the process of using technology to study technology.

Changes in Teachers' Concerns

Reflecting on the ten years since ACOT began, we recognize the importance of studying teachers' experiences in technology-rich classrooms over a number of years. Had we examined teachers' experiences for only a year or two, our conclusions would have been significantly different. Frequently, those funding or evaluating innovative programs expect to see measurable progress in a short time. Our longitudinal analyses continued to illustrate that, even when classroom environments are drastically altered and teachers are willingly immersed in innovation, change is slow, and sometimes includes temporary regression. Moreover, commitment to the innovation will not occur until teachers see a positive impact on their teaching. Four main areas of teachers' concerns in ACOT classrooms changed over time. These included: beliefs, management issues, instructional strategies, and student assessment.

Changes in Beliefs

As volunteers in the ACOT project, teachers were eager participants in an ambitious program aimed at changing instruction and learning. But each teacher also had considerable experience in traditional classrooms and brought deeply held beliefs about schooling. Over time, the addition of technology served as a catalyst for change, bringing the teachers' beliefs into conflict with what they witnessed in their classrooms.[2] The process was gradual, prompting teachers to reexamine their beliefs about both teaching and learning.

Throughout their careers, teachers had taken the role of expert in the classroom. But technology-rich classrooms undermined that role as some students quickly became more knowledgeable than both their peers and their teachers in using particular computer applications or hardware. Eventually, teachers not only accepted students' expertise but capitalized on and expanded the roles of student experts in their classrooms, relinquishing their emphasis on teacher-directed activities.[3] Moreover, they discovered that students who had been perceived as slow or reluctant learners often blossomed when given an alternate means for displaying their abilities.

These types of changes, however, brought other beliefs about instruction into question. For example, many teachers, long accustomed to a quiet, orderly classroom where students raised their hands for permission to speak, naturally questioned whether learning could occur in a noisy environment filled with movement and peer interaction. When students worked in groups, some teachers felt guilty, feeling as though they weren't really teaching. Others wondered whether students could stay on task and actually accomplish serious work in a group setting. As the students spent increasing amounts of time on computer activities, teachers confronted concerns about whether they were appropriately covering the required curriculum. When students became more proficient and interested in the layout and cover design for a project, teachers wondered if the time spent making a project visually appealing detracted from the time spent on content.

Over time, teachers in ACOT classrooms moved toward child-centered rather than textbook-centered instruction; toward collaborative rather than individual tasks; toward active rather than passive learning. However, during the process of change, teachers continually questioned their beliefs and actions.

Changes in Management Issues

The thirty-two ACOT teachers represented in our database, though primarily experienced teachers, discovered that managing a technology-rich classroom was significantly different from many of their previous experiences.[4] Initially, teachers were preoccupied with their own adequacy and concerned with their abilities to maintain control over the classroom and the students. Teachers frequently found themselves unable to anticipate problems in their high-technology classrooms and grappled with issues such as controlling student behavior, organizing the physical environment, and defining their roles in the classroom. Faced with such problems, teachers often focused on changing their management strategies rather than on becoming instructionally innovative.

Later, teachers began not only to anticipate problems but also to develop strategies for solving them. To combat student misbehavior, they restricted computer access and used the technology as a motivational tool. To save themselves time, they capitalized on students' technological expertise. They found ways to organize the room to create a better working environment and obtained resources to eliminate other physical problems. Teachers became increasingly able to troubleshoot and repair the equipment and to change plans when last-minute problems arose. As teachers became more knowledgeable about and confident with the technology, they witnessed positive changes in student engagement and motivation, further decreasing management problems.

Eventually, teachers focused on the effects of their teaching on students and began to employ technology to their advantage in managing the classroom. Rather than just troubleshooting, teachers developed technological supports for monitoring student work, keeping records, grading tests, developing new materials, and individualizing instruction. As teachers learned more about computers and software, they discovered that technology could save them time rather than create additional demands.

Changes in Instructional Strategies

In the early years of the project, instruction primarily remained unchanged even though the physical environment had been radically transformed. Gradually, new patterns of teaching and learning emerged. We identified five stages of instructional evolution in

ACOT classrooms and labeled them: entry, adoption, adaptation, appropriation, and invention. In this evolution, text-based curriculum delivered in a lecture-recitation-seat work mode was first strengthened through the use of technology and then gradually replaced by more dynamic learning experiences for students.[5]

In the entry stage, teachers had little or no experience with computer technology and demonstrated little inclination to significantly change their instruction. Teachers focused on changes in the physical environment and typical first-year-teacher problems such as discipline, resource management, and personal frustrations. Teachers began using their technological resources but simply replicated traditional instructional and learning activities.

As teachers moved into the adoption stage, their concerns shifted from connecting the computers to using them. However, they adopted the new electronic technology to support their established text-based drill-and-practice instruction. Teachers continued to rely on whole-group lectures, recitation, and individualized seat work.

The adaptation stage brought changes in the efficiency of the instructional process. Teachers increasingly incorporated technology in their instruction, and their reports focused on ways in which students' productivity increased. For example, teachers noticed that students were able to complete a self-paced math curriculum in significantly less time, allowing teachers to engage students in higher-order learning objectives and problem solving. Many students now could type faster than they could write, thus preparing assignments more quickly and with greater fluency. In addition, they willingly reworked their papers. Teachers also noted improved student engagement in classroom tasks.

As teachers eventually reached the appropriation stage—in which they came to understand technology and used it effortlessly as a tool to accomplish real work—their roles began to shift noticeably and new instructional patterns emerged. Team teaching, interdisciplinary project-based instruction, and individually paced instruction became more common at all of the sites. To accommodate more ambitious class projects, teachers even altered the master schedule. In a critically important shift that typically occurred in this phase, teachers began to reflect on teaching, to question old patterns, to speculate about causes behind the changes they were seeing in their students.

The invention stage is essentially a placeholder for continuing development by teachers and the new learning environments they will create. In this stage, the expectation is that teachers will implement an integrated curriculum, make balanced and strategic use of both direct teaching and project-based teaching, and integrate alternative modes of student assessment.

Changes Related to Student Assessment

As teachers began using different instructional strategies, they discovered that traditional forms of assessment were not always adequate. Moreover, technology-rich classrooms increasingly generated new situations related to student assessment. For example, teachers noticed vast differences in students' technical abilities. They found that students with the highest grade point averages were frequently not those with the most technological expertise. This situation raised questions about the meaning of various forms of assessment. In addition, some students came to know more about technology than their teachers, placing teachers in an unusual situation with respect not only to instruction but also to evaluation.

Students' increased interest in computer activities brought up additional issues related to time management, curriculum, and ultimately assessment.[6] Teachers questioned how long students should be allowed to work on the computers, wondered whether they were covering the mandated curriculum, and puzzled over how to judge student learning in meaningful ways. Moreover, students' high levels of engagement while working with computers led many to go beyond the requirements of their assignments, leaving teachers grappling with questions of whether to and where to draw boundaries. While some teachers attempted to keep students from going too far, others purposely developed assignments that allowed students with the interest and ability to go beyond the minimum requirements. This approach raised more issues about evaluating students' work and determining how to acknowledge the extra efforts of some students.

When teachers began to incorporate more computer-based projects, they found that many students began to invest larger amounts of time on layout, design, and visual appeal of their work. Although teachers appreciated students' enthusiasm, they wondered about the implicit time trade-off and its effect on content coverage. Moreover, having traditionally focused on evaluating content, they struggled with how to assess students' creativity and resourcefulness in experimentation as well as the new technical skills being acquired.

Technology-rich classrooms also resulted in higher levels of student interaction and peer collaboration.[7] As students began spontaneously teaching each other, typical definitions of cheating dissolved. As teachers increasingly allowed and encouraged students to openly share information with one another, the customary forms of measuring student knowledge and achievement became inadequate. In addition, students who were the most successful at peer tutoring didn't necessarily perform well on traditional assessment measures. Teachers struggled with how to translate students' teaching skills into a grade on a standard report card.

While questioning traditional forms of assessment, teachers also knew that their students would still be required to perform on standardized tests in other situations. Solutions to these and other assessment issues have lagged behind the instructional changes and continue to be a serious concern. Recently, the ACOT project has focused more attention on assessment and worked to support teachers who are struggling in this area.

Support for Teacher Change

Regardless of the number of years of experience that ACOT teachers had in technology-rich classrooms, they invariably needed a high level of support. However, the type of support shifted over time as teachers gained experience in the classrooms. For example, in the early stages of implementation, teachers' greatest needs were technical support and training. Later, teachers increasingly needed opportunities to think about instruction and learning, discuss their experiences with others, and develop alternative learning experiences for their students. Teachers required training and support to successfully integrate technology, rather than simply use it.

Support from ACOT

Early in the project, ACOT hired a full-time coordinator at each site to provide ongoing technical assistance, instructional support, and training. For a number of years, Apple funded training workshops as well as week-long summer institutes where ACOT teachers learned about the latest technologies and shared instructional ideas. Teachers also had opportunities to attend and present at professional conferences.

The fact that ACOT is a research project also served as an indirect source of support for teacher change. The audiotapes and written weekly reports, used as one of several means of data collection, also cultivated teacher reflection. Although some teachers grumbled about the time necessary to comply with data collection requirements, many recognized the value of the experience and found the process of sharing their stories therapeutic. As one teacher commented, "These tape requirements that you have given us were the pits at first. Now I am really into them as a means of mental release. Anyhow, I'll stop beating around the bush. My tape recorder is broken. I now have nothing to talk into every day and I am feeling very panicky. Is there any way you could bring a new tape recorder to the MECC conference? I would really appreciate it."

The database itself also provided a means whereby ACOT staff could monitor teachers' needs, and, when possible, offer assistance. The database template included a follow-up code that could be marked whenever an episode warranted further attention by ACOT staff. For example, when audiotapes reflected teachers' ongoing problems with a team-teaching arrangement, we apprised ACOT staff members about the teachers' frustrations.

At the end of each school year, we provided teachers with a chronological record of their audiotape contributions. The flexibility of the database made extracting individual teachers' contributions simple and provided teachers with a diarylike account of their classroom experiences. Teachers enjoyed receiving these diaries because the chronological record gave them more opportunity to see for themselves the changes they were making in their classrooms.

In some cases, individual teachers worked closely with university-based investigators on issues such as student empowerment, multimedia instruction, and mathematics software. Although this aspect of the project was time consuming for the teachers, we found that the research process further encouraged them to confront their own beliefs about teaching and learning, and also validated their efforts to change.

School and District Support

Schools and districts also provided support for ACOT teachers. When ACOT began, one of the selection criteria was the level of school and district support for the project. Teachers often had opportunities to meet during the school day for joint planning. Whenever possible, administrators permitted daily schedules to be flexible, allowing for peer observation and team teaching. At some sites, teachers attended technical and instructional workshops organized by their schools or districts. One site, with school and district approval, altered the master schedule to accommodate teachers' instructional innovations and interdisciplinary approaches. These forms of contextual support also promoted change by decreasing teacher isolation.

Collegial Support

Perhaps the greatest support for ACOT teachers came from each other. As teachers grappled with difficult issues, they wanted to share experiences with others in similar situations.[8] Each ACOT site had access to telecommunication services, so teachers could communicate not only with project staff members at Apple, but also with each other. Teachers often sent direct queries to their colleagues and generally received prompt responses. All ACOT teachers could read the weekly reports posted on line by each site, and they frequently made unsolicited offers of assistance to each other.

At the beginning of the project, interaction via telecommunications was infrequent and focused on emotional support. Teachers typically shared their frustrations and successes, and provided one another with words of encouragement. Over time, teachers' interactions over telecommunications shifted to include technical assistance. Teachers sought and received advice about managing and using specific types of equipment, locating appropriate software, and troubleshooting. Later still, when teachers ventured beyond using the technology for text-based drill-and-practice instruction, discussions about instructional topics emerged. Their instructional experimentation motivated them to share their endeavors with other teachers and sites.

Teacher Professional Development

Over the first decade of the project, ACOT staff learned a tremendous amount from project teachers about professional development and the supports needed to successfully integrate technology into instruction.[9] ACOT teachers' willingness to share their triumphs and tribulations provided insights that were invaluable when ACOT joined the National Science Foundation and three school districts to create the ACOT Teacher Development Center project in 1992. The primary objectives of this project were to help teachers learn to integrate technology into their instruction and move toward a more constructivist method of teaching.[10]

Four features that were built into the program can be directly traced to lessons learned by studying the experiences of ACOT teachers over the past decade. First, we learned that teachers need ongoing emotional, technical, and instructional support during the change process. Therefore, schools wanting to participate in the project were required to send at least two teachers at a time, rather than single individuals, to the center. To facilitate teachers' support of one another, principals agreed to provide teachers with common planning time as well as time for reflection. We also recognized that teachers would need additional support beyond what they could offer each other. Consequently, after coming to a center each teacher received at least two follow-up visits from the center coordinator.

Second, we discovered that teachers who are learning to use new technological tools want to use their new skills as soon as they return to their classrooms. Too often, new skills become rusty while teachers wait for new equipment to arrive. The project stipulated that participating teachers should have access to technology in their classrooms as soon as they finished their training.

Third, we found that teachers value learning from other teachers. Consequently, the program included time for visiting teachers to discuss and share ideas. Coordinators encouraged program participants to teach each other, and often asked them to make presentations and lead discussions. At the centers, ACOT teachers were frequently released from regular classes to conduct technical training and mini-workshops on topics such as alternative assessment. However, one of the most critical contributions by ACOT teachers was allowing visiting teachers to observe and work in ACOT classrooms. This aspect of the program, which we call "situated learning," allowed participants to see veteran ACOT teachers modeling a variety of teaching strategies, including the use of technology in project-based, interdisciplinary instruction. We believe that the opportunity for teachers to see their colleagues in action was perhaps the most valuable aspect of the program.

Finally, we learned that contextual changes in the teaching environment create new challenges for even the most experienced teachers. When ACOT teachers first faced the prospect of becoming involved in teachers' professional development through the Teacher Development Center, we were surprised at the trepidation some expressed about working with adults. Teachers who had willingly relinquished their role as experts in their classrooms now worried that they didn't know enough to teach their peers. Some ACOT teachers wanted more technical training, even though most had been using technology for years. Others wanted to learn more about mentoring, so ACOT staff organized a workshop on this topic. The teachers' anxiety reminded us that even the most accomplished teachers need opportunities for personal growth and professional development.

Using Technology to Study Technology

The ACOT teachers were pioneers, and we were too, because the techniques we used to study their experiences had not been widely used before that time. When ACOT started, the guiding question of our research was simply put: What happens when teachers and students have constant access to technology? Since there were few if any studies investigating this type of learning environment, we really didn't know what to expect, much less how to capture and describe the complexity of what was happening in these teachers' and students' lives. We did, however, have an ongoing pipeline into ACOT classrooms through the audiotapes and written reports that were often so rich in detail that we felt like we were on the front lines with the teachers.

Differences in Data Sources

ACOT teachers were asked to reflect on their experiences and record their thoughts on audiotape every few weeks. In these audiotape journals, teachers recorded their personal observations of events in their classrooms and their reflections on those events. Rather than asking teachers to comment on any particular aspect of their teaching, instructions about content on the tapes were purposefully left vague, giving teachers freedom to report what was most salient to each of them at the time. They often used the tapes to vent their frustrations and share their triumphs, giving the tapes an emotionally charged quality. Although the thirty-two participating teachers differed with regard to how many tapes they made over the course of a year, each teacher produced, on average, two sixty-minute tapes per month.

In contrast to the audiotapes, the written reports we received were much less personal and introspective. Weekly reports communicated major events and were electronically distributed among all project participants, including administrative staff and teaching colleagues. Site links, typically short messages from one teacher to another or from one site to the ACOT project staff, often focused on relatively mundane issues such as missing cables, troubleshooting advice, or other logistical matters.

Challenges in Creating a Database

Our goal was to create a database that did not reduce the data to mere codes, but instead provided an indexing and retrieval system allowing interaction with the rich qualitative data in teachers' audiotapes and written reports. Similar to a table of contents of a book, we wanted our indexing system to direct us, and other researchers, to episodes illustrating specific content where the original textual data could be studied. We also needed a system of data management that would allow for evolving questions. In essence, we wanted to create a way to systematically query what became the equivalent of five thousand single-spaced pages of prose.

At that time, analyses of massive quantities of qualitative data were typically carried out on mainframe computers and often required the assistance of a programmer. Databases, once built, were unchangeable. If mistakes were made in structuring the database, making subsequent additions or corrections would be impossible.

Since we wanted to keep the process of data coding, retrieval, and analysis in our own hands rather than having to rely on a programmer, we decided to use a desktop computer and newly released software entitled Double Helix. This software allowed us to modify the database structure as our understanding of the data emerged. This feature was unique at that time. We used a Macintosh II computer with 2 megabytes of RAM, an internal hard drive with 40 megabytes of memory, and an external drive with 40-megabyte removable cartridges. Back then, this equipment was state-of-the-art for desktop computing.

Our first challenge was to develop a template with appropriate codes for categorizing the data. We made a number of false starts. We didn't anticipate the complexity of what we were trying to do. We also discovered that it's difficult to come up with a coding scheme for data that are constantly changing. As teachers adapted to their new environments, their concerns changed over time—and our template had to reflect these changes. We struggled to find categories that were broad enough to capture the richness of teachers' experience, but narrow enough to be useful.

Early on, we realized just how fortunate we were that Double Helix allowed modifications to the database. And modify we did— more times than we care to remember. Some of the changes were minor, more or less fine-tuning. Other changes were not quite as simple and ultimately required reindexing literally thousands of episodes. Our final template consisted of forty-seven fields. Our first had only four.

Limits in Using the Database

Over time, the sheer quantity of data pushed the limits of the available hardware and software, as well as the limits of our technical abilities. We wanted to develop tools for graphically representing the content of the database as a whole while allowing comparisons among subjects, sites, and grade levels. Unfortunately, the database grew too large to be used effectively with even the most powerful types of graphing software that existed at that time. In the mid 1980s, processing large amounts of data on a mainframe was routine—but led to unforeseen difficulties on desktop computers. Although we were not able to systematically graph and display the data, our system eventually allowed us to quickly organize a vast quantity of text data and retrieve them by variables such as grade level, school, teacher, content theme, and context, as well as combinations of these variables.

As the database expanded over the years, we increasingly relied on the help of an expert in the use of the relational database, and our roles shifted from database design and indexing to analysis and report writing. We used the database to investigate a variety of topics, such as changes in teachers' beliefs and concerns, classroom management strategies, and teacher and student roles.

New Today, Old Tomorrow: Does It Really Matter?

Ten years later, we can't help but reflect on what would be different if the ACOT project started in 1995 instead of 1985. Would teachers' experiences be vastly different? Would our experiences as researchers change?

Certainly, creating the database on teachers' experiences would be much simpler given the technological advances in hardware and software over the last decade. Now that people can routinely store gigabytes of information on personal computers, our 120-megabyte database doesn't seem so huge. And now that more powerful software has been designed, we could no doubt complete (probably in a matter of minutes!) the graphical analysis of our whole data set that eluded us just five years ago. Despite the challenges that we faced while capturing teachers' voices, we see the value of the work. We believe that what we learned about teachers' struggles to integrate technology in spite of incredible changes in the technology itself provides valuable information for those who are learning to use technology in their classrooms both now and in the future.

In our recent work in classrooms outside the ACOT project, we have heard teachers who are learning to use technology express the same concerns as their pioneering ACOT colleagues. Unlike the equipment used in the ACOT project's early years, the lessons we have learned by examining teachers' experiences have not become obsolete. In the long run, learning to integrate an Apple IIe into classroom instruction is not much different from learning to integrate a Macintosh II, Quadra 700, or a Power Mac 9500. Although teachers of this decade may be able to create glitzy presentations, ask students to create multimedia reports, and download files from a telecommunications network in the blink of an eye, they still find themselves confronting their beliefs about instruction and their roles as classroom teachers, just like ACOT teachers did when learning how to use Apple IIes. They must still learn new skills, not only with the technology, but also in instructional design, classroom management, and student assessment.

Unfortunately, people sometimes expect teachers to appropriate technology at a more rapid pace than in the past simply because the tools themselves are changing so quickly. While new users of technology have no doubt benefited from what educators and re-searchers have learned in the last ten years, one issue that does not change, no matter how sophisticated the technology has become, is that teachers need time to learn how to use new technology. They need time to think about appropriate ways to integrate it into the curriculum, reflect on the outcomes of their instruction, and share what they have learned with their colleagues. Computers may be faster and more user-friendly, but the learning curve for appropriate classroom integration will not change as rapidly as the technology.

Teachers learning to use technology need ongoing support in order to grow professionally, and the type of support they need changes over time. Typically, districts investing in technology ear-mark the majority of their funds for hardware and software, and neglect to budget sufficient resources for teacher development. They often look at teacher training as a one-shot deal, as if the need for training will end once teachers have computer basics under their belts. In reality, the more teachers learn about technology, the more training they typically want, especially since technology seems to change at a breakneck pace.

We close with a quote from an ACOT teacher who, early in the project, commented about students' using telecommunications to do homework: "We really should be keeping a log of all the excuses that are given for not doing bulletin board homework. Students are the same: it does not matter if they are doing their homework by candlelight or telecommunications, only the tools and technology change. Excuses remain. Here are the three best ones for this week: 'My telephone cord is too short.' 'Momma gave my adaptor away.' 'My modem messed up and erased all my messages.'"

It reminds us that, though we believe that technology clearly can improve education, some things never seem to change.[11] Age-old problems may simply reemerge with a slight technological twist.

Notes

1. A pseudonym.

2. Dwyer, D. C., Ringstaff, C., & Sandholtz, J. H. (1991). Changes in teachers' beliefs and practices in technology-rich classrooms. *Educational Leadership, 48*(8), 45–52.

3. Ringstaff, C., Sandholtz, J. H., & Dwyer, D. (1994). Trading places: When teachers use student expertise in technology-intensive classrooms. *People and Education, 2*(4), 405–430.

4. Sandholtz, J. H., Ringstaff, C., & Dwyer, D. (1992). Teaching in high-tech environments: Classroom management revisited. *Journal of Educational Computing Research, 8*(4), 479–505.

5. Dwyer et al., cited in note 2.

6. Sandholtz et al., cited in note 4.

7. Ringstaff et al., cited in note 3.

8. Sandholtz, J. H., Ringstaff, C., & Dwyer, D. (1995). The relationship between technological innovation and collegial interaction. *People and Education, 3*(3), 295–321.

9. Dwyer et al., cited in note 2.

10. Additional perspectives on ACOT Teacher Development Centers are presented in Chapters Fourteen, Fifteen, and Sixteen.

11. Sandholtz, J., Ringstaff, C., & Dwyer, D. (in press). *Age-old concerns in new-age classrooms: Teachers' experiences in technology-rich environments*. New York: Teachers College Press.

The Contributors

Eva L. Baker is professor of psychological studies in education at the University of California, Los Angeles. She directs the UCLA Center for the Study of Evaluation and co-directs the National Center for Research on Evaluation, Standards, and Student Testing. She holds a Ph.D. in educational psychology from the University of California, Los Angeles (1967). She has published on a wide variety of topics related to educational evaluation.

Robert A. Carpenter is a veteran teacher in the Columbus Public Schools in Columbus, Ohio. He has taught instrumental music at the elementary, middle school, and high school levels. For the past eight years, he has participated in the ACOT project at West High School in Columbus. He received a Ph.D. from Ohio State University (1986) and since then has published and presented on a variety of topics concerning the application of technology to teaching and learning processes.

Allan Collins is a principal scientist at BBN Corporation, and professor of education and social policy at Northwestern University. He earned a Ph.D. in psychology from the University of Michigan (1970). His extensive contributions to education include work on inquiry teaching, cognitive apprenticeship, situated learning, and applications of technology to learning.

Jere Confrey is an associate professor of mathematics education at Cornell University. She holds a Ph.D. from Cornell University (1980), and before returning as a faculty member she was a senior researcher at the Institute for Research on Teaching at Michigan State University. She is the primary developer of several innovative software products for undergraduate and precollegiate mathematics learning. She has published widely on mathematics education.

Jane L. David is director of the Bay Area Research Group in Palo Alto, California. She holds an Ed.D. in education and social policy from Harvard University (1974). Her research and publications focus on the connections between school improvement and education policy at all levels of the educational system.

David C. Dwyer is a Distinguished Scientist at Apple Computer. He earned a Ph.D. in educational innovation and policy from Washington University (1981). Dwyer twice gained national recognition as a public school science teacher. His research and writing focus on educational change, school leadership, and uses of technology in teaching and learning. Dwyer directed ACOT's research and managed the program for most of its initial decade.

Charles Fisher is senior research scientist in the School of Education at the University of Michigan. He earned a Ph.D. in educational theory at the University of Toronto (1973). His research on teaching and learning processes has focused on the uses of instructional time in a variety of classroom task structures and social organizations.

Maryl Gearhart is a project director for the Center for Research on Evaluation, Standards, and Student Testing at the University of California, Los Angeles. She holds a Ph.D. in developmental psychology from the City University of New York (1983). Her research and writing focus on mathematics and language arts assessments and on the roles that assessments play in effective teaching and learning.

Richard Greenberg is professor of planetary sciences and of teaching and teacher education at the University of Arizona. He holds a Ph.D. in planetary sciences from the Massachusetts Institute of Technology (1972). Since 1990, he has directed the Image Processing for Teaching project. Greenberg is also a member of the imaging team for NASA's *Galileo* Jupiter-orbiter spacecraft.

Jan Hawkins is director of the Center for Children and Technology at Educational Development Center. She received a Ph.D. in developmental psychology at the Graduate Center of City University of New York. Hawkins has been studying uses of technology in education since 1980. Her research and writing focus on issues related to technology and educational reform, new forms of assessment, diversity, and gender.

Joan Herman is associate director of the National Center for Research on Evaluation, Standards, and Student Testing at the University of California, Los Angeles. She holds an Ed.D. in learning and instruction from the University of California, Los Angeles (1977). Her research and publications explore the design and effects of assessment systems that support school improvement.

D. Midian Kurland is a senior scientist at Apple Computer. He earned a Ph.D. in educational theory at the University of Toronto (1981). He has developed several computer-based tools for writers that are widely used in educational settings. His research and writing have focused on various aspects of computer-supported learning.

Brian Reilly is a researcher at Apple Computer. His research focuses on the use of interactive digital photography, video, and multimedia in schools. His interactive video *Bell High School Portfolios* won three national awards in 1994.

Cathy Ringstaff is an independent consultant to school districts, universities, and foundations on educational evaluation. She holds a Ph.D. in educational psychology from Stanford University (1989). Her research and writing focus on teacher change.

Judith Haymore Sandholtz is director of the Comprehensive Teacher Education Institute at the University of California, Riverside. She holds a Ph.D. in curriculum and teacher education from Stanford University (1989). Her research focuses on collaborative teacher education, professional development schools, and technology-rich classrooms.

Robert J. Tierney is professor and chairperson for the department of education theory and practice at Ohio State University. He holds a Ph.D. in literacy from the University of Georgia (1974). He has published widely on teaching, assessment, and the construction of meaning in the context of literacy acquisition.

Decker F. Walker is professor of education at Stanford University. He holds a Ph.D. in education from Stanford University (1971). He has published widely on curriculum issues in education.

Kristina Hooper Woolsey is a Distinguished Scientist at Apple Computer. She holds a Ph.D. in cognitive psychology from the University of California, San Diego (1973). She co-founded the Apple Multimedia Lab and served as its director from 1987 to 1992. She is currently interested in media-rich computing, particularly for casual communication in early idea development. Woolsey has developed and published a variety of highly acclaimed multimedia products.

Keith Yocam is program manager of the ACOT project at Apple Computer. He joined ACOT nine years ago, after eleven years as an elementary school teacher specializing in science and computer instruction. He also directs the ACOT Teacher Development Center project. His research examines the impact of situated teacher development on teacher change.

Index

A

Access, to technology, 2, 215–216
Accomplished practice, and professional development, 240–245, 248
Addison-Wesley, 168
Afamasaga-Fuata'i, K., 148
Alexander, 94
Alkin, M., 126
Allen, C., 10
Alluisi, E. A., 200
American Association for the Advancement of Science (AAAS), 94
American Astronomical Society, 226
American Education Research Association, 4
Anderson, J., 11, 55
Anderson, R. E., 105
Animation: innovative, 211–213; in interactive learning, 57
Anti-intellectualism, 77, 145
Apple Classrooms of Tomorrow (ACOT): affiliated classrooms for, 104; approach of, 98; aspects of, 1–12; assessment of, 185–202; beginnings of, 2–3; and computer appropriation, 169–183; developmental efforts of, 6–7; in elementary schools, 109–127; evaluations of, 98; focus refined for, 4–7; goals of, 191–192, 205; hindsight on, 21–28; history of, 2–7;
ideological flexibility of, 97–99; improving, 103–105; international interest in, 4, 6, 12; and learning tools and tasks, 107–234; mission of, 1–2, 93; partnerships for, 7, 12, 245–247; and physical sciences teaching, 59; and professional development, 118–121, 235–299; research on, 3–7, 9–12; support from, 289–290; teachers for, 116–118, 265–266, 281–299; and technology, 13–106; Writing Institute of, 159–163. See also Teacher Development Centers
Apple Computer, Inc.: and assessment, 191, 193; multimedia interfaces at, 71, 76; and professional development, 245–246, 250, 253–254, 258, 269, 289; projects of, 1, 2, 118–119, 168, 234; StartingLine materials of, 12, 263
Applebee, A. N., 168
AppleWriter, 153
Apprenticeship, for video production, 211
Appropriation. See Computer appropriation
Arizona: field trip in, 6; weather analysis in, 232
Arizona, University of, 11, 222, 225, 230

The Editors

Charles Fisher is senior research scientist in the School of Education at the University of Michigan. He is coeditor of *Perspectives on Instructional Time* and coauthor of *Openness in Schools*.

David C. Dwyer is distinguished scientist at Apple Computer, working in the Advanced Technology Group.

Keith Yocam is program manager of the ACOT project at Apple Computer.